The King of Swings

The King of Swings

Johnny Goodman, the Last Amateur
to Beat the Pros at Their Own Game

Michael Blaine

HOUGHTON MIFFLIN COMPANY

BOSTON · NEW YORK   2006

For information about permission to reproduce selections from
this book, write to Permissions, Houghton Mifflin Company,
215 Park Avenue South, New York, New York 10003.

Visit our Web site: www.houghtonmifflinbooks.com.

Library of Congress Cataloging-in-Publication Data

Blaine, Michael.
The king of swings : Johnny Goodman, the last amateur to
beat the pros at their own game / Michael Blaine.
p. cm.
Includes index.
ISBN-13: 978-0-618-51464-9
ISBN-10: 0-618-51464-3
1. Goodman, Johnny, 1909–1970.   2. Golfers—United
States—Biography.   3. Golf—United States—History—
20th century.   I. Title.
GV964.G66B53 2006
796.352092—dc22   2005031536

Printed in the United States of America

Book design by Robert Overholtzer

QUM 10 9 8 7 6 5 4 3 2 1

For John and Helen Goodman Jr.,
and for Jack Atkins

I'd rather play golf than eat.

—JOHNNY GOODMAN

CONTENTS

AUTHOR'S NOTE

While most of the dialogue in this story is derived from primary sources, I have taken the liberty of reconstructing conversations in a limited number of scenes in order to communicate the flavor of the time and bring the principal figures to life. Although these bits of dialogue are my own invention, they are based on documented incidents.

In addition, in order to give the reader insight into the thinking of key characters, I have attributed certain thoughts and feelings to them that were consistent with their public statements and well-known attitudes toward the game and themselves. Although I have exercised a certain dramatic license in order to make the material come alive, I have not strayed far from the essentials of what is widely known about the central figures in this story.

PROLOGUE

IN THE BEGINNING, trains tell the story. Cattle trains. Mail trains. Gleaming Pullmans. Private cars with all the appointments. And a freight train that ran through the heart of a Midwest golf course.

On August 18, 1929, just before dawn, nineteen-year-old Johnny Goodman stepped out of L. B. Webster's modest home at North Thirty-eighth Street in Omaha, Nebraska. On his own since his early teens, Johnny had been living with the Websters for several years. In return for room and board, he stoked the furnace and did yard work for the family, but Mrs. Webster was a kind woman, and it hadn't taken her long to draw the shy young man into the family circle. Johnny had become fast friends with her son Wendell.

The blade-thin Goodman stood a bit over five seven. With hair slicked back tight to his skull, and his hollow cheeks, he had an undernourished look. A prominent nose added to the narrow, birdlike shape of his face, but he had a generous mouth and striking blue eyes.

The son of Lithuanian immigrants, Goodman had grown up in South Omaha on a street hard by the city's teeming stockyards and meatpacking plants. When he was fourteen his mother, Rose, died in childbirth. The infant, also named Rose, was her thirteenth child. The baby lived for little more than a day. In the midst of this crisis, Johnny's father, William Goodman, abandoned the six children still living under his roof. The older boys were renting rooms elsewhere. Clinging to jobs in the packinghouses and factories, they couldn't offer much support.

Johnny and his sixteen-year-old sister Anna, who was working as a maid, pooled their meager resources and tried to keep the family together, but when county authorities discovered the children's plight, ten-year-old Mary was farmed out to do housework and the three youngest boys, Mike, Pete, and Tommy, were bundled off to St. James Orphanage.

Johnny was left to "paddle his own canoe," in the picturesque language of the *Omaha World-Herald*. First the Zadalis family took him in, then the Websters. He scratched out a living caddying at the Omaha Field Club, working as a Western Union messenger, a printer's devil, and, for one summer, in one of the vast packing-houses. Still, he had managed to graduate from high school with honors.

Whenever he could, he stole a few hours to practice his golf game. By nineteen, he'd transformed himself into the best golfer in Omaha. Now he was headed for the 1929 U.S. Amateur at the far-flung California links, Pebble Beach.

Gripping his cardboard suitcase in his left hand, he bent down and swung his golf clubs over his right shoulder, then paused, gazing at the empty lot across the street. For untold hours he'd pitched golf balls from the Websters' front yard, lofting shots over the asphalt into the dusty field.

Turning away, he headed for the train station, stopping once to straighten his tie. He was wearing a V-neck sweater and a dark blue blazer, the first new jacket he'd ever owned. Out of his trainee's wage at the sporting goods store where he was clerking, he had squirreled away a few cents a week until, after seven months, he had accumulated enough to buy the garment. In his suitcase he had a second sweater he called his "dressy number."

To reach the train station, he boarded a streetcar that ran down Dodge. Setting his clubs down, he slipped into a seat and watched the neatly kept houses drift by. Residential blocks gave way to office buildings, and then at Tenth Street the wholesale district swam into view.

Finally, the streetcar rolled up to Union Street Station. The old station had been pulled down, and work on the new building had barely begun. Meanwhile, a temporary wooden structure had been thrown up at track level in the middle of the gritty train yard. It wasn't much to look at.

On line for his ticket Johnny felt constricted, so he slipped out of his jacket and set it down on a bench next to the makeshift booth. Mostly, he kept his eye on his new clubs, the irons gleaming, the woods polished to perfection. He'd bought them at a discount from the sporting goods store. For years he'd played with a ragbag of castoffs, woods stripped of varnish, hickory shafts peeling like old skin. Now he even owned a MacGregor Chieftain driver with a weighted ivory back. He told the ticket agent with the brush mustache where he was going.

"Fast Mail, you said?"

The Fast Mail train was the cheapest. It had only one passenger car. "Yes, sir."

After the agent passed him his ticket under the grille, he wandered down the rough-hewn platform. Waiting, his leg jiggling with nervous energy, he stared at the Union Pacific's gorgeous brochure, an illustration of the Grand Canyon of the Platte on its cover. He shot through the pages, barely grasping the inflated copy about some explorers plunging over a hidden waterfall. He shuffled his feet and then straddled his bag. Where was the damn train?

He craned his neck, looking for the Fast Mail's grimy cars. The brochure advertised a free reclining chair, but he'd been told that after Ogden, Utah, they'd try to clip him for the adjustable seat. He'd make sure he chose one that didn't tilt back. When you were tired, you could sleep sitting straight up.

When he heard the steam locomotive rumbling in, he gathered up his suitcase and his clubs and raced for the last car of the sooty train. In his excitement, he left his brand-new jacket folded neatly on its perch.

Montana. Arizona. Wyoming. Once they were just colored boxes on a map. Soon they would take shape before him. He'd seen plenty of westerns, with their endless plains, rocky monoliths, and hanging trees. These silent thrillers featured Indian raids, train robberies, and heart-pounding rescues. Johnny's native sense told him that

Hollywood exaggerated to make its stories more exciting, but out beyond Nebraska and Kansas, civilization petered out to nothing. You never knew what might happen.

~~After storing his clubs, he loosened his tie and tried to get comfortable.~~ The seat was hard, but he couldn't afford to get soaked in a Pullman dining car, where they charged an arm and a leg just for coffee and pie. His older brother George had given him a piece of ham from the packinghouse where he worked. Armour, Swift, and Cudahay all granted discounts to their workers. George said it was a good deal.

Settling in, he went over his plan to play Pebble Beach. Although he'd never laid eyes on the oceanside layout, he'd read hole-by-hole descriptions of the treacherous course, and in his mind's eye he saw how he would attack each tee shot, each approach, where he would have to be disciplined and steer away from danger and where it was worth going for broke.

Before every competitive round he played, he planned his strategy step by step. He'd start concentrating long before he reached the first tee; he hated to make mental mistakes. When he drifted into these reveries, he'd stop talking, stop listening, and get a faraway look in his eyes that his friends said was downright spooky.

After envisioning each of Pebble Beach's eighteen holes, he flipped the pages of the brochure and ran his eyes down the schedule. Cheyenne. Granger. Butte. Portland. Ogden. Salt Lake. San Francisco.

These cities had always seemed impossibly far away, and now he was flying along the rails to see them. He pressed his nose against the glass and watched the flat plains whip past. When it got cold, he started groping for his jacket. Somehow, it had disappeared.

On August 17, 1929, Bobby Jones prepared to board a private railroad car at Atlanta's Brookwood Station for the first leg of his cross-country trip to the United States Amateur Golf Championship at Pebble Beach, a recently remodeled course little known back East. Before departing, Jones offered a few modest words to fans and reporters about his chances. A solidly built twenty-seven-year-old, he had soft, boyish features that fit his diffident manner perfectly. His black hair, parted in the middle, sometimes strayed to his broad forehead. One sensed that he was faintly embarrassed to be Bobby Jones, to be so handsome, to have won so many championships, and to look so good in a pair of pinstriped flannel trousers. His shyness was genuine and made his personality all the more appealing.

In June, Jones, the amateur, had pummeled Al Espinosa, the professional, in a two-round playoff for the United States Open at Winged Foot in New York. Jones had posted 72 and 69, the shaky, overawed Espinosa 84 and 80. With his effortless, powerful drives, and the help of a putter he called Calamity Jane, Bobby had been steamrolling the opposition, amateur and professional, since he had taken the U.S. Open from Bobby Cruickshank in 1923. In 1926 he had triumphed at both the British and U.S. Opens, and in 1927 he'd repeated in the British with a record score of 285.

Now Jones, who had also dominated in the U.S. Amateur, securing championships in 1924, 1925, 1927, and 1928, was pointing toward winning another to become the first simultaneous holder of U.S. Open and U.S. Amateur crowns since Chick Evans had pulled off the rare feat in 1916.

Accompanying Bobby were his wife, Mary, his two children, Clara and Bobby junior, his parents, Mr. and Mrs. Robert P. Jones, and family friends, Mr. and Mrs. Charlie Black Jr. and Mr. and Mrs. Sherwood Hurt. The party planned to spend a day sightseeing at the Grand Canyon and then go on to Los Angeles, where Jones was scheduled to play an exhibition with George Von Elm and the British stars Cyril Tolley and Angus Storey. The cowboy humorist Will Rogers had invited Bobby to stop by at his ranch along the way.

In the parlor car's well-appointed stateroom, with its walnut paneling, English mohair upholstery, silver trays, and brass ashtray stands, Bobby tried to relax, but as the train rolled west, the atmosphere grew stifling. He stretched and fidgeted, but nothing seemed to help. His neck was stiff. His shoulder ached. In the intense heat, he felt drained of energy.

A complex and fiercely intelligent man, Jones was feeling the stress of living up to his idealized image, and to his own expectations. He had been playing major championships since he was four-teen years old, and over the years he'd acquired a host of chronic aches and pains. His finicky digestion defeated one remedy after an-other. As a young man, he had even had an operation to treat a vari-cose vein condition. While spectators, in awe of his towering drives and courageous finishes, believed that Bobby pulled off his miracles without strain, every major championship left him weak and ex-hausted.

His wife had grown increasingly disturbed by Bobby's condition. Mary was also tired of their marriage being fodder for romance magazines and of the lonely stretches when Bobby went out to win just one more championship. From a conservative Atlanta Catholic family whose parents regarded Jones as faintly racy, and the Jones clan as "new money," the former debutante was becoming insistent that her husband spend more time at home.

Mary's mystical streak, and her taste for tarot cards, also led her to raise questions about her husband's life beyond the fairways. What exactly did all of Bobby's struggles mean?

Jones didn't simply want to appease Mary. Conservative by na-ture himself, he wanted to live the same family-centered life his wife craved, and he planned to stay home for good sometime in the neb-ulous future. After spending years in college earning an engineering degree from Georgia Tech, a master's in English literature from Har-vard, and topping it off with a year at Emory Law School, Bobby Jones knew it was time to go to work and earn a living. He couldn't keep changing his mind; he couldn't keep shifting careers.

In fact, he had recently entered his father's lucrative law practice and argued his first case in federal court. Although he had won, re-covering a small loan for an Atlanta firm, he found the experience distasteful. He didn't like arguments. He didn't like putting himself on display. How could he tell Big Bob, his father, that after choosing the law, he never wanted to appear in court again?

The tall, heavyset Big Bob sat just inches away from him, but Bobby couldn't bring himself to confront the man. Big Bob loved the law, and especially the Coca-Cola account he'd secured as a young man on his way up in Atlanta. Wouldn't it be better to put off that conversation?

In the evening, father and son stepped out to take the air and share some of Big Bob's corn liquor. As the stark Southwest landscape rolled by, Bobby tried to find the right words to explain his reservations about the legal profession. He didn't like pretending to be aggressive. He didn't like sticking his hand in another man's pocket. He didn't like twisting the rules. In the end, he talked about the field at Pebble Beach, and the new links by the sea.

"Sounds tricky to me," Big Bob observed. The elder Jones also offered his opinion that Bobby would sweep the field yet again.

Jones couldn't help nursing a few more dreams of glory himself. In fact, his greatest achievement, the Grand Slam, was still ahead of him.

As Bobby made his stately progress across the country, the procession took on the air of a coronation. In San Francisco, after a brief stay, he inspired competing arias of praise. The *San Francisco Chronicle* claimed that Californians had fallen in love with the golfing idol's "slow, boyish smiles and marvelous golf shots." The *Examiner,* not to be outdone, claimed that Jones had "made a million friends."

In the wider world, strange and marvelous changes were taking place. The papers were advertising a "novel, all-talking movie" called *Side Street* featuring all three Moore brothers. Clara Bow was starring in *The Wild Party* and Joan Crawford was searching for true happiness in *Dream of Love.* J. E. Smith of the National Radio Institute reported that canned music from phonograph records was becoming increasingly popular on local stations and that it was impossible to tell the recordings from live broadcasts.

At a hangar in Lakehurst, New Jersey, the Capital Electric Company's sales manager presented the *Graf Zeppelin*'s crew, in honor of its around-the-world excursion, with forty Majestic radios. Pepsodent toothpaste sales had gone through the roof since the company had begun advertising on *Amos 'n Andy.* In the white-hot stock market, margins were so generous that investors could buy fifty thousand dollars' worth of stock for five hundred up front.

Down on the Monterey Peninsula where the Pebble Beach golf course was being readied for the tournament, nervous officials were taking every precaution. The tight course, snaking along the edge of

Carmel Bay, presented unusual crowd-control problems. Worried that galleries, incited by the presence of the magnetic Jones, might get out of control, the hosts had hired one thousand men, many to serve as marshals.

Weeks before the tournament, every room in Monterey and Carmel had been snapped up, and despite the astronomical price of twelve dollars a day for accommodations, the fashionable Del Monte Hotel was packed. The Calcutta betting pool, in which gamblers bid for the player of their choice, had swollen to record proportions.

The *Monterey Peninsula Herald* warned that motorists would descend on the area in staggering numbers, and suggested intricate alternative routes to the Pebble Beach links. Thousands of Jones worshipers were expected to migrate to the Monterey Peninsula by train, and more than a few would sail down in their yachts.

After motoring to town for the matches, Mr. and Mrs. William Randolph Hearst were staying at the coffee magnate James Athearn Folger's home. Ethel Barrymore was being feted by the Crockers at the Del Monte. The screen comedians Harold Lloyd and Oliver "Babe" Hardy were racing down from Hollywood to catch the competition. Wishing to capture the action on film, Lord Charles Hope, a British entry, brought a movie camera with him all the way from England.

A photograph in the *Monterey Peninsula Herald* pictured former United States Open champion Willie McFarland leaning on a luxurious Pierce-Arrow straight eight. Crowing that the automobile would be conspicuous among participants and spectators alike, the ad copy concluded: "Bobby Jones, the world's greatest golfer and winner of last year's tournament, is also a Pierce-Arrow enthusiast."

Whether or not Jones was being compensated by Pierce-Arrow — he was scrupulous in observing the letter of the United States Golf Association's code — the appearance of his name in a commercial context was sure to get under the skins of other great amateurs like George Von Elm, who bridled at Jones's ability to maintain a "simon-pure" image while simultaneously keeping an eye out for the main chance. From the perspective of Jones's competitors, the

USGA's Brahmins held to a double standard when it came to cashing in on amateur golf fame, a flexible one for Robert Tyre Jones Jr. and an unbending one for the amateur game's mere mortals.

The amateur ideal had a powerful allure in the 1920s. As the press endlessly proclaimed, the true amateur played the game for the sheer joy of it. His motives were unstained by the pursuit of fame or money. In fact, he played with a certain careless grace. He never committed the cardinal sin of wanting to win too much. If a cup came his way, it was all very fine, but the real amateur didn't covet glory any more than he lusted after riches. The talent that brought him to the top of the game was somehow inborn. He deserved to win because of who he was. Any labor he put in to hone his skills took away from the purity of his achievement, so he rarely labored at all. If practice became absolutely necessary, he made the necessary adjustments to his swing in private.

Bobby Jones was the incarnation of this amateur ethic. The press never tired of pointing out how little he practiced, and how golf for the gifted Atlantan was simply a sideline. Of course, no one would have been talking about Jones if he didn't beat the professionals in the great tournaments year after year. Every time Bobby Jones took another U.S. Open, he proved to an admiring mass media, and to the public, that amateur golf was the premier form of the game. In Jones the powerful United States Golf Association had proof of its unshakable belief that amateurs were superior to the professionals, who, after all, were just performing a species of cheap vaudeville.

At a time when purses at professional tournaments were pitifully small, when there was no organized tour, and exhibition matches offered the best way for a golf pro to scratch out a living, it is no wonder that the United States Amateur was still the most prestigious prize in all of golf.

Beginning as an eleven-year-old caddie, Johnny Goodman had virtually grown up at the Omaha Field Club, whose upper-class membership revered Bobby Jones and the amateur ethic. As a teenager, Johnny, too, had developed a deep admiration for Jones, and a profound respect for the amateur ideal. He had devoured Bobby's articles and his book, *Down the Fairway,* and he saw no reason why he shouldn't rise in the amateur game himself. He didn't give much thought to the fact that he didn't have quite the background that golf's eastern establishment figures had in mind when they envisioned an amateur golf champion.

In fact, the United States Golf Association's Executive Committee held a jaundiced view of impecunious golfers who tried to barge into the amateur ranks. Usually, the game's ruling body handed down its decisions in neutral, opaque language, but A. H. Gregson, editor of *Golf Illustrated,* often gave voice to the private opinions of the famously tight-jawed USGA officials. On the subject of talented golfers who lacked a sufficient fortune, he took a hard line. "A young man with no means should not be wasting his time at a golf club to which he cannot afford to belong, and to such a one the temptation to capitalize his capabilities without honestly setting up as a professional, which in spirit is what he really is, may be very strong. Such a one should be at work."

As Johnny Goodman rolled west on the Fast Mail, he thought of greens jutting out above the sea, and ball-eating dunes that sprouted tall, silvery grass. His imagination was full of the vagaries of the Pacific winds and the twists and turns of doglegs. The USGA's power was the last thing on his mind.

In mid-August of 1929 Johnny Goodman was virtually invisible as far as USGA officials and sports fans were concerned. Instead, the West Coast's golf devotees were waiting impatiently to catch their first glimpse of one man, Bobby Jones, who was passing the time with Douglas Fairbanks, Mary Pickford, and other assorted Hollywood royalty. Finally, the time for amiable practice rounds at the Los Angeles Country Club came to an end.

As Jones approached Pebble Beach's dramatic links for the first time, every major paper in the country had its correspondent in place. One of the last glamorous events of the Roaring Twenties was about to begin.

PART ONE

On the Rails

1

THE FIFTH CHILD of William and Rose Goodman, Johnny Goodman was born in South Omaha, Nebraska, on December 28, 1909. For most of his childhood he lived in a single-story frame house at 4128 South Thirty-sixth Street, in close proximity to Omaha's great stockyards and meatpacking plants.

Johnny Goodman's name first appeared in the Omaha papers in 1916, when he contracted diphtheria. Alerted to the situation by neighbors, health workers discovered the feverish boy in a bed he shared with three other siblings. In the same room, four more Goodman children slept in a single bed. Suspicious of the officials' motives and fearful of hospitals in general, Rose Goodman refused to allow the authorities to take her son away for treatment. In response to her intransigence, the city quarantined the entire family.

Today, Rose's resistance to medical intervention would be viewed as irrational, bordering on child abuse. But for an illiterate immigrant whose knowledge of hospitals was limited to the unsanitary poor wards of Lithuania, her actions can be seen in a different light. However misguided, she was taking a stand to protect her son. Miraculously, none of Rose's other children caught the disease and Johnny eventually recovered.

Johnny's father worked in one of the city's meatpacking plants. Every morning William Goodman would join the masses of men and animals pouring toward the looming slaughterhouses, never knowing if there would be work that day. Over the years he labored in the pickling room, where meat was hauled out of vats of salty water, and the boning room, where the air contained fine bits of bone that lodged in workers' lungs. If he was lucky he'd catch on with the hog-killing gang — a man could breathe better on that job — but there were always accidents. If you got cut, you wrapped a rag around the wound and kept on slicing.

He stood all day long in blood and water up to his ankles. On the killing floor in the winter his feet would grow numb with cold, and he would wrap them in layer after layer of cloth until he felt as if he were walking on frozen hooves, but he was thankful for the job; back in Lithuania, there was little work for a man like him. Eventually he became a butcher and earned a little more an hour. It was a dangerous job — during "speedups" on the line the exhausted men sometimes cut one another accidentally with razor-sharp knives — but you stuck some plaster on the wound, you laughed it off, and cut some more.

He worked hard and provided for his wife and children. In fact, he managed to buy his own home. By then he had nine children, all of whom attended school. He made his mortgage payments and fed his family.

Despite his punishing job, William learned to read and write English. For a number of years he was the picture of an upwardly mobile man, able to feed and clothe his sprawling family. But hacking away at steer carcasses ten hours a day left him worn out and hungry for release. At the end of his shift he began joining the other meatpackers in the local saloons. At first it was just for the free pea soup and boiled cabbage, for the raw talk about who almost fell into which vat, who skinned himself good, and what the bosses were going to pull next. There was nothing unusual about downing a few beers after a hard day's work, but William Goodman's taste for liquor grew, and soon he was staying out later and later.

There were joints that would serve you after hours too, and if you didn't get home in time to sleep, you could still make the next shift. If you were a minute late, the company docked you an hour's pay. And if you didn't get home on payday, you could always show up the next day as long as you had a few dollars to throw down on the kitchen table.

Johnny learned to stay out of his father's way on the nights he came roaring home. He learned the telltale sounds that meant trouble, the scraping of a key that missed the lock, the low muttering, the uneven shuffle of uncertain feet, and he learned to make himself small. Sometimes Anna and Mary and Johnny would skitter out to the yard and wait for things to quiet down. It was better to stand outside in the cold than to catch the back of his father's hand, but then the neighbors might see you and guess what was going on. The thought of strangers looking down on his family made him squirm.

More often than not, he prayed his father would never come home. At the same time, he wished he would come home, but sober and quiet. In the perfectly still mornings after one of his old man's sprees, his mother never said a word. Johnny learned it was better not to talk about these things. He would gather his books, tiptoe over the wreckage, and make his way out to the street.

In school, the desks were lined up in strict order. The walls were whitewashed and the floors smelled of fresh wax. Subjects came one after the other at the same time every day. No matter what was happening at home, Johnny got his homework in, and his teachers praised his precise, perfectly slanted handwriting. When complimented, he would look at his shoes — he never said much when teachers praised him — but he liked the kind words more than he'd admit.

His father couldn't touch him in school. He didn't even know that Johnny was doing better than his brothers and sisters had ever done, and he probably wouldn't have cared. But in school Johnny felt as good as the next kid, and sometimes better.

William Goodman maintained an ominous silence when he wasn't drunk. He brooded or slept half the day. Then he was gone again. Over time, his absences grew longer. He would disappear for weeks at a time, then turn up at the table for a bowl of mushroom barley soup with bacon and carrot baba, a queer dish that Johnny's mother insisted on making even though the kids thought it tasted strange, foreign. Maybe she thought good Lithuanian cooking would keep her husband coming back.

Other fathers Johnny knew went on binges, too. Other fathers sat in the corner of overheated kitchens and never said a word. At least on the surface, the Goodmans weren't all that different from the other immigrant families who lived cheek by jowl in his neighborhood. You just kept your mouth shut about the bad times, and you didn't stick your nose into other people's business.

On a warm June day when he was eleven years old, Johnny went wandering down the tracks and clear out of South Omaha. He was accompanied by his younger friend, Matt Zadalis. The boys passed out of the confines of the stockyards and slaughterhouses into the more genteel precincts of the Omaha Field Club. The golf course's rolling hills framed the roadbed, but they had only the haziest idea of what the men and women waving clubs were doing.

At four separate points, golfers had to cross the railroad tracks, but when Johnny and Matt saw a foursome sauntering across the roadbed, they didn't think much of it. For all they knew, every golf course in the world was split by a set of rails.

Then they saw the ball nestled outside the fence, right between the tracks. Johnny picked the thing up and brushed off the grit. It was smaller than a baseball, and it didn't have any stitching on its strangely slick surface. What was it made of?

On schedule, a steam locomotive whistled. Before they even saw the train, the boys could feel the tracks vibrating. They weren't frightened. They had half a minute to hop out of the way. Every kind of car flashed by. Boxcars, cattle cars, flatbeds, a dusty tanker.

Johnny flipped the ball a second time. There was something appealing about it, but he couldn't explain it. He wondered how high it would bounce.

Then a man appeared on the other side of the fence. He was wearing pants bunched below his knees. Knickers, they called them. Approaching, he offered an easy smile, but the boys were wary.

The closer the golfer came to the fence, the more the boys pulled away. They were suspicious. Adults were always telling you what to do.

Then the man made a proposal. He would give them a nickel in return for the ball. It sounded like a good deal, but the boys still had doubts. Maybe the man was trying to trick them into doing some chores. On the other hand, maybe he was on the level. Johnny wanted to see *Shark Monroe,* starring the movie cowboy William S. Hart. The four-reeler was playing downtown. Movies cost money.

To be safe, Johnny stepped back from the fence and made the man repeat the offer.

Finally, with an easy motion, Johnny tossed the ball over the fence. A moment later the coin came sailing down. Johnny snatched it out of the air.

Then the man told them something even more intriguing. For carrying a player's golf bag around the field, they could make fifty cents. The man called the job caddying.

You had to be eleven. Johnny was old enough, and Matt swore he was, too. Johnny could imagine his mother's face if he came home with fifty cents.

In a few days Johnny and Matt were looping at the Omaha Field Club. At first it wasn't easy. Johnny had to ask the other boys what to do, and more often than not they hooted at his ignorance. Once in a while, in a voice barely above a whisper, he questioned the stern caddiemaster about the names of the clubs. They all sounded funny. Niblick, mashie, spade mashie, midiron, brassie, spoon, driver, putter. Didn't you *dig* with a spade? Didn't *cars* putter?

He watched the players to see how high and far the balls hit with each club went, and how high and far each member could hit each specific club. By observing the other bag haulers, he learned where to stand — close enough to dispense the right club but far enough away to keep from catching the eye of a golfer in deep concentration over his ball.

During the first few weeks, he wondered if he would ever get the names of the clubs and the arcane rules straight in his head. Early on in Johnny's caddying education, one old man snarled at him for stepping on his line on the second green. What was a line? Johnny stared and stared at the green, unable to make the damn thing out. When the round ended, the old buzzard stiffed Johnny without a word. Johnny would have to find out what a line was or work for nothing.

The caddies called the cheap members snakes and the generous ones snags. A snake would always find fault; a snag would be free with his money even if you made one or two mistakes. Johnny learned to make himself scarce when a snake was looking for a caddie.

Every Sunday Johnny hauled bags around the carefully tended Field Club layout twice, but sometimes he showed up late because his mother made him attend Mass. He was a bright, eager boy, though, so the members didn't make a fuss. More often than not, caddies were devoted to worse pursuits.

Johnny and Matt didn't forget the five cents they made on the man's golf ball, either. Hunting lost balls became a fever. They found them in clumps of grass on the edges of railroad ties. They found them under scraggly bushes near the country club. They found them sunk in mud puddles and once in a while just sitting out there in plain sight like dimpled eggs. If one ball was worth a nickel, how much would ten, twenty, thirty get them? After three weeks, Johnny and Matt built up a huge hoard, one hundred balls on the nose.

They carried them in a gunnysack to the caddiemaster, who sent them to the pro, an avuncular man in tweeds who hoisted the bag of balls and tossed it behind the counter. They waited eagerly for the money to pour from his pocket, but instead he pulled a battered mashie — a five iron — out of a barrel.

The boys didn't know what to make of the thing, but they were sure they'd been cheated. The club had a scarred hickory shaft, and the clubface was studded with a pattern of small holes — the reason, they figured, that the man was throwing it away. In a shy voice, Johnny spoke up. Couldn't they get some money for the balls instead?

The caddiemaster gave them a severe look. Hadn't he given them a good golf club? What more did they want?

Disappointed, they retreated with their dubious prize in hand. Matt had secreted one cut ball in the pocket of his short pants. When they passed through the club's gates, he tossed it into the air.

The boys exchanged glances. There was a farm a couple of miles away. They'd be safer hitting the ball there. The cows wouldn't mind. Nervous excitement ran through the boys now. Maybe it hadn't been such a bad deal.

They slid under the farmer's fence and placed the ball on a tuft of grass. Johnny splayed his feet the way the toffs at the club did, but there was something wrong. The clubface was turned backward. The pro had slipped them damaged goods. Johnny took a mighty swing, but the ball dribbled away, never leaving the ground.

In silence the boys examined the mashie, turning it this way and that. Then Johnny had an idea. If the clubhead was screwed on backward, then he'd line up backward too. He reversed the position of his hands, placing the left below the right, and set himself up on the other side of the ball.

Now the clubface was aimed in the right direction. Could he swing left-handed, though? Why not? He knew a kid who threw righty and batted lefty. Johnny took a long backswing, swayed back, got up on his toes, and whaled one. Veering left in a screaming slice, the ball barely rose ten feet, but it did get up in the air. Now he was running after it, Matt whooping at his heels.

Soon they developed their own game. Whoever hit the ball farthest in an afternoon got to take the club home and practice with it. Years later spectators marveled when, blocked against a tree, Johnny Goodman would make a miraculous left-handed recovery, but Matt Zadalis knew how long Johnny had labored to perfect that swing.

2

I N 1 8 8 5 S O U T H O M A H A was incorporated "in response to a petition from concerned citizens who wrote, 'We are exposed without any protection against tramps and murderers — having no jail, no church, one school house . . . one saloon for every twenty inhabitants, one gambling house, two houses of ill-fame, one justice of the peace, one deputy sheriff, one post office, and no constable proper here.'" One of the deputy's instructions was to "run in obstreperous cowboys," according to the Omaha historian Neil Johnston.

By the late 1890s, a transformed South Omaha was home to booming stockyards and the country's largest meatpacking plant. Early town boosters floated the slogan "South Omaha: The Magic City," but reality got the upper hand. More often than not, local residents called their hometown "Porkopolis."

Omaha proper had similarly raucous beginnings. According to an 1870s Kansas City reporter, the Great Plains city was a roaring town, and more than a little bent: "It requires but little if any stretch of the imagination to regard Omaha as a very cesspool of iniquity . . . Mobs of monte men, pickpockets, brace faro dealers, criminal fugitives of every class find congenial companions in Omaha, and a comparative safe retreat from the officers of the law . . . If you want to find a rogue's rookery, go to Omaha."

At the same time, Omaha was led by canny and aggressive business leaders who helped make the city the Union Pacific Railroad's base of operations when the road was being built in the 1860s. Eventually, Omaha secured the Union Pacific terminal and a key bridge over the Missouri River. Droughts, economic busts, and plagues of insects came and went, but by the turn of the century, the city had transformed itself into the booming gateway to the West.

Omaha's industrialists took a hard line against unions, especially after packinghouse workers won pay increases in 1903. In 1909, when the streetcar workers tried to organize, the Omaha Traction Company imported strikebreakers to crush the union. The company's chief ally, the banker and promoter Gordon Wattles, the head of the Businessmen's Association, called his strikebreakers "a jolly lot of disreputables . . . always ready for a fight."

The public took the side of the fledgling Street and Electric Railway Employees Union, and when the cars manned by the armed strikebreakers rolled out of the barns, mobs destroyed a number of them. The company refused to negotiate, and when desperate workers started filtering back to their jobs a few weeks later, they were forced to sign yellow-dog contracts. The company had killed the union, but under the surface, in the car barns, in the packinghouses, on the railroads, and in the factories, a seething resentment against Omaha businessmen's hard-nosed tactics simmered for decades.

Central to Omaha's resurgence at the dawn of the twentieth century was the Trans-Mississippi and International Exposition, a Midwest "world's fair" engineered by a coalition of the city's businessmen and the failed presidential candidate William Jennings Bryan, who became a great booster of Omaha's potential as a trading center. The exhibitions drew huge crowds and stimulated Omaha's image as a commercial boomtown.

By design the exhibition did not reflect the lives of the western Nebraska sod house farmers or the meatpackers, who were crammed into cheap tract housing. Instead, it presented fantasy structures: a Venetian lagoon complete with gondoliers, plaster of Paris Renaissance buildings, copies of nude classical statues, nymphs, cupids, and an Indian warrior in an improbable chariot.

On the midway, better attended than the uplifting "white city," dancing girls performed in a "Streets of Cairo" fantasia, until the prudish city fathers shut it down.

In the gritty world of the real Omaha, professional women had been big business for years. At the turn of the century, four square blocks of the Third Ward known as the Arcade were devoted to wide-open prostitution. The women, scattered among the ramshackle houses and tarpaper shacks, paid two dollars per night for their "cribs." While 1911 legislation forced the more lavish houses to close, the oldest profession continued to thrive under the machine politician Tom Dennison, "the old Gray Wolf," who made a quiet alliance with Mayor James C. Dahlman.

Dennison, a former dancehall bouncer and professional gambler, summed up his philosophy this way: "Some people are good. Some people are bad. Laws can't change them. Laws that people don't believe in can't be enforced if whole armies tried it . . . People are always getting excited about little things, like minor lawbreaking and misdemeanors. Take gambling, for example. A dinky crap game or penny-ante poker causes a hell of a racket. But the stock market gambling was all right."

Johnny Goodman's South Omaha neighborhood was composed of one-and-a-half-story cottages and cheap rooming houses. Lured by employment in the stockyards and packinghouses, immigrants poured into the cramped dwellings. They came from Poland, Croatia, Czechoslovakia, Lithuania, Ireland, and Mexico. The Catholic Church encouraged the development of ethnic parishes so that immigrants would feel comfortable in their new country. The strategy also kept antagonistic groups apart to some extent. Ethnic societies and churches thrived as well.

Despite the breathing room that ethnic parishes provided the various immigrant groups, there were inevitable tensions. In 1909, a Greek resident killed an Omaha policeman, the newspapers fanned the flames of hatred, and the entire Greek community was driven out of town.

South Omahans divided themselves into ethnic enclaves: L Street was populated by Poles; on Q Street, Lithuanians clustered together; east of the Lithuanians, a large Irish community thrived. (Due to the purportedly primitive behavior of its inhabitants, the Irish neighborhood was dubbed Indian Hill.) The various nationalities gave birth to their own gangs, which jealously guarded their turf.

African Americans found their own portion of grief in Omaha. In 1919 a black man, an itinerant packinghouse worker named William Brown, was accused of assaulting a white woman, and a mob of five thousand men looted sporting goods stores and pawnshops for weapons and ammunition, then stormed the city jail.

In a heroic stand, the mayor, Edward Smith, blocked the mob's way and was almost lynched himself. Soon after, Brown was beaten unconscious, castrated, tied to the bumper of a car, and dragged through the streets. The rioters pumped hundreds of bullets into his body, then hung him from a light pole at Eighteenth and Harney Streets.

When Johnny Goodman's parents came to the United States after the turn of the century, they settled first in Pennsylvania, but by 1904 they had joined the small Lithuanian community in South Omaha. Only a few dozen strong, the Lithuanians founded their own church, St. Anthony's, at Thirty-second and S Streets. After World War I over eight hundred Lithuanian immigrants made their way to South Omaha, taking up residence around this house of worship. Boasting a band and a theatrical troupe, the Lithuanians clustered together in the South Omaha neighborhood called Golden Hill.

Johnny's early childhood was colored by his immigrant roots. Lithuanian was spoken at home. His father always made a point of reminding the family that the Goodmans were "good Lithuanian," not to be confused with Poles. After years under the Polish yoke, Lithuanian nationalism still burned bright in the New World.

A steady churchgoer, his mother, Rose, took him regularly to the Lithuanian church, which had its own distinct rituals — an Ash Wednesday with a Mardi Gras quality; Christmas featuring fortune-telling games; Easter distinguished by "verbos," reed-and-flower constructions carried in a procession to honor Christ's rising.

Two meatpacking plants, O'Neill's and Rothchild's, did a strong business a few blocks from Johnny's door. Defiant South Omahans liked to joke that late at night, if you were stinking drunk, you could always smell your way home. Residents got used to the some-times rancid, sometimes sickly sweet odor, but outsiders were al-ways struck by the atmosphere, thick with the stink of animals being slaughtered by the thousands.

Johnny played in the streets like the rest of the boys. They ran up to Crispey Park or Farmers Hill. On vacant lots they played sandlot baseball or kittenball, Omaha's version of softball. Another juvenile pastime involved tossing washers into tin cans. South Omaha didn't offer a wealth of diversions.

When the boys were bored, there were more exciting places to ex-plore. They could peek into the taverns that choked Q Street near the packinghouses. Ethnic bars ran card games; over at the Dock-yard Exchange Building, dice was king. A kid could get an eyeful in the Gully, the red-light district where women very different from their mothers lounged in doorways and made enticing offers to boys just out of short pants.

Overall, however, the parish system worked well. Immigrants dis-oriented by a strange new country found comfort within their eth-nic enclaves. Despite the predictable frictions, South Omaha also had a more peaceful, day-to-day reality. Remembering the city years later, many South Omahans spoke about a safe, warm environment of extended families and hard-working mothers and fathers.

Bob Astleford, eight-time Nebraska Amateur golf champion, grew up in South Omaha during the Depression. Despite the hard times, Astleford didn't feel particularly deprived. Instead, he later re-called a South Omaha where everyone struggled through the same difficult times. "Everybody was kind of in the same boat, and everybody pulled for each other as best they could with what they had. Life was tough, but it seemed to be in some way easier. I re-member very well hauling coal from the street in chunks. You just did things. That's all."

Johnny Goodman's father and older brothers made their way into the packinghouses every day. In a world bounded by penned cows, sheep, and hogs on one side and slaughterhouses on the other, Johnny had little prospect of escaping a similar existence.

One of his father's drinking buddies, also a meat cutter, was missing the tip of his finger. The purplish wound had been tied up like the end of a sausage. Johnny heard jokes about meatpackers falling into boiling vats of acid. The men worked long shifts and returned home bone tired. They were out of work and out of sorts for weeks and months on end. A bright and observant boy could not help but recoil at the thought of filing through the packinghouse doors himself one day.

The Omaha Field Club must have seemed like a glorious oasis to Johnny Goodman. The city's most distinguished and affluent citizens drifted in and out of the lavish clubhouse. Johnny also caught glimpses of holiday festivities, charity affairs, and tea parties for women who flounced around in the latest fashions. Among themselves, the caddies gossiped about the faster, younger women who sneaked a smoke or had a taste for strong spirits or didn't mind flashing an ankle.

The caddies loved to watch the parade of automobiles that rolled up the Field Club driveway, a prewar Stanley Steamer, a Detroit Electric, and several rickety Hupmobiles among them. Some boys swore by the Stearns Knight, whose sleeve-valve engine ran quiet and fast.

Almost immediately after becoming a caddie, Goodman developed a deep fascination for golf. After learning the names of the clubs and the rules of the game, he studied the slopes and grains of the Field Club's greens. He became expert at discerning a putt's break and speed, and which pin placements held hidden dangers for the unsuspecting golfer. He learned to get down on his knees and shape sand tees just right, and to ferret out lost balls in the tall grass. Within a year he became the preferred bag-toter of accomplished golfers like perennial state champ Sam Reynolds. Goodman also caddied for the Field Club's talented women golfers, Mrs. Mark Levings and Mrs. Russell Fowles. They were charmed by his energy and enthusiasm and — although he was shy, especially with fashionable, well-heeled adults — by his infectious grin.

It was nice to get praise from his teachers, but he knew he'd never be tops in the classroom. At the Field Club, he stood out. He didn't say much at home about how well he was doing there, but secretly, he flushed with pride every time he was singled out to carry Sam Reynolds's bag. At the golf course, nobody knew about his old man's latest rampage, or how many times he'd had to eat potatoes for supper. Clearly, Johnny had found a safe haven at the Field Club.

On a late autumn afternoon in 1922 a chauffeured Cadillac touring car ground its way up the club's driveway. It featured a leather-covered visor and nickel-plated headlights. For this new model, the manufacturer had tucked the horn away beneath the aluminum hood.

A man in a fawn-colored coat stepped out, grinding the gravel under his handcrafted cordovan shoes. About five feet ten inches tall, and weighing no more than 175 pounds, he was not a physically dominating presence, but he carried himself with the air of someone who expected to be recognized. His name was Walter Hagen, and at twenty-nine years of age, he had just captured the British Open crown.

On his return to the United States, Hagen — dubbed Sir Walter by the American press — planned to enjoy himself, but he needed his usual fuel to light up the party. To get around Prohibition, "the Haig," as he was also known, had secreted a magnum of champagne in the British Open's revered trophy, the Claret Jug, and had enlisted the industrialist L. A. Young, a fervent teetotaler, to smuggle it into the States for him.

With Young's help, Hagen had been sufficiently oiled to enjoy the festivities celebrating his Open win, a parade along Broadway to New York's City Hall. Only President Harding, another hard-drinking golfer, was missing from the welcome-home-Hagen affair at the 650-acre Westchester-Biltmore Country Club.

In the early 1920s, the Professional Golf Association sanctioned all of seven tournaments, and the pickings were decidedly slim. As far as golf's eastern establishment was concerned, the professional game was a cheap carnival and its practitioners a sideshow attraction. More significantly, the golfing professionals' leading lights had decidedly suspect origins. Hagen's father had begun as a blacksmith. Gene Sarazen, born Eugene Saraceni, was the son of an immigrant carpenter. Mike "King" Brady sprang from a blue-collar Boston family. Far too many golf pros had learned their trade as caddies.

The best way for a professional to make money was to barnstorm, which usually meant following a brutal regimen of one-day stands at every far-flung course that could scare up a gallery at one dollar per head. Two bucks on weekends. Immediately after his British Open victory, Hagen arranged an exhibition tour with the Australian professional and trick-shot artist Joe Kirkwood. Sir Walter's original plans were typically grandiose. The two men would demonstrate their gifts on every continent. Hagen meant to cash in.

His first stroke of genius involved hiring the Associated Press sportswriter Bob Harlow to act as press agent. The cool-headed Harlow talked Hagen out of trying to straddle the globe, reducing the barnstorming itinerary to a swing through North America.

When Hagen appeared at the Omaha Field Club, he offered his usual endorsement of the layout, the same one he repeated at every track west of Garden City, New York. "Sporty little course you got here," the Haig opined. He made only one request of the Field Club's caddiemaster: "Gimme the best boy in the shop."

The barefoot bag-haulers crowded around the caddiemaster, imploring him to choose one of them to carry Sir Walter's clubs. Johnny positioned himself off to the side, where he could be seen. Many of the boys were older and taller than he was, and he didn't want to get lost in the crowd. His expression didn't reveal a trace of need, but inside, he was pleading his case as hard as the next kid. If you showed how much you cared, though, you'd have to admit how much it hurt if you were passed over.

The caddiemaster didn't hesitate. He sent Johnny Goodman out to manage Walter Hagen's bag.

3

WHEN JOHNNY PEEKED out of the caddieshack, he saw a man with a nut-brown face, a high forehead, and a rounded dome of a head. Pasted to his skull, Walter Hagen's jet-black hair glistened with pomade. He wore a pale blue cashmere sweater, a white silk shirt, a pigeon's blood tie, and black-and-white golf shoes. The Haig was ready to shoot some golf.

Johnny watched, fascinated, as Sir Walter opened a small packet, extracted a red wooden peg, and stuck it behind his ear.

"You the kid?" he asked.

Elated but speechless, Johnny nodded. He feared he wouldn't be able to cough up a single word.

"Well, let's shove off." Hagen nodded toward his boat of a golf bag. The hand-rubbed leather affair was monogrammed in silver.

It was late October, and a cutting breeze rattled the dun-colored leaves. Walter Hagen strode, shoulders back, chin up, exuding confidence in the icy air. He'd grown up in Rochester, New York, and he knew something about bitter-cold winds.

Johnny seized the bag, staggered a bit, and followed Hagen to the first tee. Over two hundred people were gathered there, quietly jostling one another for a better look at the great man. Smiling and shaking hands, Hagen made his way through the gallery. Waiting for the Haig were Joe Kirkwood, his partner; Sam Reynolds, the Field Club's ace; and Blaine Young, a former Nebraska State Amateur winner.

Johnny handed Hagen his driver and got down on his hands and knees to form a sand tee.

"No need, sonny," Sir Walter instructed, producing the wooden peg from behind his ear. "In my hand is a new item, the Reddy Tee. You just stick it in the ground and balance the ball. Like so."

Hagen proceeded to perform the hitherto-unknown procedure. "Then you give it a good whack."

Feet splayed, shoulders slumped, Hagen took his stance. Then, swaying back, he made a full-shoulder turn, lunged forward a bit, and unwound, knocking the ball low and dead straight down the fairway. "That'll do," he commented. "Now, this Reddy Tee is the latest innovation in the golf field, and I am certain that sand tees will soon become obsolete."

Listening to this pitch, anyone who knew Walter Hagen would have assumed that he was making a paid announcement. And he was, for a dentist named William Lowell. After his invention had failed to catch on, Lowell had given Hagen fifteen hundred dollars to flog the new product.

Magnanimously, Hagen handed his caddie one of the shiny pegs. Johnny carefully hid it away in his overalls.

Omaha was an important stop on Hagen's extensive 1922 barnstorming tour. Sir Walter needed every dime he could make to support his lavish tastes. Most professionals scraped out a living as hired hands at country clubs, but Hagen had spurned such servitude. Tournament purses being pitiful, he was forced to live by his wits alone. This arrangement suited Sir Walter's temperament perfectly, but he also knew how precarious his situation was. "Pro golf is a parasitical business," he once remarked, "and they can do without us." Of course, against all odds, Hagen aimed to become indispensable.

Hagen played the game to the hilt. To keep his Cadillac touring car in tiptop shape, to pay his chauffeur, to guarantee a supply of bonded whiskey, and to satisfy the whims of various "nice numbers" he entertained in various roadhouses, he had chosen to barnstorm rather than defend his PGA title. This decision had angered his fellow professionals, not to speak of the tournament's promoters, who paid dearly at the gate for Sir Walter's defection, but for Hagen it was sound business. There was more money to be had beating the bushes in Nebraska and California than in winning one more PGA championship.

Hagen's refusal to defend his crown also solidified the professional game's low reputation. Even its top star didn't respect its most important prize. Walter Hagen may have been the 1922 British Open champion, but to the USGA's Executive Committee, he was nothing but a mercenary.

Amateur golf was still regarded as the higher calling. Amateurs played for love, after all; professionals bore the stigma of commerce. Better still, amateurs were, almost to a man, members of the white Anglo-Saxon upper class. Jerry Travers, Bob Gardner, Max Marston, Jess Sweetser, George Dunlap, and Charlie Seaver, among many others, had the luxury of taking up golf in their early years. They were instructed by the finest teachers and had all the leisure in the world to hone their skills.

Not only did the well-off and well-born hold neoaristocratic views about the superiority of amateur golfers. Ironically, so did the mass media, which would demonstrate its allegiance to the simon-pure practitioners all through the 1920s in a torrent of articles, radio programs, and newsreels extolling that most unblemished of amateurs, Robert Tyre Jones Jr., who would soon dominate amateurs and professionals alike.

Sir Walter had heard it all, and he couldn't have cared less. The USGA's social secretary wasn't about to pick up his bar tab or the price of his snow-white pleated slacks. After Omaha it was on to Kansas City, and when the chill settled down on the prairie states, he and Kirkwood were slated to roll through sunny California, where the pickings were said to be fine.

As a seven-year-old caddie, Walter Hagen had been mesmerized by the grand affairs taking place at the Rochester Country Club. From a distance, he had watched the parade of well-dressed gentlemen and their wives as they made their stately way up the hill to their exclusive affairs. He longed to get closer, to see exactly what went on inside the grand clubhouse, but he knew it was forbidden territory. As he grew, the longing became more intense.

Hagen was "the best boy in the shop" at the Rochester Country Club. The most accomplished players chose him to carry their bags, and while watching how they stroked their brassies and spade mashies, Walter conceived a passion for the game. As he practiced and improved, members took notice and gave him special privileges. While the other caddies were barred from using the facilities, Hagen's well-placed admirers allowed the youngster to play some holes at odd hours. When school was out, Walter would slip onto the course early and race through a round, then spend long mornings and afternoons looping. Before sunset, he'd fit in a few more holes for himself.

Although he was a talented baseball player who could hit and pitch equally well right-handed and left-handed, Hagen was more fascinated by golf. By the seventh grade, he found it extremely difficult to sit still in class, especially considering the alluring view. As Hagen recalled, he found himself "looking out the window, feeling the nice warm air and sunshine on my face. I could see the golfers on the course at the Country Club of Rochester. Suddenly I could take it no longer. When Mrs. Cullen, the teacher, wasn't looking I jumped out the window. I never went back to school regularly after that."

Having shrugged off the dusty schoolroom, Hagen threw himself into the world of golf. He was free to work at the game he loved, but he was also free to exercise his restless intelligence and sharp eye.

While caddying during a club championship playoff, Hagen was instructed to commit an act forbidden to every other caddie. He was sent to the clubhouse to ferry back a round of drinks. As Hagen recounted, "The playoff was most important to me because it gave me the unusual opportunity of seeing inside the beautiful and exclusive clubhouse of the Country Club of Rochester. No other caddie had been able to wrangle that!"

It was the first time Hagen had penetrated the citadel on the hill, and it only whetted his appetite. Yet, even after he rose to the rank of assistant professional, his home course denied him the dining room, the bar, and the locker room, where members changed into their golfing togs. In Scotland and England, golf professionals had long been classified as "the help," members of the serving class, and in America, the tradition lived on.

Hagen's brief stint as head pro at the Owesco Country Club in Auburn, New York, tells a similar tale. Not only did he give lessons and run the pro shop, he also acted as greenskeeper, bartender, and club manager. His day began before dawn and didn't wind down until eleven at night.

Although the twenty-one-year-old professional was greeted warmly by his home course backers after he won the U.S. Open in 1914, he soon had to get back to his usual routine, "with little more panache than a factory hand punching a time clock in the morning," as the Rochester newspaperman Henry Clune put it. "His brief vacation was over; he went back to instructing club members in the niceties of the game in which he had won supreme honors."

Hagen had to make a living, but he didn't accept his position without a prickly awareness that he deserved better.

In 1919 Hagen snared the U.S. Open title for the second time, and when he invaded England for the 1920 British Open at Deal in Sandwich, he expected respectful treatment. Strolling into the clubhouse with Long Jim Barnes, one of the leading American professionals, Hagen's progress was halted by the distraught locker steward, who directed them to the narrow confines of the pro shop, the only place they would be allowed to change.

Hagen decided to strike back. On the first day of the tournament, he glided up to the clubhouse door in a chauffeur-driven Daimler limousine. As he was barred from eating lunch in the clubhouse — the professionals were supposed to take their nourishment in a makeshift tent — Sir Walter had pheasant under glass delivered to the back seat of his luxurious automobile, where he ate and drank with ostentatious relish.

An absolutely miserable performance at Deal did not humble Hagen in the least. He headed for the continent, his sights set on the French Open, taking place at La Boulie near Versailles. There Hagen and the English professionals Abe Mitchell and George Duncan were directed to use an active stable as their locker room. "The vile odor and the hundreds of flies swarming about added to the disgust I felt," Hagen recalled.

The British players "were long accustomed to acceptance of the rigid ruling, which barred pros from using, or even entering, the clubhouse of the famed old British golf courses. But we had a meeting, and they agreed with me that it was an impossible situation," the Haig concluded.

After Sir Walter threatened to withdraw, and take Mitchell and Duncan with him, the club manager acceded to their wishes. For the first time in French history, golf professionals entered the grand clubhouse and locker room, where they were allowed to change their clothes in peace and comfort.

For good measure, Hagen beat the Frenchman Eugene Lafitte in a playoff, and walked away with the 1920 French Open crown. At the reception, Sir Walter appeared resplendent in white tie and tails.

As preparations for the 1920 U.S. Open at Inverness, in Toledo, Ohio, progressed, USGA and Inverness officials fretted that Hagen would repeat the flamboyant protest he had staged at Deal. At first they considered making an exception for the reigning U.S. Open champion, but they didn't think Hagen would leave the rest of the professionals out in the cold. Finally, resigned, they chose the path of least resistance and flung the door to the clubhouse open wide.

Walter Hagen did not win the 1920 U.S. Open. Instead, Harry Vardon's sidekick, the pipe-smoking English basher Ted Ray, fought off Leo Diegel and Jock Hutchinson for the title. After the tournament ended, however, Hagen's fellow pros presented him with an eight-foot-tall cathedral-style chime clock. With Sir Walter leading the way, they marched into the Inverness clubhouse, where the Haig, planting the clock in a prominent place in the foyer, pointedly recited the lines inscribed on the timepiece.

> God measures men by what they are
> Not what in wealth possess
> The vibrant message chimes afar
> The voice of Inverness

Hagen kept up his assault at Royal St. George in 1922. Before the British Open, he was asked why American golfers were threatening to dethrone their British counterparts. "First, we have more tournaments at home. There's no substitute for competition," Hagen replied. "Secondly, and perhaps more important, in America the golf professional . . . is respected far more than he is over here. He is encouraged to rise in the social as well as the financial scale."

Compared with the rigid class barriers in England, American strictures against professionals may have seemed more flexible to Sir Walter. More likely, he was playing to the American press, which liked a good jab at John Bull.

Hagen's first priority was to rectify the miserable impression he had left behind in the 1920 British Open at Deal. For two years he had worked hard on hitting the ball under the wind, the key to mastering the gusty British courses. To keep his tee shots low, he had picked up a pair of straight-faced drivers. Bernard Darwin observed how Sir Walter "had shortened his swing," which helped him hit the low runners so necessary on British links. "As a patriotic Briton I do not at all like the look of him," Darwin added. Darwin's fears were well-grounded.

Having mastered the strong and capricious British winds, Hagen showed he could survive a downpour, too, turning in a brilliant final-round 70 in the rain to beat Jock Hutchinson by two shots. After his victory speech, he turned over his five-hundred-dollar check to his caddie, Hargreaves. His gracious acceptance speech was well received, but his largesse offended the British, many of whom thought five hundred dollars was more than a simple caddie could handle. Other English observers wondered aloud whether Hagen was simply violating good taste by turning his back on their generous prize money. Even when he was on his best behavior, Sir Walter seemed to be thumbing his nose at the English gentry.

Like many of Hagen's egalitarian gestures, this one was both sincere and shrewd. He genuinely liked his caddie, Hargreaves, who had made such meticulous notes for him on the British courses, and he felt nostalgic about his bag-toting days. But the publicity he gained from his generosity was more than worth the modest British Open check.

Hagen knew the American papers would love him more now, and

the real cash was in barnstorming tours. Poking a finger in John Bull's eye could only drive up attendance in the American hinterlands.

Johnny Goodman observed carefully as Hagen took his wide stance, set his strong grip, and lashed away, swaying on every tee shot. Somehow, Hagen managed to hit his drives in the fairway, most a full 250 yards. Johnny also noticed how Sir Walter placed — or attempted to place — every iron at a given spot.

Several times Hagen let loose with wild midirons that put him in the soup, though, and Reynolds even outdrove him twice. Johnny couldn't understand why Hagen looked so ordinary sometimes. He'd expected the great man to walk — or at least golf — on water. On the other hand, the Rochester native was producing one birdie after another with his unerring putting. Long ones, short ones, uphill, sidehill. It didn't seem to matter. Sir Walter would grasp the line with a quick once-over and give it a ride. More often than not the ball rattled into the cup.

"How far from that bush?" Hagen asked Johnny on one hole.

"I'm not sure," Goodman replied uncertainly. The blood rushed to his face.

"You gotta know how far, kid," Hagen said, but there was no malevolence in his tone. Smiling, he added, "I'd say it's 122."

Not 120, or 125. The way Hagen put it stuck in Johnny's mind. So did Sir Walter's short iron, which shot straight as a string to the pin, bit, and, the steam taken out of it, trickled to the hole, one foot away. He noticed that with a niblick in his hand, Walter Hagen did not sway one-quarter of an inch.

Soon Sam Reynolds, the cream of Omaha's golfing elite, was in a deep hole. Blaine Young was coming apart at the seams. Dimly, Johnny noticed that Joe Kirkwood was scoring a few birdies of his own, but no one seemed to dominate the Field Club layout like Hagen. His game didn't look spectacular, but his results were. He made birdies with a casual air, but he made them in bunches.

"You broke the course record," Reynolds informed Hagen as they walked off the eighteenth. "Sixty-seven."

"You don't say," Sir Walter replied.

Before long, dollar bills were changing hands, but Hagen immediately offered to stand his victims to drinks in the clubhouse. The Omaha Field Club wasn't about to deny its facilities to golfing royalty, professional or otherwise. Before setting off on this all-important mission, Sir Walter dug into his pocket, glanced down at the coins he'd fished out, and tossed several quarters to Johnny, who snatched them out of the air.

Johnny got up his courage. "What does it take to be a great golfer, Mr. Hagen?" Hagen laughed, patted him on the head, and then headed toward the clubhouse bar.

Johnny Goodman had a stubborn streak. Hagen would have a few drinks and head for his touring car, he figured. He decided to wait him out and ask his question a second time.

While squatting near the clubhouse, Johnny noticed a commotion off the first tee. Another crowd was gathering, bigger than the gallery that had followed Hagen around the course. Johnny wandered over and squirmed to the front, where he recognized Hagen's playing partner, Joe Kirkwood, a black-haired, handsome man who was swinging two golf clubs, one in each hand.

"Now, watch carefully, ladies and gentlemen, and you will see two shots, struck simul-tan-e-ously, two shots which will trace the same arc and come down within yards of each other."

In quick succession, Kirkwood struck the golf balls, with one hand, then the other, each shot acting precisely as he'd predicted, sailing high and descending one hundred yards away, almost in the same spot. Before Johnny could absorb this feat, the trick-shot artist was on to something else.

"Do I have a watch face? Any nice crystal will do." A brave soul offered up his watch and Kirkwood proceeded to clip a mashie right off the glass, without leaving a scratch.

The crowd burst into spontaneous applause.

Johnny was transfixed. Walter Hagen had performed a more subtle form of magic on the golf course, but Joe Kirkwood was a sorcerer.

"Nice trick, but it ain't golf," an older Field Club member observed.

"They're like trained seals," his companion agreed. Johnny knew this man, a generous tipper.

The remarks made Johnny think. Kirkwood's act was swell, but did hitting a ball off a watch face mean he could get it into the hole any better?

Watching Joe Kirkwood was fun, but Johnny hadn't forgotten that Walter Hagen had won two U.S. Opens, and the British Open to boot. Kirkwood continued making golf balls dance, but Johnny kept half an eye on the clubhouse and Walter Hagen's roadster.

Hagen was a swell guy — hadn't he given his check to that caddie in England? He might answer one or two questions.

For another half-hour, the chauffeur lounged in the front seat, smoking a Turkish cigarette. Finally, Sir Walter emerged under the porte-cochère and wove his way, faintly unsteady, to his gleaming automobile.

Johnny knew that walk. When his father came home weaving like that, it always meant trouble. But Walter Hagen didn't seem to have a mean bone in his body. He wasn't nasty like the old man. Johnny approached him, diffident but determined.

"Mr. Hagen, can I ask you something?"

"Sure, what is it, kid?"

"What's it take to be a great golfer?"

Hagen paused and looked down at the earnest boy. "Well, when you hit it in the cabbage, just keep on smiling," the Haig said with a laugh. It was a line he'd repeated, with small variations, a thousand times.

The chauffeur raced around to the passenger side, flung open the door, and Sir Walter tumbled into the dark, padded interior. As Hagen's Cadillac rumbled away, Johnny puzzled over the great man's gnomic pronouncement. Finally, he translated Sir Walter's remark into his own terms. If you get in Dutch, don't worry. Just stay in there and keep on pitching. Maybe that was the secret.

After meeting Walter Hagen, Johnny Goodman began taking golf more seriously, working on his game by slipping onto the Field Club fairways just after dawn, or just before twilight, always fearful he would be caught violating the club's strictures against caddies setting foot on the course except for Monday afternoons. After he and Matt picked up a few discarded clubs, they practiced hitting balls in fields and rough lots in their neighborhood, too.

Of course, like every other caddie who ever picked up golf on the side, Goodman never took formal lessons, but when he wanted to know something about the proper grip or how to refine his swing, he overcame his shyness and asked the best players in the club. Mary Levings was free with advice, and Sam Reynolds, too.

Stanley Davies, the big Scottish pro with the hound-dog face, was struck by how penetrating Johnny's questions were, and how carefully he observed the technical aspects of the game. Davies had a marvelous pedigree, having studied club-making under J. H. Taylor, a member of the great British triumvirate that included Harry Vardon and James Braid. At nineteen he borrowed money to make his passage to America and quickly found a home at the Field Club. Davies couldn't help offering a couple of tips to the kid, whose grave expression amused him.

Goodman had soon adopted the Vardon grip Davies recommended. It felt funny at first. Wouldn't it be easier to hold the club like a baseball bat? Davies also told him to keep his left arm straight when he drew the club back, but that felt worse than the grip. The stiff left arm seemed to restrict how far he could take the club back, but he kept at it stubbornly until it felt natural. Davies said a crooked left arm hit the ball crooked.

More often than not, Davies was too busy to answer questions. Johnny knew that he shouldn't pester the pro, so he took to watching Davies's swing instead. Johnny didn't know the word *tempo*, but he noticed that Davies seemed to swing at the same speed with every club, and without strain. And he played fast, hit-and-march golf.

Forced to learn through observation, Johnny came to his insights slowly, through painstaking trial and error. He collected old, gouged-out balls and performed experiments. What happened if you played the ball forward? Back? How about an open stance? Closed? He liked fooling around with shots, and hitting balls put him in a pleasant trance. When an experiment worked, and he struck a soaring mashie, or a stone-solid brassie in some secluded field, the pleasure was all the more deep for being hard-won.

Mastering technique was one thing, but then there was the sheer thrill of hitting a fine shot. Johnny Goodman was a bright, analytical boy, but he was also a kid discovering an exciting game. Hitting golf ball after golf ball was no mechanical task: it was exploration, tension, and release, a physical pleasure that created the need for one more pure hit, and another still.

Johnny hit golf balls, chased after them, and hit them again. Practice became its own reward. Before Ben Hogan "found it in the dirt," Johnny Goodman was scratching his own patch of ground.

Over time, Johnny developed a swing that would repeat and withstand the pressures of tournament play. Often it was described, somewhat condescendingly, as a "caddie's swing," implying a short, stabbing motion lacking in grace. In fact, his was a highly athletic stroke, as long and fluid as any modern swing. If it lacked the loops and dips of early-era golf swings, so much the better.

His setup was pure geometry. Standing ramrod straight, he bent from the hip, forming a perfect angle to allow his arms to swing freely. With his weight on his toes at address, he extended farther from the ball than Bobby Jones, feeling he could swing the club more freely that way. Goodman favored a one-piece takeaway; he did not pick the club up with his wrists. He employed the tremendous hip turn common for his time, and a powerful shoulder turn coming through the ball.

Perhaps because he was self-taught, he hit the ball in a slightly unorthodox fashion. Contemporary observers believed that he actually caught the ball at the last possible second, on the upswing. More likely, he didn't hit down at the usual angle but rather made contact just as his swing bottomed out.

Goodman's accuracy was built on a left side as solid and unmoving as a stone pillar. At impact, his left leg did not give a fraction of an inch.

Johnny was a confirmed hooker early in his career — he compensated by sending his drives far right and curving them back into the fairway — but over time he began fanning open his clubface while taking it back, eventually trading in the right-to-left trajectory for a slight fade. In a sense, his development foreshadowed Ben Hogan's early struggles with the duck hook, and his eventual movement toward the power fade.

Like Walter Hagen, Goodman's trump card became the short iron from one hundred yards, which he hit with tremendous consistency and accuracy. In fact, he could strike this shot so straight so often, a myth grew up around Omaha that on his walks to the Field Club he practiced hitting balls all along the Union Pacific tracks, aiming to keep every shot between the rails. It may as well have been true.

4

OBBY JONES WAS HARDLY an aristocrat, but he came from a well-to-do family whose roots were deep in colonial Georgia's soil. In the aftermath of the Civil War, his grandfather, the original Robert Tyre Jones, ran his father's modest farm near Covington and clerked at his cousin's general store. R.T. was a huge man, six feet five and 230 pounds, and a pious one as well. He took his religion seriously enough to be baptized twice, first as a Presbyterian when he was seventeen, and then seven years later as a Baptist.

Hardscrabble Reconstruction times shaped R.T.'s business values, which were every bit as severe as his views of earthly delights. Although he farmed during the day and worked at his cousin's store when he could make the time, he also burned the midnight oil resoling his neighbors' shoes.

A married man at thirty, he moved to Canton, Georgia, with his wife, Susan, and immediately invested his life's savings of five hundred dollars in a general store of his own, which he named the Jones Mercantile Exchange. The business prospered, and R.T. helped found the Bank of Canton, and in 1899 the Canton Textile Mills. In time he became one of the richest men in the county.

R.T. was convinced that business success and Christian piety were intertwined. In an article he wrote for the local paper, the *Cherokee Advance*, titled "Christianity as Related to Business," he laid out his creed. "There is no question in my mind but that the scriptures plainly teach that if, when we as Christians enter into any line of commendable business . . . we do so with a view first of service to our Lord that He will enter into that business with us. For a business to succeed . . . Christianity should be the dominating power."

R.T. did not drink, smoke, or chase women. In fact, he refused to take a single sip of that seductive new drink, Coca-Cola. He had little tolerance for frivolous pursuits like dancing, parties, or games. Wasting time chasing a ball around violated his Bible-based moral code.

His son, Robert Permedus, Bobby Jones's father, developed different leanings. From R.T.'s perspective, Robert had a suspicious taste for sticks and balls. In fact, the young man was revealing quite a talent for baseball. When Robert voiced ambitions to join the Brooklyn Dodgers, his father barred the way. And when a knowledgeable baseball man praised Robert's ball-playing talents, his father snapped, "You could not pay him a poorer compliment."

Evidently, R.T. threatened to disown his son if he pursued his dream of making it in the big leagues, and though Robert bent to his father's will, attending university and eventually obtaining a law degree, his personality could not have been more different from his father's.

The ebullient Robert did not openly break relations with R.T., but his very character repudiated his father's implacable fire and brimstone. R.T.'s son told jokes, played games, liked a friendly drink or two, and, as his son Bobby remarked, was "an expert at profanity."

Robert married a delicate beauty named Clara Thomas. Five feet tall, she weighed no more than ninety pounds, but she was strong-willed, a trait her confident new husband found appealing. After the couple's firstborn son, William, died at three months of age, and she became pregnant a second time, she prevailed on Robert to move the family to Atlanta. In the hub of the New South, the young lawyer quickly found work defending the Coca-Cola Company's patents, but initially his one-man operation yielded no more than a middle-class income. Robert had a talent for making useful friends, however, especially at the Atlanta Athletic Club, chief among them George Adair, later a power at the East Lake Country Club.

Robert's intelligence and gracious manner helped him make his way into Atlanta's power structure. Eventually he would become an intimate of Coca-Cola's owners, as well as representing some of Atlanta's wealthiest and most influential families.

On March 17, 1902, Clara gave birth to Robert Tyre Jones Jr., a sickly child they named after his more-robust grandfather. In biographer O. B. Keeler's description, Bobby was "an almost shockingly spindling youngster with an oversize head and legs with staring knees. Few youngsters at the romper age have less resembled, without actually being malformed, a future athletic champion."

Afflicted with a digestive illness, Bobby couldn't hold down solid food until the age of five. Big Bob Jones opened his wallet to a succession of doctors, whose least harmful suggestion involved "a diet of egg whites."

Every summer the family escaped Atlanta to a house across from the East Lake Country Club, five miles out of town. In 1908 Tom Bendelow carved out the club's original golf course on the site of a former amusement park, which had featured a beach, hot dogs, popcorn, and a peep show of the 1889 Paris World's Fair and its bloomer-flashing bathing beauties. Built around the sparkling East Lake, the course was surrounded by a dense forest of loblolly and Virginia pine, and white and red oak with a generous sprinkling of dogwood.

The Old Course had its peculiarities. Only two par threes offered relief to the weary golfer, who otherwise faced a fifteen-hole stretch of par fours and par fives in his journey around East Lake's often steep terrain.

Donald Ross redesigned the layout in 1913, developing a new routing plan and adding variety to the somewhat monotonous Old Course. His imaginative renovations, which reflected European influences, turned East Lake into a championship course. (In the 1920s Ross would earn greater celebrity when he created a private nine-hole course on Douglas Fairbanks and Mary Pickford's estate.)

Having suffered under R.T.'s ascetic regimen, Robert became an indulgent parent. Naturally, he was not averse to his own son perfecting the frivolous pursuit of golf. Here was a father a boy could love.

Some of Bobby Jones's earliest memories involved watching foursomes toddle past his house. When he was seven years old he asked his lawyer father, "Dad, what do people do on Sunday that don't play golf?" In the Jones household, golf seems to have superceded theological concerns.

The athletic Big Bob took up the game and turned into quite a golfer himself. If not pious, Big Bob's approach to the game was certainly serious. As Bobby, with typical dry humor, put it, "I shudder to think of the artistic profanity with which my father would respond to your calling him a duffer." His petite mother adopted golf, too, and became quite adept.

Although Bobby never took formal lessons, he followed the club pro, Stewart Maiden, of Carnoustie, Scotland, everywhere.

From O. B. Keeler's perspective, Bobby couldn't have had a better model. "Stewart Maiden's conversational style was always monosyllabic — but his golfing style was as fine as ever came out of Scotland." As Jones explained his entry into the sport, in *Golf Is My Game,* "There was nothing very conscious or contrived about the whole procedure. The game was there, I liked it, and I kept on playing."

In fact, Jones was a gifted mimic. To entertain his friends, Big Bob often called on his son to imitate the swings of various club members, which Little Bob would proceed to do with hilarious accuracy. Not only did Bobby love the game for its own sake, he discovered that swinging a golf club in a certain way elicited a river of praise. If he was a bit of a showoff, there was no harm done. Performing before an audience seemed as natural as the confidence that flowed through him every time he waved his sawed-off golf club through the air.

Wisely, though, Bobby spent most of his time simulating the club's sweetest stroke, Stewart Maiden's. Bobby adopted Maiden's simple takeaway and equally simple, unhurried downswing, but slowly his swing became all his own. From a narrow stance he made a full hip turn, a long, relaxed backswing and then a strong move forward with the lower body. Always in perfect balance, he finished his follow-through with his hands held high and the club pointing down to the ground. As one observer put it, Jones moved "up and down instead of to and fro" like the lunging Walter Hagen. Overall,

Bobby's swing had a "drowsy rhythm," as Bernard Darwin put it, a languid quality that veiled great resources of power. Depicting Jones's swing, the sportswriter Grantland Rice wrote: "One might as well attempt to describe the smoothness of the wind as to paint a clear picture of his complete swing."

Play was at the center of Jones's golden childhood. His father encouraged him to try baseball, tennis, and fishing, but golf held a special fascination for the boy from the beginning. For Bobby Jones, love of the game preceded ambition. That his demonstrative father enjoyed golf so much was all — or mostly — to the good. Big Bob's admiration and support gave his son an inherent belief in himself and his talent.

To Bobby, loving his father and loving golf were barely distinguishable. On the one hand, the boy's emotional attachment to the game couldn't have developed in more fertile soil. However, growing up as an instrument of his father's thwarted athletic ambitions translated into internal pressures he could not understand. Bobby soon found failure intolerable. Easily frustrated, he would burst into sudden rages.

"I do not recall the first time I hit a golf ball . . . The game did not make much of an impression on me except that I used to get mad enough to dance in the road when a wild shot went under a little bridge covered with briars."

Jones always had a charming way of putting things, and his affectionate recollections of a sunny childhood on the links have the ring of truth, but golf meant too much to Big Bob, and Bobby learned the lesson only too well.

When he arrived at the Merion Cricket Club outside Philadelphia in 1916, fourteen-year-old Bobby Jones stood all of five feet four inches tall, and tipped the scales at 165 pounds, extra weight he would shed in the coming years. The teenager was riding a hot streak that had made him feel invulnerable. He had successfully defended his Birmingham and ACC titles, and then gone on to Tennessee to take the Cherokee Country Club's championship. He capped this run off a win in the first annual Georgia State Golf Association crown.

Founded in 1865 along the Main Line, the route Philadelphia's moneyed class took on weekends to pursue suburban pleasures, the Merion club was established as a playing field for that most English game, cricket. Its renowned East Course, designed by a former Princeton golf team captain, Hugh Wilson, took full advantage of the rolling landscape. Giving free play to his sense of drama, Wilson set the East Course's three closing holes around a huge stone quarry.

As much a seat of eastern golf power as the Country Club in Brookline, Massachusetts, the Merion Cricket Club had a way of inspiring regional jealousies. When East Coast reporters commented that had the Massachusetts native Francis Ouimet entered the Amateur, he would have been favored, Chicago's pride, Chick Evans, the reigning U.S. Open champion, retorted, "In the West it is generally understood that when a leading player fails to enter an event, he has little chance to win it. There is a certain provincialism about the East."

Bobby Jones had his own regional difficulties to negotiate. He had never putted on anything but the coarse Bermuda grass favored in the South, and at first Merion's glassy greens puzzled him. But not for long. On the less-difficult West Course, he reeled off a 74, the lowest score in the first qualifying round. His second round was less successful. On the more-challenging East Course, he shot an execrable 89, but he still managed to qualify for match play.

Before match play began, Grantland Rice, sensing a good story in Jones's progress, took the boy to breakfast. Rice, who had captained the Vanderbilt baseball team, stood six feet tall and carried over two hundred pounds with the ease of a former college shortstop. With his broad, open features and his syrupy southern accent, he immediately put his subjects at ease. When Rice conducted an interview, his pure, natural curiosity was transparent. Without strain, he drew people to him. As Red Smith put it, "Wherever Grantland Rice sits, that's the head of the table."

A one-man sportswriting tornado, Rice covered everything from the New York Giants to Notre Dame football to tennis on the lawn. At a time when sports editors thought golf coverage belonged on the society pages, he popularized the game with his accounts of the great tournaments and his column, "Tales of a Wayside Tee."

In the years before World War I, Rice's interest in golf was met with puzzlement. His *New York Mail* editor, Frank Albertini, refused to let the reporter cover the 1913 U.S. Open in Brookline. "In Albertini's book, golf was something played by sheep herders and coupon clipping stiffs," Rice recalled. When he was told that businessmen were flocking to the game, Albertini replied, "Then put it on the financial page."

Rice, a scratch golfer himself, persevered, and by 1916 he was writing for the *New York Tribune,* a paper whose upper-class readership was interested in the more-genteel sports. No doubt Bobby Jones's precocious talent would have caught Rice's eye no matter what, but the reporter, who had written for the *Atlanta Journal* just after the turn of the century, had met Big Bob several times. The two southerners had both been gifted baseball players whose fathers had thwarted their professional ambitions. They were both outgoing, and they shared the courtly southern manner. Naturally, Grantland Rice was favorably disposed to Big Bob's son.

At breakfast Rice watched Bobby closely and sensed that he was meeting someone with social graces beyond his years, not to mention extraordinary golfing talent. Rice vowed to keep an eye on Jones as the tournament progressed.

In Bobby's first match, though, he played abominably, and he responded the way he always did at East Lake. After hitting a bad shot, his face darkened. Muttering curses under his breath, he stamped his feet and shook his head. Clearly, the ball wasn't obeying his wishes. Then he exploded, hurling his club as far as he could down the fairway and picking it up along the way. He found this method of letting off steam satisfying and repeated it as often as necessary.

His opponent, the oldest competitor and former U.S. Amateur champion, Eben Byers, was playing poorer still. In a rage, Byers began flinging clubs as well. "Players in the match directly behind them said later that it looked like a juggling act on stage," O. B. Keeler, Jones's friend, observed. "At the twelfth hole, Mr. Byers hurled a club over the hedge and out of the golf course and would not allow his caddy to retrieve it. Bobby explained whimsically that he had defeated Mr. Byers only because he had run out of clubs first."

What Keeler didn't report was that Jones also let loose, more than once, with a stream of profanity as fluent as his golf swing. When he made a mistake, his bursts of anger were not quite as charming as O.B. rendered them in retrospect. In a post-Victorian society, Bobby's invective sounded particularly raw, but a prudish and protective press insulated him from the harshest criticism. In fact, the fourteen-year-old's tantrums were predictable, the fits of a pampered perfectionist who had never been exposed to public scrutiny.

In the second round, Frank Dyer knocked Bobby flat, taking five of the first six holes. In response, Bobby went wild again, muttering under his breath, cursing, and tossing clubs. In the grip of pure rage, Jones was threatening to fly completely out of control.

George Adair, the president of the East Lake Country Club who had accompanied Bobby to Merion, interceded. "Bob, you are playing bad golf because you are not in the right mood. Now just get your mind on the game and play for all you are worth or I'll send you right back home."

To the young man's credit, he managed to rein in his anger, but his purple-faced outbursts revealed the rage that was lurking beneath Bobby's polite, sweet-swinging exterior.

Chastened, Bobby got off the canvas and reeled off his hottest streak of the tournament to win 4 and 2. After Jones fought his way into the quarterfinals, Grantland Rice wrote: "Considering the personal equation and all other intimate details, a chunky, chubby broth of a lad, just fourteen years old, with a pink, round face and big, blue eyes, gave the greatest exhibition of golf today that we have ever seen."

The third round pitted the adolescent Jones against the six-foot-one-inch former Yale track and field star Robert Gardner, the defending U.S. Amateur champion. Attracted by the precocious Atlantan's run at the title, the largest crowd ever to gather for a third-round match assembled on the first tee.

The two competitors looked almost comical standing together. One newspaper suggested that Bobby "appeared almost like a midget alongside the tall and slender Gardner."

Height aside, however, the young Georgian exuded an insouciant confidence. A picture taken shortly before the match shows Bobby in a snazzy tweed cap, a white shirt, and carefully knotted tie. The slightly crooked, sly smile on his full, handsome face is worthy of a pool hustler about to skin a mark, but it is the look in his eye, amused, yet cold, that is most striking. He is out to win, and he doesn't care who knows it.

In Gardner, Bobby was facing a talented, experienced player who knew how to win. With his athletic build, his curly hair, and his stylish, creased slacks, the titleholder looked every inch the Ivy League star.

He was also quite nervous. What could be more embarrassing than losing to a boy? Feeling the pressure, Gardner topped his first tee shot, hit his second shot out of bounds, clipped a tree with his third effort, and promptly lost the first hole. Wild off the tee, he missed the second fairway, handing Jones another hole.

Meanwhile, Bobby was swinging loose and free; he might as well have been back in East Lake, knocking the ball around with his childhood pal Perry Adair. His confidence was surging. How could he lose to such a shaky opponent?

Although his play improved as he went along, Gardner was still one down to Jones after the first eighteen. The fourteen-year-old had sailed through his first tour in seventy-six strokes, a solid, steady round.

Gardner, on the other hand, was relying on one desperate save after another. On the sixth hole in the afternoon, he blew his approach, missing the green entirely. Somehow, he managed to finesse a lightning-fast, downhill chip stiff, rattling his teenage opponent, who missed a makable birdie putt. On the next hole, the Yale man yanked his tee shot left. Jones laid his in a perfect spot, just below the hole. Facing another delicate, downhill chip, Gardner flashed his marvelous touch again, rolling the ball to a foot for another halve.

Now Bobby was growing frustrated. He was stroking the ball far better than the Yale man. He had a better, more reliable swing. A rank amateur could see that, he believed. Why wasn't he crushing his lucky opponent? Wasn't there something just a bit unfair about the whole exercise?

On the eighth, Gardner fired off another wild one, pulling his approach all the way to the ninth tee. Bobby knocked his a cool ten feet from the cup. Now he was certain Gardner was about to go to pieces. The match was finally turning his way. He couldn't suppress a crooked smile, though he tried his best to act polite. And this time, his hopes were rewarded as the defending champion's chip died fifteen feet short of the pin.

While Gardner, who was still away, surveyed the green, Bobby idly counted how many holes he needed to close out his erratic foe. Meanwhile, Gardner took a deep breath, drew his club back, and with a smooth stroke holed the fifteen-footer.

Bobby did a double take. Now he had to knock in his birdie putt to take the hole, but he was distracted by the match's inherent lack of justice. Bob Gardner was probably the luckiest man alive, he thought. In his irritation, Bobby failed to roll in another makable birdie putt. For the third time in a row he'd failed to come through.

Recalling his mental state at that moment, Jones said he felt that he "had been denied something that was rightly mine. I wanted to go off and pout and have someone sympathize with me, and I acted just like the kid I was. I didn't half try to hit the next tee shot, and I didn't half try on any shot thereafter. In short, I quit."

Bobby's assessment might have been a shade harsh, but Gardner proceeded to win three out of the next four holes. His confidence restored, the older man roared ahead and took the match 4 and 3.

The former U.S. and British Amateur champion Walter J. Travis, the cigar-chomping curmudgeon and editor of *American Golfer,* watched Jones's performance closely. Travis, who had taken up the game in his mid-thirties, was the greatest putter of his generation. After playing less than two years, he made it all the way to the U.S. Amateur's semifinals. Two years later he took his first of three U.S. Amateurs. In 1904, wielding his center-shafted Schenectady putter, Travis shocked his English hosts by winning the British Amateur. In a fit of pique, the Royal and Ancient Golfing Society outlawed the club.

When questioned as to how the Atlanta prodigy might improve, Travis remarked: "Improvement? He can never improve his shots, if that's what you mean. But he will learn a great deal more about playing them. And his putting method is faulty."

In two prophetic sentences, Travis foretold Jones's long struggle to break through to the top. Only years later, when Bobby submitted to a Walter J. Travis lecture, did his putter gain its legendary brilliance.

Still, the teenager had made an extraordinary impression with his talent — and his volcanic temper. The eastern press went mad for Jones, dubbing him a boy wonder, but also referring to him as "a hot-tempered Southerner." The *New York Times* was full of admiration: "Not even Bob Gardner, who is the last word in courage, could outgame the little fellow." In public Jones accepted defeat modestly, making a fluent speech to the crush of reporters.

But for Bobby the experience was decidedly mixed. The high-strung young man had played his heart out and lost. None of his starry-eyed worshipers could have imagined what lay ahead. With misleading grandiosity, O. B. Keeler would call it the "seven lean years."

5

O.B. KEELER HAS BEEN called Bobby Jones's Boswell. He covered Jones's exploits exhaustively for the *Atlanta Constitution*. He traveled with Jones's family and friends when Bobby did battle in the major tournaments. He shared hotel rooms with the much-younger Jones, and eventually wrote books about Bobby's exploits. On the surface, Keeler appears to be nothing more than a Jones mythmaker, a handy scribe who kept Bobby's name in the papers during his long and agonizing rise to the top.

Keeler was not simply providing a service to Bobby Jones, however. His relationship with the Atlanta prodigy gave him a purpose. When the newspaperman first met the fourteen-year-old golfer, he was going through another bad patch in the string of bad patches that distinguished his life. At the time, O. B. Keeler needed Jones far more than Bobby needed him.

By the age of thirty-four Keeler had survived financial ruin, a desultory suicide attempt, a broken marriage, a life-threatening bout with pneumonia, and a near-fatal tonsil infection.

After failing at a business venture, O.B. had made an attempt to do away with himself on a railroad bridge over the Chattahoochee River, but his efforts at suicide proved as ineffectual as his previous projects. Not long after that he made an advantageous marriage to a woman whose father owned the Georgia Marble Company, but he managed to make a hash of this adventure as well. After fathering two children, Keeler became estranged from his wife, and eventually the two separated.

O.B. just couldn't settle down. He had too many interests, among them classical literature, women, and corn liquor. At best he was fit for the dodgier professions, so he drifted into sportswriting. His talents included a marvelous memory and verbal facility, so his fall from grace into the lower depths of word-pushing suited him just fine.

Unfortunately, his fragile constitution wasn't always up to the rigors of the job. After covering a college football game in raw weather, his throat became an incubator for a colony of streptococci. Within days he was seeing double, and worse still, he lost control of his extremities. Blood from a cerebral hemorrhage, the doctors discovered, was leaking into his spinal cavity.

Twice they drained fluid to ease the pressure, but otherwise he had to recover on his own. The hungry infection damaged nerves in his hand, turning it into a frozen claw. His muscles atrophied; his reflexes faded to weak impulses. As Keeler put it, he was "pretty comprehensively dilapidated."

O.B. could no longer shoot skeet, and his amateur boxing days were long over. Unable to play golf, he somehow retained his passion for the game. Always a keen observer, Keeler now found that observation was the only sport left to him. Golf, with its protean challenges, both mental and physical, held an endless fascination for him. While he could no longer grip a club, he could analyze the subtle slope of a fairway and where to place the perfect drive; he could run a course through his mind and judge where its vulnerabilities lay, and where discretion was the better part of valor.

And he just liked to talk golf. Talking was one of the few pleasures left to him. Over time he regained some of his faculties, but by then he'd found his vocation — covering Robert Tyre Jones Jr.

Just before Bobby burst onto the national stage at Merion in 1916, he came up against his boyhood friend and golfing partner, Perry Adair, widely considered the best young golfer in Georgia, in the finals of the Georgia State Amateur. Several years older than Bobby, more experienced in competition, and quite gifted, Adair was the odds-on favorite. Bobby was still little more than a precocious tyro.

In the morning round, Adair dominated his chubby opponent as expected, finishing the first eighteen three up. During the lunch break, tournament chairman Ralph Reed, assuming Adair had taken an insurmountable lead, asked Bobby to please "play out the bye holes." He explained to the fourteen-year-old that so many people had traveled so far to witness the first Georgia State championship that they would be disappointed if it were cut short. In other words, Reed expected Adair to close out Bobby far before the finish.

"Don't worry, Mr. Reed, there aren't going to be any bye holes!" Jones snapped, according to O. B. Keeler. (Jones later denied the episode, but Keeler insisted he had witnessed the exchange.)

After letting the first hole get away and falling four down, Bobby channeled his fury into every golf swing. He hit the ball harder than he ever had in his life. He tried to knock every putt in the heart, and succeeded more often than not. From the second hole until he closed out Adair 2 and 1, Bobby Jones shot even-par golf.

Drinking in Jones's brilliant streak, O. B. Keeler thought he had witnessed something more than fine golf. He had seen Bobby going through a transformation. The stocky boy's will had broken through to the surface, a will that when wedded to his extraordinary ball-striking talents would turn him into a remarkable player. Keeler made a mental note to follow Jones closely, to get under his skin.

O.B. couldn't attend the 1916 U.S. Amateur, but after Bobby returned from his stunning debut, Keeler made a habit of chatting with him at East Lake. O.B. was always able to make friends, but this was a curious relationship, a rickety newsman and a fiery, precocious teenager.

Although Prohibition was in full swing, O.B. had no compunction about sharing his corn liquor with the boy. Of course, this was a detail he kept from the public eye.

Jones was impressed by Keeler's deep grasp of golf, as well as his access to illegal spirits, but O.B. appealed to the bright, thoughtful teenager in other ways. Keeler's conversation veered wildly between subjects. He was just as likely to expound on Aristotle as on the Atlanta Crackers baseball team, on classical sculpture as on a certain East Lake matron's voluptuous figure. The perfect bohemian uncle, Keeler offered Bobby an alternative ideal to his fun-loving but conventional father.

Doubtless, Bobby's golfing prowess would have been enough to engage the sportswriter in O.B., but as he grew to know the teenager more intimately, he discovered a young man far more complex than the run-of-the mill athlete. Instead of going blank when O.B. began spouting Greek philosophy, Bobby responded with penetrating questions. Nor was he put off by the older man's impromptu displays of erudition — O.B. was fond of reciting long passages of poetry without provocation.

It didn't take long for Keeler to realize that Bobby Jones not only possessed an uncommon intelligence, he also had a taste for ideas. This delighted Keeler, who spent the next couple of years planting the seeds of sedition, a love of literature, in the growing boy's mind. A more phlegmatic athlete would never have captured Keeler's imagination in quite the same way.

At the same time, O.B. offered absolute loyalty to Bobby's cause. As he and Bobby grew more intimate, O.B. didn't shy away from criticizing Jones's mental approach, or his taste for mounds of ice cream and pie between rounds, but his devotion was so sincere, Bobby never took offense.

As time went on, Keeler insinuated himself into the Jones family. When Bobby and Big Bob traveled to tournaments, O.B. played the role of nanny, scold, confidant, and links philosopher all in one, while pouring out reams of copy about his young friend at the same time. The quaint concept of journalistic objectivity hadn't yet seeped into the sports pages.

More than Grantland Rice, O. B. Keeler was responsible for mythologizing Bobby Jones, but his style was much less florid, and he also managed to humanize his subject. Although, like most of the sportswriters of the times, he sanitized the object of his admiration, playing down Bobby's fits of rage and hiding his taste for illegal spirits, he also reported how much Jones suffered for his artistry in plain language that rings with truth.

Despite his growing reputation, from his 1916 appearance at the U.S. Amateur until his great breakthrough in 1923, Bobby Jones failed to win a single major championship. "These seven lean years," Keeler wrote in *The Bobby Jones Story*, "constitute a chapter in the history of a world champion that very likely is without a counter-part in any sport . . . Seven years of unvaried defeat in the Big Shows."

There is truth in this account, but it is exaggerated. In fact, during these years Jones, who was still a teenager, was rising steadily in the ranks of the greatest American amateurs. His own expectations, as well as his father's and Keeler's, were simply unrealistic. For all his talent, Bobby was still too young and too undisciplined to win a big one.

His appeal was undeniable, however. Even in his teens, Bobby Jones was good copy. In 1917 he won the Southern Amateur, an important title, and when World War I began, he launched into a fundraising tour that led him all over the country. Wearing a dashing red beret, he attracted attention with his brilliant, if erratic, play, and his volatile outbursts. During one such display, at Brae Burn, in Boston, he snatched his ball off the grass, wound up, and flung it into the crowd. "I don't give a damn what anybody thinks of me," Bobby fumed.

Then he turned around and set a course record at Ekwanok in Vermont. In a second charity tour, the eighteen-year-old took on Chick Evans, the country's best amateur, in a series of matches. Sharing the stage with Evans, and holding his own, Jones raised his profile still further.

Bobby's style also attracted attention. While still in college, he began to appear in magazine spreads highlighting his dapper, southern gentleman look. In cardigans and two-toned shoes, the handsome Jones was presented as a new sartorial ideal. Of course, he had the manners to go with the fine clothes. Before the 1920s began, Bobby's adult image — scholar, athlete, social paragon — was already coming together.

In the glamorous Jones, the press could feature an alternative to the harsher reality, the disoriented and unemployed veterans streaming home from the European front. No one had a brighter future than Bobby Jones, and America wanted more than anything to look forward.

In 1919 Jones was runner-up in the Southern Open, the Canadian Open, and the U.S. Amateur. Still in his late teens, he was ranked second in the country by the *New York Times*. Not bad for a nineteen-year-old Georgia Tech student.

By 1919 American golf had emerged from Britain's shadow. The 1919 U.S. Amateur was rich in American stars. Chick Evans, who after years of frustration had taken both the 1916 U.S. Amateur and the 1916 U.S. Open; Francis Ouimet, 1913 U.S. Open and 1914 U.S. Amateur champion; and Bob Gardner, 1915 U.S. Amateur winner, led the veteran campaigners. Young, gifted players had been posting stunningly low scores all year, among them Jesse "Siege Gun" Guilford, known for his booming tee shots (Jesse had hit a drive in a tournament that carried a bunker 280 yards away, an astonishing distance for the time), Max Marston, Fred Wright, and above all, Bobby Jones.

In the weeks before the 1919 U.S. Amateur at Oakmont, outside Pittsburgh, Bobby had been wild off the tee, and Big Bob had sent his son to consult with his first and only model, Stewart Maiden, who was then a professional at a St. Louis club. When Maiden failed to solve the problem, he shrugged philosophically and suggested Bobby hit the ball as hard as he could. "It will go somewhere, and if you get off the fairway, you'll be nearer the green anyway."

Designed by Henry C. Fownes, the Oakmont course was a severe test. Fownes believed in the "penal" approach, and here he created a layout that realized his punitive dreams. Extremely long for the period, the par-seventy-three course ran 6,707 yards. Its narrow fairways were laced with an average of twenty bunkers, which were raked with ball-eating furrows. The deep rough exacted a price, too. Fownes had made good on his threat: "A poorly played shot should result in a shot irrevocably lost."

Surprisingly, Jones cut through the draw rather easily. In the finals, he faced Davy Herron, a solid golfer playing his home course. Bobby and O.B., who were sharing a hotel room, both lay sleepless the night before. There was no denying it. Bobby had a golden opportunity to shrug off his jinx and finally snare a major title.

Once play began, it became clear that the heavyset Herron had a superb touch on the greens. Herron had attended Princeton, but he had also worked in a steel foundry, acquiring a blue-collar following along the way. His fans cheered his every shot, and to Big Bob and

O.B.'s distress, they cheered again when Bobby Jones dunked a shot into a trap.

Herron was no match for Bobby from tee to green, but he more than made up for it with his delicate work with the putter. Bobby couldn't match Davy's touch. In fact, Jones's weaknesses during this period were as much technical as they were emotional. The flaw Walter B. Travis had detected in his putting stroke was undermining his best ball-striking efforts.

Jones and Herron fought to a standstill in the morning round, and the deadlock held after three holes in the afternoon. Then Herron took the fourth and began inching ahead. By the turn, he was two up.

Bobby's reputation for fiery meltdowns had followed him to Oakmont. Touts claiming inside knowledge swore that if he fell behind, the Atlanta kid would throw yet another tantrum, and toss away his chances yet again.

Three down at the six-hundred-yard twelfth, and with Herron in a bunker after an errant second shot, Jones elected to go after a two wood. Deep in concentration, he settled in over his brassie. Then he launched into his graceful stroke. As he did, a marshal noticed a wayward child far down the fairway and bellowed "Fore!" over a megaphone just as Bobby reached the top of his swing. Flinching, Jones dribbled a pitiful shot into a nearby trap.

Now the teenager's temper did get the better of him. He was certain he was the better player — Herron's ball-striking was mediocre at best. He was certain that he was the best player in the tournament, *certain* that he had already demonstrated this obvious fact as he had cruised through the field to reach the finals. And he was *certain* that only the bad luck that seemed to haunt him in every major tournament had put him in this unlikely position. That and a few measly missed putts.

Cursing under his breath, he hacked at the ball twice without escaping the sand. Eventually he just conceded the hole, which he might very well have won. Instead of closing the deficit to two holes, now he was down four. "He could have bitten his ball in half," O.B. wrote. Still in a fury, Jones gave away the next hole as well.

Bobby's latest burst of pique sent his hopes down in flames.

American Golfer commented that Jones's "temper displays and the number of clubs he broke" had been "grossly exaggerated, with the exception of one brassie." Still, the subject had become Bobby's florid rages, not his gifted stroke.

Once again, Jones was an also-ran. For a perfectionist like Bobby, second place provided no satisfaction. In his heart, he knew he was the best player in the world, and that very knowledge made losing intolerable. How could he square his feeling of invulnerability with the cold print? Second place.

He also wondered why he felt so exhausted after every tournament, and how he could lose so much weight — eighteen pounds at Oakmont — in just a few days of competition. He could play every day for weeks at East Lake and never lose an ounce. Was he suffering from some nameless weakness? If so, what was it all about?

At Georgia Tech a new, more complex Bobby Jones was being born. He was elected to two honor societies. He joined a fraternity, and soon became its most prominent member. Always intellectually curious, Bobby was fascinated by the science of angles and forces he was learning as an engineering student. Later, he brought this understanding to golf, that mystery of leverage, weight shifts, and swing planes. Although the Georgia Tech curriculum demanded almost total focus on science and engineering, he also continued his informal literary education at O. B. Keeler University. By his own admission, he was also drinking heavily, and his unpredictable bursts of rage shook him to the core.

O. B. Keeler faithfully reported Bobby's most flagrant outbursts during tournaments, and at college, among his peers, he occasionally exploded into similar white-hot furies. He had been far more disturbed by his defeat at Oakmont than he had let on. After a few extra drinks, Jones would grow angrier and angrier at himself. Alcohol only fueled the natural morbidity of his introspective character. Confused, he would lash out at everyone and no one, leaving him more confused still.

The wear and tear of tournament play had frayed his youthful sense of invulnerability. Bobby Jones was growing up.

To his father, to his family, even to O. B. Keeler to a lesser extent,

Bobby had to present a personality in accord with his precocious talents. There is no doubt that he was articulate, good-looking, and charming, but the years were rushing past, and he still hadn't delivered in the major championships. The pressure to succeed was, at times, almost unbearable. Like most prodigies, he was threatening to flame out.

In 1920 Bobby entered the U.S. Amateur at the Engineers Club in Roslyn, Long Island. By now he was all too aware of Big Bob's expectations. "My Dad was convinced that I was good enough to win a national title," Jones wrote, "and made no bones about telling me so. All of which got me to thinking about it myself, in a different way than before, when a golf tournament was simply a golf tournament, and the bigger the better."

In the semifinals, Francis Ouimet, Bobby's boyhood hero, played rock-solid golf against him, but it was a bee that finally killed Jones's innocent enthusiasm for the game. According to Jones, "As I was preparing to putt, a bee came buzzing along and alighted on the ball. I shooed it away. It returned at once. I shooed it away again . . . and a gallery official popped his megaphone down on the persistent insect, which instantly emerged from the mouthpiece and came back to me — it seemed fond of me. The gallery was beginning to giggle. I took off my cap and chased that pernicious bee clear off the green. I got to laughing myself, and the gallery fairly whooped . . .

"Having disposed of the bee, I went back to the ball myself, made a wretched putt, and failed to sink the next one, losing the hole . . . Sometimes I fancy that bee flew away with a good bit of my juvenile fancy for the game of golf. Anyway, it hasn't seemed the same since the Engineers Club in 1920."

The bee, of course, was incidental. Bobby's growing awareness of Big Bob's expectations had already stolen his sense of play. Already fixed in the glare of constant publicity, Jones now became all too conscious that his own father was dissecting him in public.

Jones's performance at St. Andrews in the 1921 British Open began on a hopeful note. He qualified as low amateur, and his two rounds on the first day were quite respectable, 78 and 74, good enough to put him in ninth place. He was overshadowed, however, by his playing partner, Jock Hutchinson, the 1920 PGA champion who had caddied at St. Andrews as a boy. A steely professional, Hutchinson had been practicing on the storied layout for four months before the tournament began, and it showed. "Set like a piece of flint to win," as Jones described him, Jock proceeded to shoot a hole in one on the par-three eighth and then lip out on the 306-yard par-four ninth. After touring the rim of the hole, Hutch's drive settled down three inches from the cup.

Although somewhat mystified by the flat St. Andrews course, with its hidden pot bunkers, Bobby found himself only six behind at the midway point. Hutchinson led the field by two. Jones had every expectation of fighting for the title in the closing rounds. On the opening hole of the third round, full of confidence, he topped his drive. A string of bogeys followed, choking his card with 5s and 6s. In short order his game deserted him completely. He smothered irons; he thinned them; he couldn't hit the ball straight. To make matters worse, his putting was atrocious. By the time the first nine's agony came to a close, the numbers added up to a stomach-turning 46.

In a fury, Bobby stalked to the tenth tee and promptly made a hash of that hole too. His self-disgust mounted after he knocked his drive into Hill Bunker in front of the eleventh green. All the years of frustration seem to have coalesced at this moment. Unfortunately, a man in a blind rage doesn't make much of a sand player. He swiped once at the ball, but it trickled back to his feet. He took a second mighty swing, but the ball refused to crawl over the lip. Grinding his teeth, he dug his niblick into the gritty sand, but this maneuver proved futile, too.

After one more wild swing, he surrendered. The great Bobby Jones couldn't get out of a bunker. Now he did something he regretted for the rest of his life. In the grip of a furious tantrum, Robert Tyre Jones Jr. quit the British Open.

In an amused commentary, the *London Times* reported that Mr. Jones "tore up his card and expressed a preference for cricket." While Jones's fit was widely reported, it was often communicated in an indulgent tone. As gifted as he was, Bobby was still immature, but he had so much charm and charisma, and he came from such an appealing background, surely he would overcome his juvenile lapses. The press found it easy to forgive Bobby Jones.

However, Jones had done something that wasn't particularly amusing: he had fled the humiliation golf visits even on its greatest players. It was a gutless performance, but not surprising.

At Merion in his very first major tournament, he had stamped, flung clubs, and cursed his head off. Under the pressure of tournament play he had broken clubs, smashed putter heads into the turf, attacked various shrubs, and vilified himself in streams of artistic profanity worthy of Big Bob himself. In fact, his self-absorbed tirades were becoming increasingly shopworn. He was too old to keep acting like a spoiled child.

6

To a casual observer, golf balls appear to be benign, inanimate objects, dimpled white spheres with no particular agenda. In truth, they have evil intentions, and mysterious powers to do the innocent player harm. They have highly sensitive sensory systems, and they can catapult themselves to precisely the wrong spot, behind the only tree in the rough, under a singular bush, or, with remarkable frequency, in the only divot for a hundred yards dead center in the fairway.

Fourteen-year-old Johnny Goodman had heard players bemoaning the latter twist of fate so often that he had come to a conclusion. It would be a good idea to learn to dig balls out of holes. For a few weeks in the summer of 1924, he concentrated on this single difficulty.

To master this shot he had to break the rules. Caddies were only allowed to play once a week at the Field Club, a maximum of nine holes. The members didn't want South Omaha boys to get the wrong idea. They warned the caddies that if they were caught stepping onto the fairways at any other time, they would be committing a crime — criminal trespass.

Johnny knew a few members who would get hopping mad if they nabbed him, but he didn't think they could put him in jail for hitting a golf ball. It was a kind of game. Sneak onto the fourth hole at dawn. Smack a few around in the rain. Chip some shots when nobody was looking. Otherwise, how could he learn to play?

After looping all day Sunday, he drifted away from the Field Club, and then under cover of near darkness, he doubled back and slipped onto the course. After a weekend's play, the fairways were pock-marked with divots: gouges, cuts, slender slices, and trenches reminiscent of shell holes.

Johnny looked around and found a good, deep one. Then he dropped his ball into it and took out a mashie. He'd teach himself the shot, he figured. The first time around, he dubbed it. He knew the right method. Stanley Davies always said, "Hit down and stay with it. Down, down, down!"

Johnny made another attempt and barely lifted the ball off the ground. Then he played it back a little. This time he made good contact, but the shot came out low and hot. His eyes narrowed as he watched it skitter all the way to the green, at least ten yards farther than he usually hit a mashie. Knock it down. That was the ticket.

He kicked another ball into a divot and performed the same operation all over again. He was inconsistent at first, but after a few days of excavating his ball from the worst lies, he started to get the feel.

Systematically, he was picking up the game. Let the other caddies bang one drive after another. He always practiced with the club he dreaded to hit. How else could he get better?

Johnny also managed a few rounds at the public course, though it was a far rougher and easier track than the Field Club. On his first tour of the Field Club's front nine, Johnny posted a stunning 37, although he'd done it the hard way, chipping in twice and sinking a sixty-foot putt. All summer he tried to match the brilliant score, but he kept falling short. Still, he could shoot in the low 40s like clockwork, and one time he'd turned in a 39. He was getting better with every stick in the bag. If he concentrated on the game, maybe he could turn pro when he grew up.

It wasn't such a crazy idea. Once Walter Hagen had been just like him, another caddie with an old man who worked with his hands. Other kids pretended they were Grover Cleveland Alexander, Babe Ruth, or Ty Cobb coming up with the bases loaded. Johnny acted out sinking twenty-footers in the last round of the U.S. Open.

Ever since he had hatched his ambitions, he had imposed a highly organized regimen on himself. First he gave up all other sports but golf, although he loved baseball and had a knack for the game. Then he divided his time into school, caddying, and golf, focusing on mastering one club at a time. He had noticed that mediocre players who learned to hit a few clubs well depended all too often on the ones they had confidence in.

He also threw himself into his schoolwork, paying particular attention to his English grammar, as he was determined to speak like the better people at the Field Club. If he was going to turn himself into an elite golfer, and make money giving lessons, he would have to use proper English.

Every act of discipline became a bulwark against the increasing chaos at home. Golf was Johnny's chief refuge. When he practiced, he didn't think about the next time his father might burst into the house in the middle of the night, stumbling into the furniture and cursing. Golf filled up his mind, leaving no space for his worries. The dread he felt — when would the old man show up? who would he smack? what would he break? — melted away in the hours he stroked shot after shot. It was easier to control a golf ball than a raging, reeling drunk.

In the winter of 1924, William Goodman made one of his increasingly rare appearances, leaving his worn-out wife, Rose, pregnant for the thirteenth time. In the ensuing months, her face grew puffy, yellow, she forgot what she was doing, and she moved around as if she were underwater. By the fall of 1924, the family wasn't eating so well, and more and more Johnny took up Matt's invitations and grabbed supper over at the Zadalises' table.

Anna, who was working full-time as a maid, complained that she was turning every cent of her paycheck over to their mother, and she was only a year and a half older than Johnny. He knew what she really meant. Why was a boy his age still in school when he could be out earning a few dollars? As his mother grew more visibly pregnant by the day, Johnny threw all his weekend caddie money into the kitty too, but it was never enough.

Although "Coolidge prosperity" wasn't trickling down to the Goodman family, Omaha, fueled by its vibrant livestock market and the country's fourth-largest rail center, was booming. With the spread of electricity, modern manufacturing techniques, and a burgeoning armada of automobiles, the city seemed to be entering a machine-age Valhalla. Downtown, the Brandeis Stores, housed in a square-block-size, seven-story building, opened its doors to reveal a dizzying abundance of goods: carpets, corsets, derbies, doilies, painted china, perfume, laxatives, fox furs, rolled umbrellas, nutcrackers, screwdrivers, and ivory-handled mirrors. Shoppers could choose from three different restaurants, all under the Brandeis roof, where they might take tea and rest from the buying frenzy.

In Omaha, as elsewhere, radios proliferated in the grander homes, and in the shabby ones too. You could spin the dial and listen to Beethoven, the A&P Gypsies, or Rudy Vallee pouring magically through the speakers of your Florentine cabinet set. On Sundays, in countless living rooms, the sportscaster Graham McNamee could be heard shouting, "And he did it! Yes, sir, he did it. It's a touchdown! Let me tell you, the Praying Colonels are one of the finest college football teams I've ever seen . . ."

Shiny black Fords ferried salesmen to the hinterlands, where they converted formally frugal farm wives to the new consumer religion. Chevies in bright new colors also made their appearance. Flappers, decked out in rayon and smoking once-forbidden cigarettes, might find all that was left of their inhibitions breaking down in the intoxicating new roadsters. John Steinbeck speculated that in the 1920s more than half the new children in America had been conceived in the back seats of Detroit's latest models.

Johnny Goodman caught glimpses of the highlife at the Field Club. Like the young Walter Hagen, he could watch the members, their wives, sons, and daughters sweeping into the clubhouse for costume parties, birthday parties, holiday parties, and affairs to introduce the latest debutante, despite the fact that he was barred from entering the inner sanctum. For four years he had caddied and gazed longingly from afar, and he was determined to find a way inside.

While they hadn't kept Sir Walter Hagen out of the clubhouse, Johnny noticed that the Field Club's professional, Stanley Davies, was treated with far less deference. While Davies was welcome at the club's bar, he had to hop to it if a member needed a bit of tape on a fraying grip, or a club head had gone a tad loose. He had to wait like a shopkeeper behind a counter, purveying golf balls and gloves and the myriad penny-ante items the members demanded. Johnny looked up to Davies, who had treated him so kindly and shown such interest in his talent, but the club's board members held the pro's fate in their hands. They treated him well, but he was an employee, after all, a hired hand.

He started wondering if the great amateurs like Chick Evans, Jess Sweetser, or the one they said would be the best ever, Bobby Jones, had a better deal than the pros. Sometimes dog-eared copies of the *American Golfer* turned up in the caddieshack. Johnny pored over articles that lionized the top amateurs, but he found the ads just as intriguing. Amateurs flew airplanes to St. Tropez, Cannes, and St. Moritz. They wore tailored English suits, English golf attire, and handcrafted English shoes. They treated themselves to spas and on a whim dropped small fortunes for the latest golf clubs. One thing was certain. Amateurs never had to bow and scrape to anybody.

In December 1924, just before Johnny's fifteenth birthday, Rose Goodman went into labor. She didn't get out alive. A few days later, her baby, Rose, died as well.

At this terrible moment, William Goodman deserted his family for good, though he took care to retain title to his property. After his brood scattered, Goodman blithely took the house back, having kept up his mortgage payments. Whatever else he made in between binges, he kept for himself, disappearing so completely from his children's lives that after their mother's death they were referred to as "orphans," a term they didn't dispute.

The whole family had revolved around Rose Goodman. She had scraped meals together out of nothing. She had insisted the children get up and go to school every morning and attend Mass every Sunday. Alone in the tight confines of their frame house, the children could barely comprehend their loss.

Johnny, who had always done his best to separate his own life from the tenuous circumstances at home, was stunned and shaken.

How would they live? How would he make his way from one day to the next? His mother's absence pervaded every room in the house. For his old man's cowardly disappearing act, he felt a mixture of rage and shame.

With their father gone, the children tried to survive on their own. As the oldest boy still living with the family, Johnny was the nominal head of the household, but Anna took on most of the responsibility for Mary, ten, Mike, nine, Pete, six, and Tommy, four. The two oldest children cobbled together a routine. During the week, Johnny kept an eye on the youngsters until Anna returned home from her maid's job. Then Anna would take over, cooking, cleaning, and trying to impose some sort of order, but she was too inexperienced and too exhausted to keep the family together.

Eventually the county authorities, apprised of the fact that the Goodman brood were living "under the wing" of sixteen-year-old Anna, concluded that the situation was untenable. The authorities decided that ten-year-old Mary was old enough to do housework for her room and board. After the younger boys were deposited at St. James Orphanage, Johnny was "left to shift for himself."

The moment came when he was completely alone. Like Mary, Anna had become a live-in maid. His little brothers were long gone. In the silence, he felt his loss in a fresh, more penetrating way. His mother had been wiped from the face of the earth, erased like chalk from a blackboard. And then there was the persistent shame of his father's desertion. He had to be quiet about that. They all did. It was nobody's business.

The county officials had told him that he had to "vacate the premises." With no definite plan he gathered his few things, his school pants and shirt, his schoolbooks, and his mongrel collection of golf clubs, and walked out of the house he had lived in for so many years. The walls fell away, and he was out on the street, wondering what he was supposed to do.

He walked down the short distance to the edge of the hill and looked down at the stockyards. A cattle train was rattling in. He stood watching the drovers water their four-footed cargo in the pond, idly wondering if he should follow his older brothers into the packinghouses. It was good money — when you weren't working short hours or you weren't getting laid off — but his stomach cramped up at the thought of spending all day hitting steers over the head or carving up carcasses. Then there were the speedups his brothers Joe and George always complained about, the foremen riding herd on the men to move faster, then faster still. He didn't have a plan except to stay away from Armour and Cudahy, and out of the Union Pacific yards too.

Nothing Johnny Goodman ever faced on a golf course rivaled the struggle he endured when he was fifteen years old. His response to the twin blows of his mother's death and his father's desertion defined his character. To survive, he sprang into action. He raced around downtown Omaha, from office to office, looking for any kind of work that would keep him out of the factories. Of course, during the winter, he couldn't caddie. Above all else, he wanted a clean job. Unlike many South Omaha boys, he could read and write quite well, and he knew how to take directions. He thought he could talk his way in.

After days of searching, he caught on as a part-time Western Union messenger. While dashing around town delivering telegrams, he observed the business world for the first time. People sat at desks and greeted visitors. They worked on upright typewriters and answered phones, while a supervisor, sitting at a bigger desk, barked out orders. It was exciting to see this previously hidden universe. Alone for the first time in his life, he had taken a small step up.

At first, he slept anywhere he could, but as shy as he was, Johnny had made strong friendships. His boyhood pal and fellow caddie, Matt Zadalis, prevailed on his family to give Johnny a bed. As he had learned to do at the Field Club, Johnny ingratiated himself to adults. He was quiet, orderly, and helpful. He didn't complain. Soon, he was a part of Matt's family.

There was little social welfare at the time, and Johnny might easily have ended up unemployed and wandering the streets. Instead, despite taking the worst possible emotional blows, he had managed to find work and put a roof over his head. Staying in school, however, proved a more formidable challenge. In fact, graduating from South

High began to seem like a pipe dream. The Zadalises could offer Johnny shelter, but they couldn't feed and clothe him. Work began devouring his time.

For a while Johnny continued walking three miles each way to school, rarely missing a day. In the afternoons and evenings he scrambled for a living. After months of this regimen, however, he was forced to drop out. His devotion to his schoolwork appeared worthless. No one else in his family had ever earned a diploma — many boys from the slaughterhouse district never did. Why should he be any different? His dreams of golfing stardom seemed equally absurd. How was he going to work on his brassie when he wasn't sure where his next meal was coming from?

At times he felt resigned to his situation, but then his natural resilience would get the upper hand. There had to be a way to get back into school, maybe at night. And, maybe, even a way to slip back onto the golf course once in a while. When the weather got warmer he could loop two rounds a day on weekends. That would keep him in touch with the game too.

Then news of Johnny's predicament began circulating around the Field Club. He had long endeared himself to the club's most influential members. When they got wind of his circumstances, they arranged a printer's devil job for him. Johnny was grateful. The work paid better than being a messenger. Of course, when spring rolled around, he started carrying bags when he could, in addition to the new job.

Just getting back on the golf course gave him hope. He had withstood loss and grief, but he hadn't crumbled. Instead, he was taking care of himself, like a full-grown adult. It didn't escape his notice that his ties to the golf world had helped him survive. Soon, his taste for the game returned.

In the late spring of 1925, Goodman entered his first competition, Omaha's informal caddie championship, which pitted bag haulers from the Field Club, the Happy Hollow, Highland, and Lakewood clubs against one another. It was a humble affair, but Johnny swept the field. It may not have been the most exalted title in the world — he could see the indulgent smiles of the Field Club elders — but golf had brought him recognition at the lowest point of his life. He just might have some talent. His hopes soared.

One more challenge remained: returning to school and catching up with his classmates. When he had time, he made his way back to South High and talked to some of his old teachers. Maybe it wasn't hopeless, after all. He could work during the day and take classes at night. He had missed the entire spring semester, but he managed to cram in a whole term's work that summer, and by September 1925 he'd earned enough credits to catch up with his class again.

Golf remained his obsession. He and Matt talked golf. Constantly. Who were the best players? What were their swings like? How did they go about winning? And they followed the Walker Cup, a new competition that had caught Johnny's imagination.

The tournament, which had been inaugurated in June 1924, pitted the greatest American and British amateurs against one another. The competition had been played at the intriguing National Golf Links near Southampton, Long Island, and it brought together the best amateurs in the country — Bob Gardner, Chick Evans, Francis Ouimet, Jesse Guildford, Max Marston, Jess Sweetser, and Bobby Jones.

The Field Club's bigwigs were always saying that amateurs had more class than the pros. Johnny admired the packinghouse managers, the doctors and dentists and politicians he caddied for. These were the people who had taught him how to act on a golf course, and they had come to his aid when he was down. He listened closely to their conversations when he was carrying their bags, and he came to agree with them. Walter Hagen was great, but wasn't he just a little too loud, and weren't his outfits a little too showy?

A man wasn't supposed to hog all the attention for himself, but wasn't that exactly what Hagen was all about? All the pros thought about was money, Johnny's mentors told him, but Walker Cuppers didn't compete for dollars and cents. They played for glory, and for their country.

The English had once lorded it over the U.S. of A., but America's amateurs were the best in the world now. Imagine how swell you'd feel winning one for yourself and your country at the same time.

Johnny thought it must be the best feeling in the world, better, even, than winning the U.S. Open.

And nobody ever kept a Walker Cup player out of the clubhouse and sent him around back to the pro shop. The amateur stars swept right in through the front door of the best country clubs in the country. It was as if they had some invisible free pass. A boy who hauled bags for a living didn't need anybody to explain that.

Bobby Jones had played brilliantly in the Walker Cup, and Johnny was mesmerized by everything he read about the smooth-swinging Georgian. Walter Hagen was a great player, but Bobby Jones was something more. Arguing for the amateur Jones's special place in golf's pantheon, the *Philadelphia Inquirer* pulled out every cliché in its repertoire. "It is not the golden glow of commerce coveted by the money-changers which Bobby Jones clutches to his bosom . . . It is gold unalloyed with selfish greed — gold of accomplishment in its virgin state."

The *Inquirer*'s overblown rhetoric was typical of the praise pouring down on Jones at the time, and Johnny Goodman couldn't help being impressed, especially because his surrogate family at the Field Club shared the *Inquirer*'s sentiments. Jones was young, good-looking, modest to a fault, and he had just married a beautiful Southern debutante. Better still, Jones's silky swing evoked arias on the sports pages. It wasn't hard to drift into reveries about Bobby Jones.

Johnny pasted pictures of Bobby on his wall. One of them showed Bobby finishing his swing, hands held high. Johnny liked to take his driver and imitate Jones's follow-through, capturing the look of Bobby's relaxed arms and his perfect balance. He did it hundreds of times, maybe more. Bobby Jones was seducing an entire country. How could the young Johnny Goodman, already under golf's spell, resist his allure?

When Johnny's buddies suggested that he enter the Metropolitan Golf Tournament, Omaha's city championship, he balked. The Metropolitan was a serious affair, the second-most-important competition in the state after the Nebraska Amateur. Naturally, the players were top-notch.

Matt pointed out that the competition this year might be a little weaker than usual, however. Sam Reynolds, cream of the Field Club crop, hadn't entered the tournament. As chairman of the American Legion housing committee, the public-spirited Reynolds didn't have time to compete. Another tough competitor, Dr. Eugene Slattery, had bowed out. The boys swore the field was wide open.

Still, Johnny wouldn't reconsider. There seemed to be no particular reason. He simply refused. Even Matt couldn't pry a word out of the taciturn Goodman. It was near the end of August, and the event was looming.

Alone with a few of his closest caddie friends one day, Johnny let the secret slip. "Look at me," he said.

The other boys looked.

"What?" Matt asked, mystified.

Johnny pinched his bib overalls in disgust.

A look of comprehension dawned on their faces as they glanced at one another. They all wore overalls and ragged shirts. Kitey wore a baseball cap with a ruptured bill, and Stan liked to tie a bandanna around his neck. Lonnie's hair stood up like dry straw; Tony had a black eye; Frank's teeth were stained with chewing tobacco. They were all just a bunch of kids from South Omaha scrambling for a few pennies. They liked to think of themselves as a band of pirates, full of spirit and a little wild, but they knew what Johnny was talking about.

His shirt was an indeterminate color. It may have once been brown. His ink-spattered shoes were nothing to write home about. How could he appear in public like that, especially among all those swells with their tweed knickers and polished golf shoes and white shirts and ties?

"I'm not gonna show myself up," Johnny said flatly.

He wasn't about to show his family up, either, but he kept that to himself. About the last thing he wanted was people talking about his old man and why he couldn't buy his kid a decent suit of clothes or about his little brothers over at St. James. That was nobody's business.

The other caddies tried reassuring him, they cajoled and needled him, but he wouldn't budge. That was it. The boys knew Johnny. If his mind was made up, he wouldn't give an inch.

But they also knew he was their best hope. Behind his back, they took up a collection. They each contributed a few cents of their hard-earned money, and they scrambled for more. A few generous Field Club members slipped them a dollar or two, and one day they presented Johnny with a complete golfing outfit, shoes and all. Gray flannel pants. A cabled sweater-vest. A fresh white shirt. A striped silk tie.

Still he resisted. "Look at the clubs we've got." He pointed to the wildly mismatched clutch of hickory-shafted implements he and Matt had accumulated.

"Driver's got a dead head," Matt concurred.

The other caddies had to agree. Their champion would be going into battle at a decided disadvantage.

The next day, an anonymous Field Club member left a message at the caddieshack. Johnny could borrow his clubs, but only for the city championship competition.

For Johnny, the chance to play with a complete set for the first time was as alluring as going head-to-head with Omaha's best players. In the past, he'd always been coaxing a few extra yards out of a mashie, or choking up on a spoon to make up for the gaps in his own bag. Some of his irons had smooth faces; only a few were grooved.

The caddies crowded around the polished set, touching the irons reverently. Johnny pulled out the polished brassie and flicked it with his wrists. It felt great, so balanced.

He started thinking about things in a different light. If he showed up in a decent outfit, he wouldn't have to worry about the gallery looking at him crooked. He wasn't stupid; he knew what people thought about him and his family. But after everything his buddies had done, he couldn't say no.

"Guess I have to play now," he told the boys in his laconic way.

"Hell, yeah," Stan agreed. "You gotta win too."

Taking the city championship would fit into Johnny's methodical plan. With his disciplined practice methods, and his discipline in his studies, he had already demonstrated an organized turn of mind. But underneath his reasoned campaign to succeed there lay a welter of emotions he could barely name: hurt, pride, fear, rage, and a longing for love.

He craved acceptance in the clubhouse, certainly, but he also longed to obliterate his wraith of a father. So when the pride of the Field Club, Sam Reynolds, offered a word of praise, he glowed inside. Despite Johnny's quiet demeanor, he burned for recognition. The idea of just being another anonymous, stick-armed teenager galled him. He knew there was more to him than that. Some kids were showoffs. They told funny stories, they had bright ideas about what to do next, and the rest of the boys followed them around. He wasn't like that. He would have to *show* people why he was worth just a little more.

Sure, his mind was fine enough to raise him up. Maybe he could become a clerk at Union Pacific, or an accountant at one of the department stores downtown. He was good with figures. But working in some office would add up to a humdrum existence. He knew that he looked like a hundred other skinny boys with pasty faces, invisible at best, all too visible at worst.

There was one thing that made him different, one thing that distinguished him from every other kid in his class, and probably every other boy in South High: his touch. It was as if a putter was an extension of his hands; he could stroke the air and sense distance, how hard to tap the ball. He could see ripples in a green no one else registered; he could divine the subtle slopes of a putting surface with a sixth sense. He believed he could predict which way a golf ball would roll almost every time. Or at least he thought so.

Maybe it was time to find out if he was right.

7

THE COMPETITION FOR the fourteenth annual Metropolitan Golf Tournament was slated for the Field Club on August 21, 1925. Among the oldest country clubs west of the Mississippi, the Field Club of Omaha's first incarnation came in 1898 when the Omaha Amateur Athletic Association was formed. At first the emphasis was on cricket, tennis, and basketball, but within two years the club developed a nine-hole layout, which was expanded to a full eighteen-hole course in 1902.

The Field Club's course quickly gained prominence. By 1905 the Omaha track was chosen for the site of the first Nebraska State championship, and in 1906 the club hosted the most important regional tournament, the sixth annual Trans-Mississippi. In 1910 the first National Clay Court Tennis Championship took place there as well, adding to the club's luster.

Dues rose quickly, from a ten-dollar annual fee in 1901 to forty dollars in 1911. Ladies paid a more modest fifteen dollars for club privileges. In the same year, the board set caddie fees at forty cents a round and urged members "not to buy golf balls from poor farm inmates," whose facilities bordered the course.

By the 1920s, the Field Club had developed into a challenging layout featuring a pair of daunting closing holes. Cottonwood, oak, honey locust, and black walnut grew in abundance on the mildly hilly terrain.

According to eight-time Nebraska State golf champion Bob

Astleford, the Field Club was as tough as many U.S. Amateur courses. "The two finishing holes were two of the best I ever played back to back. The seventeenth was referred to as Long Tom. The south is the prevailing wind here. So that hole was 622 yards, par five, of course. You had to hit a cut shot off the tee to get around a bunch of trees. Then you had to hit it over Woolworth Avenue. Then you went down to this small green." Typical for their time, the Field Club's vest-pocket greens could be swallowed whole by today's behemoth putting surfaces.

Astleford, who was known for his power off the tee, considered the original final hole at the Field Club a tremendous test. "The eighteenth was over four hundred yards into the prevailing south wind with a blind second shot if you killed your drive. If you hit your drive well you had something like a two iron to the green."

The field for the city championship included most of Nebraska's best players. Former state champion Blaine Young headed a list that included Frank Massara, Jack Hughes, and Ben Yousem, all polished, experienced competitors.

Johnny had meditated for a long time about exactly why Bobby Jones had suddenly begun crushing the competition. In the 1924 U.S. Amateur, Jones had beaten the great Francis Ouimet 10 and 11, and gone on to dominate George Von Elm 9 and 8 in the finals. For years Bobby had been called the greatest ball striker in the country. He seemed to swing slow and easy, but he drove the ball as far as any man alive. Yet he hadn't been able to win. What was the reason for his sudden transformation? Johnny leafed through back issues of *American Golfer,* breaking down Bobby's performance in the all-important championship. Evidently, Bobby Jones had discovered the art of putting.

Hagen putted fearlessly, too. Johnny had watched him with his own eyes. Slick downhillers didn't faze him. He knocked them in the back of the hole, and if he missed, he just shrugged and laughed.

Hagen was great, but sometimes he threw his whole body at the ball, ending up so far forward he looked as if he would topple over. Hagen had nerve and style, but his effort showed. From what Johnny could tell, Bobby Jones was all smoothness and style — he never broke a sweat. In golf, the way you acted seemed as important as the way you played, and nobody acted more gracefully than Bobby Jones. He never suffered over a shot, he just let it fly. That's what all the papers said, and Johnny believed it.

Before the city championship, Johnny redoubled his practice sessions, lagging long putts, snaking in the three- and four-footers. Let the other caddies bang away at brassies with all their might. He'd mind the delicate stuff, putting a bit of overspin on the ball to make sure he got to the hole on the long ones, shortening his follow-through on those baked-hard August greens, when the ball just rolled and rolled.

He didn't neglect chipping, either. He popped niblicks out of grass bunkers, he experimented with his mashie from the fringe, he cut them close from the short side, and he rolled sixty-footers dead to the pin.

Following an unorthodox format, the Metropolitan called for a round of medal play and a thirty-six-hole match-play final. The lowest scorer over the first eighteen holes would win the medal crown; the runner-up would meet him in the head-to-head finals. The site of numerous championship contests, the par-seventy-two Field Club course was familiar to many of the players, but no one knew its greens better than the caddie Johnny Goodman, who had been reading them day in and day out for years.

The galleries were peppered with rooting sections, patriots of this or that club, but Johnny's South Omaha supporters had a different cast. Most of them were caddies, who, despite being on their best behavior, couldn't help whooping when their hero approached the first tee. More subdued, but watching intently, were a few of the Field Club's stalwarts, who had a soft spot for Johnny, though Stanley Davies was off playing at the Western Open.

Goodman had to warn his raucous supporters to keep it down, but they were like an excited, buzzing hive around him. This wasn't a clash of caddies for two-bit bragging rights. Manners counted.

Johnny hadn't yet turned sixteen, but he felt as if he'd been carrying bags for a lifetime. It felt strange to be standing there, the center of attention, and not off to the side, some duffer's clubs slung over his shoulder. He expected to be fighting stage fright, but instead he felt disoriented. The first fairway looked so familiar, yet curiously narrow. The small green tilted at a new angle. His body felt off-kilter.

His throat closed. The muscles in his mouth stretched into a tight smile, but it wasn't his own. There was no denying it. The Metropolitan would tell him everything he needed to know. He might fly high, or he might end up like one of those dirigibles that drifted back to the ground, all the gas leaking out. More than anything, he wanted to smack that first drive and get going.

Then the moment came: he felt the clubhead swishing through the air, and he was off. At first he was fearful of getting the slightest stain on his pristine gray flannel trousers, but then he forgot everything but the ball at his feet and the club in his hands. With a sense of unreality, he watched himself reel off a string of pars. Soon he believed it himself. He was making a good showing right out of the box.

It all seemed strangely simple, until he started making mistakes. When he smothered a mashie niblick on the sixth, he started muttering under his breath; then he bit his tongue. But it was hard not to show how you felt when you wanted to win so much it ached. Fighting off his miscues, he strung together a few more pars, and soon he was sailing along again.

When he came out of his dream, he found himself in second place in the medal round. Ben Yousem, former Nebraska State semi-finalist, had posted a brilliant 73, one over par, but Johnny had put up a 75, which tied him with Blaine Young, who had a Nebraska State title to his credit. After his first test, fifteen-year-old Johnny Goodman found himself in select company.

Even the era's most accomplished players didn't score much lower. Breaking 70 was a rare feat on a first-rate course at the time, for a number of reasons. Without the aid of space-age metals, drivers didn't launch too many three-hundred-yarders, though it was possible for a long hitter to nail one that far on the era's hard, un-watered fairways. Hickory shafts were still the norm, and balls weren't as tightly wound.

Today, professionals routinely drop their bunker shots a foot from their targets, but in the 1920s players paid the price for dunking their balls into greenside traps. Bunker play required more finesse then, especially since Gene Sarazen had yet to invent the sand wedge. Getting close to the pin with a niblick — the equivalent of a nine iron — took great feel and dexterity.

Stymies were still allowed on the greens. If a player blocked his opponent's ball, he was under no obligation to place a marker. Golfers with three-footers were sometimes forced to chip over another ball to sink otherwise easy winners. Top players became adept at this shot, but striking the ball crisply and holing it from a mere few feet was an art that few mastered.

If a ball became clotted with mud, a player was not allowed to clean it until after holing out. Hand-mown, unwatered greens, often quite hard during dry periods, didn't roll as true as present-day manicured putting surfaces, though golfers were spared the terrors of modern glasslike affairs. All of these factors conspired to prevent even the best players from savaging par.

The playoff against Blaine Young, a medal-play affair, turned into a seesaw battle. First one player took the lead, then the other. Johnny reminded himself that Young had gone to pieces against Hagen and Kirkwood. (Apparently Young didn't recall that Johnny had carried Sir Walter's bag.) The two golfers fought tooth and nail, but by the time they reached the endless Long Tom, Johnny had edged ahead by two strokes. Then it was his turn to fall apart. He topped his drive, butchered his second shot, and finally reached the distant green in five humiliating strokes. Goodman was forced to scratch a seven on his scorecard, and after Young holed out for his par, Johnny's entire lead had evaporated.

On the eighteenth the wind kicked up, harder than usual and hungry for errant tee shots. Both players managed to cut their drives around the trees by bare margins. Young's blind long iron came up short, but Johnny's was shorter still, a full fifteen yards shy of the apron.

He took one look at the pitch, stepped up, and struck the ball. His heart stopped. He'd hit it too hard, the ball bolting fifteen feet past.

After Young chipped up near the cup, Johnny filled his mind with Walter Hagen. Walter Hagen with that secret little smile. Walter

Hagen striding up to the killing stroke. Walter Hagen playing the angles. Walter Hagen striking it crisp and clean. Johnny rehearsed every move in his mind's eye, and then closing out the muttering gallery, the rising wind, the scraps of leaves drifting across the green, he took a fluid swing and hit the putt square.

His expression didn't reveal a thing, but his heart clenched, a muscle spasm in his chest, as he tracked the ball's slow progress. When the putt poured into the cup for a par four, the pain between his ribs dissolved.

Young sank his putt and the match stayed deadlocked. Officials set the playoff for 8:30 the next morning, and Johnny hurried off the course, boiling over with anger. How could he have thrown it all away on Long Tom?

"I played like a goddamn hacker," he muttered to Matt, who caught up with him on Woolworth Avenue.

"What're you, kidding? You win one hole tomorrow morning and you're in the finals."

Johnny stopped dead in his tracks. Matt had a point. What would Hagen think in the same spot? He'd probably figure he was in the catbird seat.

The next morning, Johnny appeared at the first tee in the same outfit he'd worn the day before, aware of every grass stain and smudge of mud on the cuffs of his gray flannels. Under the armpits of his shirt, half-moon-shaped stains were clearly visible. Painfully self-conscious, he did his best to put these imperfections out of his mind. Once he waggled his driver on the first tee, though, his sense of awkwardness evaporated. All he could think about was ripping one down the center.

On the short uphiller, not much more than three hundred yards, Johnny struck his tee shot with everything he had, catching it pure. The ball ended up only forty yards short, but he caught his pitch a hair fat, and the ball died twenty-five feet from the pin. Despite his flub, he saw the line as if it were a distinct, painted arrow on the slope. After Young missed his birdie putt, Johnny hit his solid and smooth. It held the break and ducked into the hole.

Just like that, he'd vaulted into the finals.

As the rules dictated, the match-play finalists would contest one round in the morning and a second after lunch.

None of the experienced players had ever heard of Johnny Goodman, but after the slight fifteen-year-old nudged Blaine Young out of the competition, a curious gallery numbering close to two hundred onlookers coalesced around him. Goodman's opponent, Ben Yousem, the recent Nebraska Amateur champion, was trailed by his own entourage.

In the deciding match, Yousem competed with a smile, but Goodman played with grim concentration. He didn't seem to see his friends anymore; he didn't respond to their advice on which way a putt would break or how to handle a fried egg lie in a trap. He had such a serious expression on his face, the other boys fell silent for the first time.

After fighting back from a three-hole deficit, Goodman still found himself one down after eighteen. In the final afternoon round, Johnny hooked his drive into the trees on the first hole, dropping two back. He fell further behind when Yousem birdied the second. Off the third tee he lost complete control of his drive, the ball sailing onto a cinder-covered road adjacent to the third fairway.

Despite this setback, Johnny's expression never changed. He looked over the rocky, loose ground, pulled a midiron from his bag, and picked the ball clean off the difficult lie, landing it ten feet from the pin. When Young posted a shaky bogey, Johnny picked one up. He'd turned a potential disaster into a win.

The *World-Herald* set the stage: "As he walked to the fourth tee he [Goodman] remarked to one of the numerous caddie friends who were following him: 'I'm going to win now. I'm only two down.' His confidence was still there."

Although Johnny promptly lost the next hole when Yousem dropped a thirty-footer for a birdie, he fought back, taking the sixth with a tough par, and sinking a birdie putt for a four on the seventh. Suddenly, he was only one down.

The pressure was on Yousem. How could he lose to a nobody, and a kid from South Omaha, no less? Rattled, he three-putted the eighth. Meanwhile, Johnny made an easy par and evened the match.

From that point, the struggle seesawed until Yousem sank an eight-footer for a birdie three on sixteen to go one up with two holes to play.

Now Goodman faced the Field Club's monstrous closing holes with one foot already in the grave. Teeing off on the backbreaking par-five Long Tom, Johnny tried to steer his drive around the trees to cut off the dogleg, but he came up short. Now he had to knock it out and get some distance or be devoured by the hole's 622 long yards. Taking a midiron, he slashed out of trouble, leaving himself a daunting but makable approach shot. Doggedly, he ripped a second midiron, which sailed right and nestled in the rough.

When Yousem sliced his third behind a stand of trees, Johnny had an opening. Reminding himself to cut through the long grass with a firm swing, he recovered to four feet.

How many times had he read this putt as a caddie? He crouched like a catcher. There was a spike mark on the edge of the hole. The putt would flow against the grain. A slight rise on the left suggested a left-to-right break, but he couldn't give away the hole. He felt strangely double-minded, both caddie and competitor in the same body. Then, with a simple, resolute strike, he knocked the ball in. After thirty-five holes, the antagonists found themselves dead even.

Barely 130 pounds, Goodman packed a decent punch. Nailing yet another long iron approach, he reached the distant par-four eighteenth green in two. Off to the right, Yousem threaded a brilliant spoon through a narrow opening, reaching the edge of the putting surface. After halving the hole and still deadlocked, both golfers dragged themselves back toward the first tee.

Johnny had already come out on top in one sudden-death playoff that day, and he'd birdied number one twice during his matches.

Taking advantage of a fairway baked hard and dry, Goodman almost drove the green. Shaken by his inability to put his opponent away, Yousem popped one up barely 180 off the tee. Then he flopped his approach weakly to the fringe. Now Johnny needed one more nerveless chip. He thought of Hagen's rhythm with the short clubs, the way Sir Walter accelerated through every shot. Crisp and clean, crisp and clean, he told himself. Don't tighten up. Setting himself slightly open, he took one long look and flicked the ball at the hole. Five feet from the pin. Good enough.

Yousem lagged to ten feet and the door was open.

Johnny's putt looked like a left-to-right breaker, slightly uphill. He had to follow through, make sure he got it to the hole. If he ran it by a few feet, so be it. Just don't quit. When he took his backswing, he sensed it was too long. If he followed through with it, he'd blast it way by. If he quit, he'd stub it. It was amazing how many thoughts could flash through his mind before his club tapped the ball. Surrendering to the momentum of the clubhead, he heard the ball click and drop into the cup.

The contest was over. It was a strange feeling. He'd almost thought it would go on forever. For a moment, his knees turned to water. Prickles of heat broke out on his cheeks. Flat caps flew in the air. He heard the cheers as if they were at the other end of a tunnel.

As the *Omaha Bee's* publisher presented him with the victory cup, Johnny blinked at the spectacle of dozens of boys in overalls shouting, bouncing up and down, whistling through their teeth. One of their own had won something, for once.

Goodman was the youngest winner in the history of the Metropolitan. Taking the trophy in his hands, he couldn't help smiling. Maybe he shouldn't show how happy he was, maybe he ought to act the way Bobby Jones always did, shy and modest, but he couldn't help himself. The caddies hooted and whistled. Johnny kept smiling.

"Never in the history of the metropolitan association . . . has a champion been given such a demonstrative and straight-from-the-heart ovation," the *World-Herald* declared. "John was and still is a Field Club caddie and now, more than ever before, he is the hero and the idol of the hundred or more youngsters who work with him."

For his efforts, the sponsors rewarded Johnny with a few cases of pop. He tossed the soda bottles to his caddie friends, who swarmed around him.

Johnny's victory eclipsed what would have been Omaha's biggest sports story of the day, local boy Roy Luebbe's first appearance with the New York Yankees. Luebbe had caught a full nine innings for Bob Shawkey, but Goodman's unlikely victory relegated the catcher's breakthrough to a small box. Accounts of Goodman's gritty performance filled whole columns.

That night Johnny went back to his room, but seized with a fear that burglars would steal his trophy, he asked Matt's mother to lock it in her cedar chest until morning. When he woke up at five, he ate a Spartan breakfast and then traveled across town to Fort Crook, where his sister Anna was working as a maid for an army officer. For a few minutes he let Anna admire the cup, then he set out for the St. James orphanage, where he shared his good fortune with his younger brothers. He had to explain what a golf tournament was, and what he'd won, but in the end he wasn't sure they understood at all.

8

BY 1921 THE STIGMA of unrealized expectations was weighing heavily on Bobby Jones. Although his fame, fed by Grantland Rice and other worshipful sportswriters, was growing, he hadn't come through. His renown only added to his burdens. It was no small feat to live up to the media's idealized version of Bobby Jones. He had the dark good looks, the style, the clothes, and the ever-present entourage, but he didn't have much to show for his celebrity except celebrity itself.

In fact, Bobby Jones came of age when modern celebrity was being born. Taking advantage of the latest technologies, mass culture was creating new heroes and villains, and in the process undermining the old verities. It started with the Dempsey-Carpentier fight. Three men at ringside offered play-by-play over telephones, their accounts transmitted through the ether to eighty sites around the country. The experiment, an exercise in "wireless telephony," didn't get much notice, but a few months later, in the winter of 1921–22, radio was everywhere. In a state of wonder, people tuned in concerts in their own living rooms. They picked up signals from as far away as Havana. President Harding had a receiver installed in his study, and members of the Dixmoor Golf Club had church services piped into the clubhouse.

Popular fare didn't stay chaste too long. Newspapers, increasingly dependent on sensational stories, gobbled up radio stations, giving the mass media more capacity to tell the tales of terrible and terribly fascinating crimes. When the Reverend Edward Wheeler Hall and Mrs. James Mills, who led the choir, were shot to death and left in a suggestive embrace in an abandoned farm in New Brunswick, New Jersey, a delicious thrill ran through the pages of Mr. Hearst's newspapers and the rest of the tabloids as well.

There was never a shortage of new crimes and fascinating new monsters. Within this vast landscape of pictures, stories, and breathless wireless announcements, clearly labeled forces of good and evil waged perpetual war, driving circulation through the roof. After hemlines rose to nine inches above the ankle, the *New York Times* boomed its disapproval, fixing yet more attention on the delicious iniquity. Tabloids joined the chorus of moral censure, selling more copies with every blast of disapprobation. Immune to the bombast of papers and preachers alike, hemlines rose several inches higher. Bright young women adopted short-sleeved, gauzy dresses. Some took to rolling their stockings down to expose forbidden knees and ankles.

Cosmetics, previously the preserve of actresses and other women of questionable virtue, took the place of fashionable pallor. As the novelist Dorothy Speare put it in *Dancers in the Dark,* "The intoxication of rouge is an insidious vintage known to more girls than mere man can ever believe."

Adding to the dangers of lipstick and eye shadow, speakeasies sprang up in the cities and, in the midst of Puritanism's greatest triumph, Prohibition, everybody was drinking. An invasion of vamps and bootleggers threatened to undermine the American way of life.

Naturally, the mass media's hunger for heroes grew too. Baseball players, who at one time were regarded as little more than harddrinking, brawling thugs from the slums, were now elevated to the moral highlands. College football stars took on the stature of biblical scourges when Grantland Rice compared the Yale backfield to the Four Horsemen of the Apocalypse. Fighters were transformed into noble gladiators, none greater than Jack Dempsey.

After Grantland Rice invented the art of play-by-play when he broadcast the 1922 Yankees-Giants World Series, radio was able to inflate athletes to heroic proportions. With his earphones tucked under his fedora, Rice spoke into a slender device that looked a bit like a telephone, first waiting for each play to wind down before re-creating it in bursts of lyrical language. Soon after, Rice launched a newsreel company, Grantland Rice Sportlight Films, magnifying the faces of Dempsey, Ty Cobb, and Red Grange on towering movie screens before a gaping public. In the mid-1920s, in a second news-reel venture, Rice used film to elucidate every sporting pursuit under the sun, idealizing along the way skeet shooters, crocodile hunters, lion hunters, moose hunters, and saltwater game fishermen.

In this new pantheon, no one shone brighter than that white knight, Bobby Jones, though his canonization was not completed until the mid-1920s. Just as the public was fed a Babe Ruth who lived to pat little boys on the head, rather than the real Babe Ruth who lived to binge on hot dogs, booze, and amenable women, the mass media offered up a matinee idol Bobby Jones whose charming manners, perfectly tailored clothes, cowlick of black hair, and sweet Georgia accent represented the last word in class. The pleasure he took in telling an occasional blue joke, his taste for corn liquor, his lacerating fears, in short, everything that made him human, was wiped from the canvas.

Meanwhile, in the messy real world, Bobby Jones was losing his nerve. On his way to St. Louis for the 1921 U.S. Amateur, Jones shared his creeping doubts with O. B. Keeler, openly expressing his concern that he might never win a major championship. He had been banging his head against that wall since 1914 with nothing to show for it.

Keeler fired back, as only Bobby's closest confidant could. Jones's problem now was mental. He had to *believe* he was the finest golfer in the world before he could become the best.

Bobby was dubious. He had started looking around, and he'd noticed to his distress that some of his competitors were pretty damn good. There might be an objective reason he hadn't won a big one yet, he thought — there were subtle cracks in his gorgeous game and under pressure they always began to show. Despite O.B.'s reassurances, Bobby's confidence was leaking away.

He couldn't quite get his balance when the pressure was on. In the

1921 U.S. Amateur, held at the St. Louis Country Club, Bobby made a brilliant start, brushing aside his first two opponents. In the third round he came up against Willie Hunter, the reigning British Amateur champion.

After his poor performance in the British Amateur, Jones was looking forward to getting a shot at the twenty-eight-year-old Hunter, whose father was head pro at Deal. Recalling his emotions on the eve of the match, Jones remarked, "How I pined for a chance to get at him! Now (thought I) we've got some regular greens that will hold a pitch and not skid a putt off into a bunker . . . we've got some regular turf, and Willie can't run his drives a hundred yards . . . after they hit the ground."

Outdriving the diminutive Hunter by thirty to sixty yards more often than not, Jones played the front nine in one under but found himself only two up. At the end of the morning round, the tenacious Hunter, relying on his putter to level the playing field, was sticking close to the gifted Atlantan, despite Jones's superb performance.

Jones grew nervous. During the lunch break, in an uncharacteristic burst of superstition, he changed into a "luckier" pair of pants, pinstriped flannels. Despite O. B. Keeler's constant lectures on diet, he ate too much. The worm of doubt crept deeper into his consciousness. There were eighteen holes left to play.

In the steamy Missouri heat, the two combatants played spotty golf for the first seven holes, with Jones clinging to his lead. At the time, Bobby subscribed to the old Scottish saying, "When you get him one doon, get him two doon; when you get him three doon, get him four doon."

Inspired by this homespun wisdom, he conceived a brilliant idea, one sure to crush his pesky tormentor. From the elevated eighth tee, Bobby considered the sharp right dogleg. A towering stand of trees protected a small green from direct assault, forcing the prudent player to play safe into the fairway.

But Bobby had carried these sentinels in practice more than once. Wouldn't one more powerful drive to the apron knock the wind out of Hunter, putting him three down and breaking his will? In a rush of adrenaline, Bobby pictured the killing blow. His old sense of superiority surged through him, but it was a sensation tinged with self-doubt. If he didn't strike the ball absolutely perfectly, if he tightened up the slightest bit at the top of his backswing, he wouldn't get the distance he needed.

But couldn't he prove, with one glorious blow, that all the years of frustration had been a mirage? That only a few petty impediments had prevented the world from seeing the obvious: that he was the finest player on the planet? Why not do something spectacular to prove his point?

Succumbing to this siren song, Bobby took his languid backswing, screwed up every ounce of power he could summon, and ripped his tee shot. In his hands, he could feel it was a solid hit. He'd caught it flush, absolutely pure. The ball soared as high as the treetops.

As Keeler recounts, "It was an extremely perilous maneuver . . . Caught at the peak of its flight by the topmost branch of the tree, the ball came down like a wounded bird into a ditch full of stones and underbrush."

Climbing down into this pit, Bobby fought off a wave of shame. How could he have been so stupid? But he had hit a glorious shot. One more foot of elevation and he would have pulled it off. Hadn't he been cheated again?

Attempting to concentrate, he swatted at his half-buried ball but failed to move it from its nest. On his second swing, the ball skittered out, followed by a terrified rabbit, which, with its ears pinned back, fled in a serpentine route out-of-bounds.

His face flushed, Jones took three putts to get down, having turned a simple hole into his Armageddon. Hunter dropped a thirty-footer for par on the thirty-second hole. It was the Herron match all over again. On the thirty-third, Bobby tried to focus on an eighteen-inch putt, but he couldn't keep still. Self-disgust swept through him in gusts. With a jerk of his right shoulder, he yanked the ridiculously simple putt left, blowing yet another hole.

Jones felt so foolish he could barely stand it. But there was more golf to play, more humiliating public exposure to come.

On the decisive thirty-third hole, Jones misplayed his approach and, in frustration, tossed his club aside. Unfortunately, it bounced off the fairway and struck the leg of a woman in the gallery. Bobby still couldn't live up to the amateur ideal — under pressure he hadn't yet learned to mask his raw, competitive instincts.

The newspapers, which had been lauding Bobby's determination to control his temper, didn't report the incident. The spectator hadn't been seriously injured, but word of Jones's careless behavior got back to USGA president George Walker. Compared to Bobby's explosion at St. Andrews, the episode seemed insignificant, but it would have serious repercussions.

Crumbling before Hunter's killing short game, Jones was forced to concede on the next-to-last hole.

In a postmortem, O. B. Keeler told Bobby that his ill-considered gamble on the eighth hole had sent him down to defeat, but Bobby was still too young to absorb the lesson.

"I can play this game only one way," Jones swore. "I must play every shot for all there is in it. I cannot play safe."

Stubborn to a fault, the young man was wedded to his dashing style. It was a perfect prescription for failure.

After his defeat at the hands of Willie Hunter, Bobby Jones returned to Atlanta to find an unwelcome notice from George Walker, president of the USGA. "You will never play in a USGA event again unless you can learn to control your tantrums," Walker informed him. The USGA had finally lost patience with its mercurial star.

As far back as 1918 Jones, after a blowup during a charity exhibition for the Red Cross, had vowed to put a lid on his temper. "I resolved that this thing had to stop. It didn't overnight, but I managed it in the end, at least in tournaments." He added that "to the end of my days I encountered golfing emotions which could not be endured with the club still in my hands."

Yet it wasn't until Walker issued his demands that Jones finally suppressed his all-too-public rages and began the process of turning himself into the epitome of the amateur game's ethic. The transformation would take time, and it came about, at least partly, under duress.

The confrontation with Walker precipitated a crisis for Jones. Privately, he wondered to Keeler whether the price of competition, the strain on his nerves, the sudden weight losses, the frustrations of repeated defeat, were really worth it. He spent more time with his fiancée, the Atlanta debutante Mary Malone, and he also applied to the Harvard English Department, a startling decision for a twenty-year-old who had just earned a degree in mechanical engineering.

Slowly, Bobby Jones was maturing. He was involved in a serious relationship with a woman. He was renovating his Latin by picking his way through Cicero. Jones admired the orator's philosophy of modesty and restraint. He also wished he had a similar confidence in his gifts. Still a young man, he was already fighting the breakdown of his body. To repair the swollen veins in his left leg, he endured four operations. In June, bandages still wrapped around his stitches, he swept the Southern Open. By the time he entered the 1922 U.S. Open in Skokie, Illinois, he had mastered his explosive temper enough to keep it out of the public eye.

But he was still acutely aware of criticism. He heard the whispers; he knew what the sportswriters said. Despite his great shotmaking, he lacked the will to win. In fact, he was burdened more and more by the drive to succeed. He felt it like a pressure in his chest. He read the disappointment in Big Bob's eyes. Rather than bucking him up, O. B. Keeler's pep talks left him with questions he could not answer.

Sometimes being a carefree amateur golfer seemed too damned serious.

Skokie had been upgraded by the leading golf architect, Donald Ross, and baked hard by the sun. Along with many other competitors, Bobby didn't find the track too demanding, and he hoped that he might finally capture a major after seven years of frustration. Big Bob, sensing that he was putting too much pressure on his son, absented himself from the tournament.

Instead, the monosyllabic Stewart Maiden, Bobby's original mentor at East Lake, joined Keeler in Jones's entourage. The babbling O.B. and the stony-faced Scot, who did his best to ignore the sportswriter, made a comic duo, with Maiden doing a perpetual slow burn as O.B. inundated him with questions about his own broken-winged swing.

In the first round Bobby was paired with Walter Hagen, fresh from his British Open win at Royal St. George in Sandwich. In the first round at Skokie, Sir Walter ripped off one of his brilliant runs, posting a 68 the first time around, but in the second round he toured so many bunkers his score ballooned to a 77. Bobby played steadily, putting up a 74 and then a strong 72. In his third trip around the track he shaved off another two strokes. His 70 was good enough to tie him with Wild Bill Melhorn for the lead.

"The Skokie course was pretty easy, I fancied," Bobby wrote, calculating that all he needed to do was slice another two strokes off his third-round performance to take the crown.

Only a few years earlier Bill Melhorn, his closest competitor, had been crawling through the Florida circuit peddling *Golf Illustrated* and preaching the virtues of the Wright and Ditson rubber-cored Black Circle ball. Wild Bill sported a cowboy hat and a hayseed manner, just the right disguise for a man with a formidable memory and a talent for bridge.

At Skokie, Wild Bill had played rock-solid golf, posting 72, 73, and 71 to tie Bobby for the lead after the third round. A stroke behind stood John Black, a pipe-smoking, forty-three-year-old Scotsman. An old-school type, Black refused to wear the newly fashionable knickers, preferring the traditional trousers and cap. When he drew on his ever-present pipe, his caddie had to turn away to dodge the foul clouds of dark smoke.

Jones was sure he could take the championship if he could shoot a final-round 68, a task that didn't seem all that daunting after he had improved in each of his first three rounds. Losing had been an excellent mentor. He was playing a disciplined, steady game that had eluded him up until then.

When he made the last-round turn with an indifferent 36, he didn't panic, and he didn't lose his head when he heard the bad news at the tenth tee. The twenty-year-old professional Gene Sarazen, who had been playing far ahead of him, was in the clubhouse with a 68. The screws had turned another notch. Bobby needed to shoot 35 on the back to take his first major championship.

His game in high gear, he responded, stroking a perfect drive on the par-four tenth. Pumped up, he blasted his approach over the green. He took deep breaths and gave himself a talking-to, but a poor chip left him a ten-footer for par. Still he maintained his poise. He tapped the ball smoothly, and it rolled straight for the heart of the cup. Only at the last second did it curl away, catching the lip and spinning out.

"Kiltie [Stewart Maiden] and I looked at each other under the long, moaning sigh the gallery exudes on such occasions," O.B. recounted. "The little Scot was ghastly under his tan. He shook his head slightly. Bad business."

A short, husky young professional, Gene Sarazen played a free-swinging, ebullient game. Bernard Darwin likened his smile to the Cheshire Cat's. When he was on a roll, the smile on Sarazen's olive-skinned face grew wide, and with every succeeding birdie, wider still. His sunny personality belied his personal struggles, however. If Bobby Jones went through his most painful experiences on manicured fairways, Sarazen found his in less-exclusive environs.

During World War I Sarazen, the son of Italian immigrants, had pounded nails into roofs at a new induction center, sold hot dogs, and worked in a munitions factory that sent shells to the Russians. Plugging away on the assembly line, he came down with pneumonia so severe a priest administered the last rites. After he languished in the hospital for five weeks, doctors finally bored two holes through his back between his ribs and drained his lungs. It took him months to recover.

For a time he worked the night shift at Bridgeport Hospital. "My job was a grim one," Sarazen recalled. "Clad in robe and mask I would follow after the doctors who checked the beds marked with a red light, the notification that the patient was not expected to survive the night . . . I wheeled these bodies down the halls of the top floor, onto the elevator, and out into the morgue in the cellar. I still shudder when I think of the solitary descent into the silent morgue in the dead of night."

By the time he was seventeen, Sarazen had almost died, barely survived an operation, and spent months wrapping the dead in winding sheets. "When I reflect on those months at the Bridgeport Hospital, I think that this exposure to real tragedy accounted for the comparative coolness with which I could take competitive golf when other young men my age, who had led sheltered lives, were shaking at the knees."

After walloping a driver off the fairway to reach the par-five eighteenth in two — the go-for-broke maneuver was typical Sarazen — Gene two-putted for a birdie and a two-stroke lead. Sarazen, who was playing for a living, also played for the sheer joy of it. The young pro swaggered straight to the bar, where Walter Hagen himself bought the elated golfer a drink and told him he had a good chance of winning.

Then a "locker room jockey" shattered Sarazen's calm by pointing out that Jones and Black had plenty of holes to play and they could easily overtake him.

By now Jones knew the "iron number" Sarazen had put up on the board. He thought of medal play that way. In his mind, shooting for the lowest score had a rigid, sterile quality. Match play was rich in the interplay of character. You could see your opponent's small gestures, the way he set his mouth, the uncertain look in his eye when he lined up a putt. Medal play was an industrial thing, hard and unyielding.

Needing to find a birdie someplace, Bobby dug himself a deeper hole after pitching over the twelfth and going another stroke over par. Jones describes the almost unbearable strain of the moment. "I was working as hard as I ever did in my life, and when I sank a thirty-five-foot putt for a birdie three at the fourteenth, I found myself flat on the turf as the ball dropped."

His hopes revived, Jones calculated that all he needed was one more birdie to tie Sarazen, and the eighteenth, reachable in two shots for the long-hitting Bobby, was the most vulnerable hole. He almost picked up a stroke at the fifteenth, his birdie putt rimming the cup, but his confidence was soaring now. After a booming drive on the seventeenth that sailed over a distant mound, he strode after his ball, preparing to knock the next one close.

Unfortunately, he hadn't seen the perverse kick his drive had taken, leaving him a tough lie on a roadway under a tree. Instead of swatting at the ungrateful ball in a snit, Bobby simply examined his situation. In the past, bad breaks had made him feel like a victim of malevolent forces. This time he accepted his misfortune and went on to the next shot. Hacking at the tight lie, he managed to bang the ball to the front edge of the green, where, after hanging for a tantalizing moment, it rolled back off the putting surface all the way to the fairway.

Then Bobby's stroke tightened up. He dumped his chip short of the hole. When he failed to get his putt to the hole as well, he'd lost another stroke to par.

All hope was not lost yet, though. An eagle on the eighteenth wasn't out of the question. Straining, Jones pulled his second shot and ended up on the back of the green. While he got up and down from there, his birdie wasn't enough to best Sarazen. Bobby Jones had fallen short again — by a single stroke.

Still, he had played some of the best golf of his career. The *Chicago Tribune* called his performance "immaculate," and Rice claimed Bobby's play had been "the greatest display of his brilliant career." The well-oiled Jones bandwagon rolled on, but privately Bobby admitted to his intimates, "This championship quest was getting a bit thick."

However, Bobby did not see himself as a victim anymore. He had gained more distance on his quest by now. He understood that winning was all that mattered to the press, and to a certain element in American culture, and that viewing golf that way denigrated the game itself. A bad bounce here and there had beaten him, but he realized that a lucky bounce, equally arbitrary, could make him a winner. Golf seemed too rich and complex to restrict its meaning to wins and losses.

"I now feel more than ever that the popular value of a championship is a factitious rating," he explained, "and that golf is too great and too fine a thing, and too much an epitome of life itself, for such a ranking to do it justice."

With these words, Bobby Jones defined everything that was appealing about the amateur ideal. Turning the game into a commercial enterprise reduced it to "the leading money winners" lists we see in the sports pages today, all style, skill, and courage obliterated by dead columns of dollars and cents.

What Bobby Jones left out of his meditation, however, was the idea that above all else, the amateur played the game for the sheer joy of it. For all his business acumen, Gene Sarazen knew how to let go and ride the rapids of the game. When he applied a businesslike approach to a round of golf, he stifled his best instincts and became just another golfer. But when he threw caution to the winds and let his natural athleticism take over, Sarazen could play like the swashbuckling Hagen himself.

At Skokie, Bobby Jones played with the grim intensity of a professional. Gene Sarazen played with the amateur's supposed careless sense of freedom.

Back in Pittsburgh, Sarazen made a grand appearance at a William Tell Hotel banquet in his honor. Crouched inside a giant papier-mâché golf ball, he waited until the band struck up "The Star-Spangled Banner." On cue, Gene, grinning from ear to ear, popped out of his hiding place and hoisted his U.S. Open Cup over his head to thunderous applause.

It's safe to say that Bobby Jones would never have gone along with this stunt, or ever had so much fun.

9

I N THE FACE OF HIS SETBACKS, Bobby Jones was becoming more and more philosophical. O. B. Keeler encouraged this stoical view of the game. To O.B., with his taste for classical literature, accepting "the rub of the green" had much in common with accepting the irrationality of the ancient gods. Golf punished its acolytes for no reason at all. That was its nature.

Bobby understood O.B.'s point on an intellectual level, but he continued to berate himself. And he couldn't get his doubts out of his mind. If he was such a great stylist and shotmaker, why couldn't he win? He longed to go back to the days when golf was simply a happy pastime, not a neurotic obsession.

The fact that the twenty-year-old Jones had a life outside golf helped him forget his torments. After entering Harvard in the fall of 1922, his intellectual curiosity led him through a curriculum that included European history, Dryden, Swift, Shakespeare, composition, and comparative literature. He intended to finish his degree at Harvard in a single year. After he finished his education and found some way to support himself and a family, he intended to marry Mary Malone.

Mary was anything but a flapper. A slender, retiring beauty, she preferred formal dances to the peculiar gyrations of her own generation. It is striking that Bobby became involved with such a restrained young woman when his good looks and celebrity would have given him license to run riot in the openly licentious culture of the time.

In the fall, Jones pressed on with his studies and did his best to forget that small, white, dimpled balls even existed, but major tournaments have a way of coming around like the seasons, and by June he was at it again in the 1923 U.S. Open on a tough Inwood, Long Island, track.

Just before the battle at Inwood began, Bobby had been grumbling about his putting woes to Stewart Maiden's brother Jimmy, the pro at the nearby Nassau Country Club. After listening sympathetically, Jimmy produced a battered implement with a slightly lofted, nicked face stippled with rust. A hairline fracture ran down its hickory shaft. Like many of the period's handcrafted clubs, this one had a name: Calamity Jane.

Legend has it that Bobby took it to the practice green, sank twenty-four out of his first twenty-five attempts, and stuck it in his bag. Permanently.

A former potato farm, Inwood, aside from its punishing length, offered the pleasures of tight fairways, impenetrable rough, and greens slick as wet marble. Not far from the steamy swamp of Jamaica Bay, the Long Island track shimmered in the summer heat. To fight the elements, Walter Hagen, off a second-place finish at the 1923 British Open, donned an African pith helmet, but the rest of the field wore more conventional gear.

Only two players in the talented field could break par in the first round; in fact, only two matched par. Jock Hutchinson posted a two under 70, and Bobby Jones, with Calamity Jane on fire, put up a 71. Hagen blew to a 77, and Francis Ouimet limped in with an 82, a testament to the course's difficulty.

Jones played an excellent afternoon round of 73 and found himself only two strokes behind Hutchinson after thirty-six holes.

Bobby Cruickshank, a native Scot, managed a fine 73 for third. Cruickshank had withstood the horrors of World War I before emigrating to the United States. In the battle of the Somme, he'd witnessed his own brother being blown apart by an artillery shell. After months in a German prisoner-of-war camp, he'd led a daring escape and returned to the front lines. Despite all its terrors, Inwood wasn't about to intimidate Bobby Cruickshank.

At the beginning of the third round, Jones took a nosedive, making the turn with a 41, but he had great experience by now — he knew a bad run was in the cards for every golfer at some point — and he didn't crumble. A hot 35 on the back gave him a 76, and to his surprise, sole possession of the lead. Hutchinson had gone in the tank, falling four shots behind, and Cruickshank, three shots back, appeared to be on the ropes.

With a healthy lead, Jones was about to put all his doubts to rest. Then in the last round, his old demons started stirring. On the seventh hole, his drive took an unlucky bounce out-of-bounds, and he had to settle for a double bogey. Struggling, he could only manage a 39 at the turn. On the other hand, he'd shot even par on the back all week, and he still felt in control of his fate.

He dropped a twenty-footer for a birdie at the short par-four tenth and birdied the par-five fourteenth. Inexorably, inch by inch, he was creating daylight between himself and the rest of the field. How could he fail now? After scrambling out of a trap for his par on the next hole, all he needed were three pars in a row to slam the door shut on Cruickshank.

Then he yanked a midiron approach out-of-bounds on the sixteenth and had to take bogey.

On the seventeenth, he cracked a fine drive, only to muscle his approach over the green and into the rough. A delicate pitch didn't quite come off, and he missed his ten-footer, losing another stroke to par. Now there was no denying it. Once again the graceful Atlantan was flying apart before the crowd's eyes. Perhaps he was too fine-tuned, too delicate a mechanism to stand these final pounds of pressure. Eyes sunken, head down, Bobby Jones trudged to the eighteenth tee.

Inwood's closing hole was considered as daunting as the eighteenth at Carnoustie. Running 428 yards in length, the tight fairway was hemmed in by deep, uneven rough and a line of trees as well. Guarding the green was a lagoon that, despite its mild appearance, was a magnet for slightly errant shots.

Strangely enough, Jones had mastered the closing hole like no other player in the field, scoring two birdies and an easy par up to this point, but his entire history of collapses was weighing him down now. After yet another excellent drive, Jones made a mental mistake, choosing to take something off a three wood instead of ripping a full long iron. The results were dismal. He hooked the ball clear over the putting surface. Now a pot bunker stood between him and the green.

Jones promptly dumped his chip into the trap. One indifferent sand shot and two putts later, he posted an inglorious double bogey. In three holes, he'd given back four strokes to par.

After Bobby staggered off the last hole, O. B. Keeler was shocked by his haggard, drawn face. Francis Ouimet tried to console him. Joining in, Keeler insisted that Cruickshank wouldn't catch him, but Jones would have none of it.

"I finished like a goddamned yellow dog," he swore.

Hollow-eyed, he returned to the clubhouse to sweat it out with a stiff drink. Meanwhile, the wispy Cruickshank had gone on a tear. After making a birdie at the twelfth, he had forged a three-shot lead over Jones. All he had to do was play two over par for the next six holes, and he would be the new U.S. Open champion. The Scot looked like a shoo-in.

Then he began his own two-step with the Dame of Disintegration. He bogeyed the thirteenth and the fifteenth, giving back two-thirds of his lead. Unable to fight his way out of the tailspin, he double-bogeyed the sixteenth. Now he faced the daunting task of playing the last two holes in one under.

It looked as if Bobby Jones had backed into his first major championship.

Now the tough Scot righted himself. First, he put up a solid par on seventeen. Then he launched a perfect drive on the threatening closer. Unlike Jones, who had tried to finesse a wood coming in, Cruickshank whipped an iron that shot straight at the flag until it landed twenty feet from the pin and rolled to a cozy six feet.

Without blinking, Cruickshank calculated the line and knocked the putt in the heart of the cup, tying Jones with his last stroke on the last hole. After four dizzying rounds, nothing had been resolved.

Emotionally drained and exhausted, the two competitors had survived but been denied. Now they faced an eighteen-hole playoff.

In the clubhouse, Francis Ouimet protected the distraught Jones from the press, leaving Keeler to invent quotes for the hungry reporters. Then the former Open champion spirited Bobby away, taking him for a leisurely drive in the country and dinner at the Engineers Club. The restrained Ouimet was a steadying influence.

Over the meal, Bobby struggled to regain his footing. Years of defeat had tempered his perfectionism, and he decided that a playoff was all to the good. Why back into the championship? A head-to-head match would give him a chance to see if he was "hopelessly weak under the belt," as Bobby put it.

On the winding road back to the hotel, Ouimet sang a few pop songs in his practiced tenor and Jones watched the landscape drift by. That night he read a few chapters of a book and fell into a deep, nourishing sleep.

Tournament organizers fretted that a Sunday playoff would offend the pious, so in a nod to churchgoers they set the tee time at two o'clock in the afternoon. The bookmakers kept working, though. In recognition of Cruickshank's coolness under fire, he went off at 10 to 7.

When Jones appeared on the first tee, Keeler was appalled: "The boy's face was drawn, and introspective, with the look of a chess player exerting all the powers of his mind."

Keeler couldn't imagine either golfer putting on much of a show. However, defying the sportswriter's expectations, both competitors played superb, nerveless golf. First Cruckshank fashioned a two-stroke lead, then Jones climbed back into the fray. By the turn, the seesaw match was dead even.

At the twelfth Jones stuck his approach two feet from the pin and tapped in for a birdie, edging two strokes ahead, but the wild swings continued. Cruickshank just missed an eagle on the par-five fifteenth, but his bird was enough to pick up a shot. Jones sagged on the next hole with a double bogey. On the sixteenth Bobby scratched his way back into the lead, only to give it back by blowing his par on seventeen. After seventeen enervating holes, the two men stood tied yet again.

With the honor on eighteen, Cruickshank tried to hit a low draw under the wind. Instead, he snap-hooked it — his only poor drive of the day — and the ball came to rest behind a tree. Stymied, he had to play up short and hope to get up and down.

By now Jones was operating on sheer instinct. "The strain had killed us off," he recalled. "Anyway, it had killed me."

Muscle memory drove his swing as he faded a towering drive that flirted with the rough and then skittered onto a patch of bare, hard ground, settling finally on some loose dirt. After Cruickshank made a perfect recovery, Jones faced a perilous two-hundred-yard shot over the water. Storm clouds were gathering now. Just over the lagoon, the flag fluttered in the breeze.

"I suppose I had to decide again whether to play safe or go for it with an iron . . . But I don't remember it. Stewart Maiden was near me. He told me later I never played a shot more promptly or decisively. He says I picked a No. 2 iron from the bag and banged it."

Dazed, Bobby let fly with the long iron. Like a shot, the ball bored into the wind, its low trajectory holding the line until the white pellet bit into the putting surface, released, rolled — and kept rolling toward the flat, where it finally came to rest six feet from the hole.

Evidently Stewart Maiden, the least demonstrative of all men, didn't know where he was, either. In his excitement he took off his new straw hat and smashed it down on a caddie's skull. But the match hadn't ended yet, despite the thunderous applause.

Cruickshank still had a chance to get up and down.

The Scot was finally spent, though. He bladed his chip into a trap, blasted out twenty feet from the hole, and took two to get down. Double bogey. Jones cozied his six-footer close and the match was over.

Bobby Cruickshank offered effusive praise for Jones's "bonnie shot" on eighteen, and Francis Ouimet told Bobby it was "the finest shot he'd ever seen," but Jones, characteristically, deflated all the mythmaking. "I don't remember what I thought. I suppose I ought to say that I made up my mind heroically to win or lose with one shot — the magnificent gamble stuff. But I can't say that and be honest. I did think of playing safe . . . But it seems I didn't do it. I just banged away at it."

With one shot, Bobby Jones had finally broken through.

10

ANALYZING BOBBY JONES'S first major tournament victory, Grantland Rice focused on the Atlantan's nerve. "The red badge of courage always belongs upon the breast of the fighter who can break and then come back with a stouter heart than he ever had before." The *Atlanta Constitution* called Bobby "nothing less than an idol to the people of the city, the state and the south." The *New York Times* called him "the shining stylist of golf."

Much of the praise circled around a more elusive concept than golfing prowess — *the immaculate amateur*. Charles Blair MacDonald sent a telegram saying that there wasn't a "cleaner, finer sportsman." The British went into transports. Not only did they approve of Bobby's Vardon-like swing but, as George Greenwood reported, "Jones is admired not merely because he is a great and wonderful golfer, but because of his attractive personality. An Englishman loves a man who is frank, boyish, and unspoiled, and Jones is all of these things."

Only two years before at the British Open at St. Andrews, Bobby Jones had thrown a tantrum in Hill Bunker. He had followed up this self-centered performance by tearing up his scorecard and quitting golf's most revered tournament. In an amateur culture that prized the stoic manner, he had acted like a spoiled child. In retrospect, it seems astonishing that he was suddenly being lauded as *the* perfect amateur.

Bobby's personal qualities had a great deal to do with this. Aside from his outbursts on the golf course, he had a modest, winning personality. He was intelligent, well educated, and articulate. Puzzled by his celebrity, he was openly skeptical of his own myth — his self-deprecating streak was sincere. His soft, dark features and his signature cowlick made a good picture for the sports pages. He came from the right class of people, he wore the right clothes, and he had chosen the right fiancée.

In an earlier time, however, his new reputation would never have grown so quickly, or to such enormous proportions. In a period of deep, postwar disenchantment, the mass media was on the hunt for heroes, the simpler and purer the better. Nowhere was it easier to tell tales of heroism than on the sports pages. Tabloid reporting, Sunday supplements full of pictures, breathless play-by-play radio accounts of big games—all conspired to build larger-than-life figures with unprecedented speed. If Bobby Jones had had a few blemishes on his reputation, those persistent tantrums a few years before, no matter. A flood of gee-whiz journalism could obliterate the past in a flash.

At a time when children of the middle class were in open rebellion, Bobby Jones was also the least rebellious of sons. His glamour derived from a natural charisma, not garish, antisocial acts. The media, which delighted in reporting the depredations of depraved youth while simultaneously professing the most pious values, could hold Jones up as an attractive but utterly conventional alternative to the dissipated F. Scott Fitzgerald set.

Before his administration collapsed in a bribery scandal, President Harding had called for a return to something he called normalcy, but that meant reverting to the natural order of things when everybody behaved properly and everybody knew his place. Unfortunately, the old order was fraying, and never more so than inside a middle class whose children were riding around in cars, drinking bootleg liquor, and engaging in unspeakable gyrations on the dance floor. As one traditionalist put it, "The music is sensuous — the embracing of partners — the female only half-dressed — is absolutely indecent; and the motions, they are such as may not be described with any respect for propriety."

Jones, on the other hand, was attached to a highly respectable young woman whose taste in music and dance wouldn't have been out of place in the 1890s. There wasn't a whiff of scandal attached to his name — his drinking was a private, clubhouse affair — and he preferred living inside a tight knot of family and friends.

Although he hadn't inherited a fortune, Jones was clearly on a path to earn a comfortable living. There was never any question but that he would make money, and plenty of it. In this sense, he blended into another ideal figure of the time, the businessman. As the 1920s wore on, the businessman came to embody American culture's highest ideals. In fact, a best-selling book, Bruce Barton's *The Man Nobody Knows*, compared the modern corporate leader favorably with Christ. According to Barton, Jesus "picked up twelve men from the bottom ranks of business and forged them into an organization that conquered the world . . . Nowhere is there such a startling example of executive success."

Another hot seller compared Moses to a real estate promoter. In fact, it was so common for ballyhoo artists to conflate businessmen and religious figures that it was hard to tell which pursuit represented the higher calling. If the business of America had become business, a stark turnaround from prewar Progressive Era values, that business had also become a religion.

No figure of the time combined business success, glamour, charisma, and conventional social values better than Bobby Jones. That he did so while playing the upper-class game of golf, and that his swing was the last word in elegance, made for a perfect package.

In other words, Jones was not simply a great athlete who played by the rules. He was a modern hero and a traditional gentleman all rolled into one. Jones himself would have laughed at these claims, but his conventional image soothed Americans who were disturbed by stunned and aimless veterans who couldn't find work, by roaring speakeasies, by strikes and crimes and the all-too-knowing girls in Fitzgerald's *This Side of Paradise* who lounged around "impossible cafes" and bragged that they were "hipped on sex."

And now Bobby Jones was a winner — and wasn't winning, and identifying with the winner, what America was all about?

Despite his breakthrough in the U.S. Open, Jones faltered in the 1923 U.S. Amateur. He knew his game lacked a certain finish, and he knew where the weakness lay: he missed too many short putts under pressure. Walter B. Travis, who had first diagnosed the flaws in Bobby's putting stroke, came to the rescue.

By then the prickly, cigar-chomping Travis had done everything possible to advance American golf. He had won major tournaments; he had invented revolutionary concepts of golf course design, and he had conceived and published the game's premier magazine, *American Golfer.*

No one alive knew more about putting than Walter J. Travis. While the Royal and Ancient Golfing Society had banned the center-shafted Schenectady putter he had used to snag the 1904 British Amateur, it hadn't managed to outlaw Travis, whose unerring sense of distance, smooth stroke, and analytical gifts had made him the last word on the flat stick.

Travis gave Jones several tips. He told Bobby to splay his feet but also to get his heels closer together, so close that they were almost touching. He also urged him to draw the club back with his left hand and take a sweeping stroke, hinging his wrists in opposition in the process. In addition, he talked Bobby into changing his putting grip. Instead of overlapping his right index finger, Jones now overlapped the left.

Travis also suggested a breath-control method that Jones referred to as "tranquilized breathing" to quell his nervousness on the putting surface. Jones took Travis's lesson to heart, and soon Calamity Jane became a devastating adjunct to his superb ball-striking. On top of the world, Bobby Jones was still looking for an edge. Now he had found it.

In 1924 the U.S. Amateur returned to the Merion Cricket Club in Philadelphia, the site of the tyro Bobby Jones's debut. The symmetry couldn't have been more compelling. Having absorbed Walter J. Travis's lessons, Jones unveiled a deadly Calamity Jane. In the early rounds, he blew away his opponents. W. J. Thompson fell 6 and 5; Ducky Corkran went down 3 and 2; Rudy Knepper 6 and 4; Francis Ouimet 11 and 10. In the finals, Bobby closed out the proud George Von Elm by a humiliating 9 and 8 for his first U.S. Amateur championship.

After Jones's victory, the *Philadelphia Inquirer* ran a biographi-cal sketch of Bobby's career. Headlined "New Golf King Is a Fine Sportsman," the article went on to laud Jones for attending public schools and then, after garnering degrees from Georgia Tech and Harvard, "pressing the asphalt as he collected rents," an oblique ref-erence to his recent work with Adair Realty. What most impressed the anonymous author, though, was Jones's "remarkably rapid rise since he made his start from the foot of the ladder." Celebrity could do anything, even turn the privileged Jones into a populist icon.

Jones mania reached its peak when Bobby returned to St. An-drews in 1927 to take his second British Open. After he dropped his last putt, the gallery, ten thousand strong, swarmed onto the green, engulfing Bobby in its ecstatic — and crushing — embrace. Bernard Darwin feared that the adoring mob might devour its hero. In ter-ror, O. B. Keeler shouted, "They're going to kill him!"

Jones disappeared among the swirling mass of bodies. For a long moment, it seemed as if he might be extinguished by this outpour-ing of love, but then he floated out of the roiling crowd, waving Ca-lamity Jane, half in triumph, half in distress. It took a half dozen Scottish policemen to rescue the golfing deity from his acolytes.

During the presentation, Jones told the crowd that he would leave the Claret Jug at St. Andrews, a gesture that endeared him to both his hosts and the English press. *Golf Illustrated* observed that Bobby was a "better man than he is a golfer." *Golf Monthly* joined the cho-rus: "The character of Mr. Jones has captured the hearts of golfers of two hemispheres with his modesty and the sincerity of a nature as honest as the sunlight." Following suit, the American dailies gushed over Bobby's unblemished character.

As usual, Jones was a better barometer of reality than the wor-shipful media. Puzzled by his virtual deification, he remarked, "Of course it's nice to have people say nice things about you, but hon-estly, when New York papers make me out such a glowing example of moral discipline, I don't know what to make of it."

11

ON JUNE 22, 1926, less than a year after he'd won the Omaha city championship, sixteen-year-old Johnny Goodman made his way across the Union Pacific tracks and into the stockyards. During the spring of his junior year at South High, Johnny had conceived an audacious idea. He'd been wondering what he could do to top taking the Metropolitan. The Nebraska State competition was the most logical next step, but why not go straight to the big time? Why not catch a train to St. Louis and try his hand at the region's most prestigious amateur affair, the Trans-Mississippi?

If he went down in flames, they'd say he was just a 125-pound kid, but if he could make a good showing, he'd turn some heads. Johnny kept it to himself, but he also thought he might win. He didn't want people saying his head was too big for his hat, but every time he stepped on the golf course now, he believed he had a chance.

An abstract curiosity drove him too. If he was flattened in the first round, he'd learn where his game was weak. He'd find out what he had to work on. More than anything, he wanted to see how he'd stack up against men who had national reputations.

Maybe he wouldn't even qualify, but he'd been shooting lights out that spring. Lately, he had been scorching his drives ten or fifteen yards farther. The greens on long par fours looked closer, and he had to hit fewer, impossibly long brassies to get on in two. He was giving himself better looks, more chances to go low.

The gaunt young man wore a worn shirt, frayed at the collar, workpants, and dusty boots to fit in with the cattle drovers he'd be traveling with. Not that he owned anything much better. He'd grown a few inches, and he was starting to look like a scarecrow in the flannel trousers he'd worn in the previous year's Metropolitan.

Shifting his clubs on his shoulder, he picked his way around the pens, the stamping, lowing cattle. The twists and turns of fencing, the rattling freight trains, the stink of great animals packed together barely registered on his senses. They were just the fabric of his world.

Ranchers watched, eagle-eyed, as their hands unloaded their precious stock from the boxcars. Cattle drovers cursed at recalcitrant steer. Two cowboys hauled a downed calf right past him. It didn't matter. He was looking for his train. He climbed over another set of tracks and waited. Soon enough a steam locomotive's roar blotted out the voices of ranchers and their hands. Billowing smoke, the engine appeared around the bend, hauling its train of cattle cars.

Johnny knew exactly where to stand to catch his ride. As the freight cars squealed to a halt, he picked out the converted caboose set just behind the engine. A Cowboy Pullman, the drovers called it. The railroad always hooked this car up right behind the locomotive to prevent the caboose's occupants from choking on the cattle train's distinctive aroma.

Just in time, Johnny's friends Jack Pollard and Frank Siedlik descended on the freight train as well. Also teenagers, they'd been caddies at Omaha's Happy Hollow golf course. Hickory-shafted clubs rattled on their shoulders, too.

The boys handed the conductor the passes that Rollie Reynolds and Ed Cahow, members at the Lakewood Country Club, had wrangled for them and climbed aboard.

As the cars pulled out, the great packinghouses swam into view. After all his resolutions, Johnny hadn't been able to resist a job at Armour. It was the best thing he could find. Over the past two weeks, he'd been spending ten hours a day, six days a week, swabbing blood from the killing room floor and shoveling entrails into a hole for the princely sum of thirty cents an hour. When he knocked off a shift at the packing plant, Matt Zadalis recalled, "He sure smelled awful."

At one end of the converted caboose, battered coach seats had been jammed in; at the far side a rack of bunks climbed to the tin ceiling. Johnny hoisted his bag and his clubs up and onto one of the tick mattresses and gazed out the window.

The processing factories drifted closer, but he barely noticed the industrial landscape. His mind was on other things. They'd been accepted into the Trans-Mississippi qualifying rounds, but the event's organizers, and the members of St. Louis's Algonquin Country Club, hadn't taken a good look at Johnny and his pals yet. Would they even allow them to tee off? Or just laugh them off the course? In Omaha they knew who he was; he had his friends at the Field Club in his corner.

The boys didn't know a soul in St. Louis. How would they find their way to the club? Would they have a chance to clean up before presenting themselves to the tournament officials?

He wondered who he would come up against if he qualified for match play. Eddie Held and Jimmy Manion, both former Trans winners, would probably be contending for the title. Maybe James Ward, the Kansas City millionaire, a real shark who had all the time in the world to sharpen his game, would turn up, too. More than one Trans competitor had made it all the way to the U.S. Amateur.

How many rounds would he have to win before he got a chance to play Held or Manion? But what if he topped one off the first tee or started shanking and couldn't stop? Quickly, he banished these terrors from his mind. He had a gift for squelching his worst fears.

Winning the Omaha city title had swelled Goodman's confidence. Johnny knew he had talent, but his dedicated practice sessions had raised his game to a new level. His feel was better; he could vary an iron shot five yards here, five yards there, just by touch. His putter had been streaky of late, but sometimes, when he got hot, the hole looked as big as a saucer and he could just roll them in, one after another.

Johnny sat quietly, listening to the drovers talk. A cowboy with a face as dark as an oiled baseball glove recalled that in the winter of '25 there had been a snowstorm in the mountains and whole herds had frozen to death. His scrawny companion remarked that the price of beef was shaky.

"What're the sticks for, sonny?" the dark-faced cowboy asked. The man wasn't acting wise, Johnny sensed. He really didn't know. In South Omaha, plenty of people had never seen a golf ball.

"Golf."

"Oh, that's gawlf, huh?"

Now the boys turned to their subject. Frank started ragging Johnny about Bobby Jones. By this time, Johnny had elevated Bobby above Walter Hagen in his personal pantheon. Bobby, he was sure, was going to keep on winning, and he had the greatest style. Frank kept at it. Why had Johnny's big hero lost in the recent British Amateur? Wasn't Jess Sweetser, the winner and first American to take the British crown, better than Johnny's precious Bobby?

"Jones is probably a flash in the pan," Frank needled. "He'll start losing all over again."

Johnny gave his usual laconic reply. "Bobby Jones is the best player in the world." Johnny didn't say he'd squirreled away a score of articles to prove his point. He didn't mention that he could close his eyes and see Bobby's liquid backswing, his half-a-heartbeat pause at the top, his dancerlike weight shift, and the blur of his shaft as it whistled through the shot. He'd read all about it, and he could see it crystal clear in his mind's eye.

He could practically recite Jones's modest speeches and the sportswriters' paeans to the Atlantan's sportsmanship. It was one thing to puzzle out the rules that the great amateurs followed, but another to mimic their polished ways. Imitating Bobby Jones's powerful swing seemed easier than aping his impeccable manners.

Jack and Frank horsed around some more, but Johnny, staring out the window, kept to himself. The flat plains went on forever, not a single farmhouse in sight. The world was mostly sky out here. Empty air, empty land. It made you feel very small.

At night, after the kerosene lamps had been turned down, he slipped his niblick out of his bag and lay in the darkness, gripping and regripping his favorite club. Sometimes, when he was right, the short iron felt like an extension of his hands, as if his nerves ran through the leather and right down the shaft.

When Goodman appeared on the first tee, a few Algonquin Country Club stalwarts muttered under their breath. It wasn't a friendly sound. The Trans-Mississippi was one of the most prestigious tournaments in the West, up there with the Western Open. Where did a kid who looked like *that* get his nerve?

Lacking a golf glove, and to the astonishment of the onlookers, the wispy Omaha youth rubbed his hands in the dirt, took a good grip, and lashed one up the right side, the shot curving into the center of the first fairway. When it hit the ground, it skittered and rolled another twenty yards.

The muttering faded away, replaced by a single low whistle.

"Sounded like a rifle shot," a man in white linen marveled.

In his qualifying round, Goodman's putter caught fire — he holed twenty- and thirty-footers as if they'd been preordained. Inspired by his short game, he proceeded to break Walter Hagen's course record. It was a shocking spectacle. Unlike the rest of the players, Goodman carried his own clubs, a sparse array of borrowed implements. Striding down the fairway alongside dapper golfers a decade or two older than he was, Johnny looked like the servant-boy who had wandered into the ball.

A *St. Louis Post-Dispatch* reporter was on hand, as well as a stringer for the Associated Press, and they smelled a story. By the time Johnny and Jack Pollard had torn through the early match-play rounds, the scribes had their angle. These kids had ridden the rods and crashed the Algonquin Club's posh party. Soon enough the papers were reporting that the boys had ridden a "cattle car," conjuring up images of hoboes stealing onto a freight train.

The reality of the Cowboy Pullman was colorful enough, but the newspapers started calling Goodman, Pollard, and Siedlik "the boxcar trio," transforming the boys into populist heroes.

Knocking off one experienced player after another, Goodman and Pollard charged into the semifinals. To gain the semis, Pollard bested Algonquin ace Roger Lord 4 and 2 in a tight match, but Goodman simply brushed aside his opponent, David Carter, 9 and 8.

"Two sterling Omaha youngsters who came here aboard a cattle train to try their luck against a field of Middle Western stars," the Associated Press reported, "tonight coveted the honor of entering the semifinal round of the Trans-Mississippi golf tournament with a pair of outstanding veterans of this section."

Now the boys had to face more formidable opponents, Eddie Held and Johnny Dawson. Playing on his home course, Held posted a 70, going four up for the morning round. In the afternoon, he swamped Pollard, closing the boy out on the twelfth hole.

Against Dawson, Johnny Goodman put up a much stiffer fight. Although he never led the match, he twice pulled into a tie, finally going down to defeat by a hair, 2 and 1. Pollard had played admirably, but Goodman was clearly the tougher competitor. The *New York Times* praised the pair's performance: "Playing in their first major tournament, both stood the gaff like veterans."

Back in Omaha, Goodman couldn't understand all the fuss about the "boxcar trio." After all, he'd lost when he'd had Dawson on the ropes. In fact, all he could think about were his blown putts, fat chips, and loose short irons. So many lost chances, so many mental mistakes. What the hell was the matter with him?

Yet his name was all over the *World-Herald* and the *Bee*. Back in school in the fall, kids in home economics and English asked him about his adventures, and he barely knew what to say. He never liked all the exaggerations the papers were peddling about him. He didn't ride the rods like a hobo. He had a ticket. He thought the truth should stand for itself. Still, he supposed he hadn't done all that bad in St. Louis.

Slowly, his new status sank in. Being the center of attention never ceased to make him squirm, but he didn't mind moving up a notch. He met a girl named Mae, who wore a cloche hat and racy stockings when he took her to a dance. She swore everybody looked up to him now, and she let him kiss her on Saturday nights. He grew self-conscious about his looks. He kept himself clean, and his hair combed just so. He was on display now.

The following spring he wrote in his high school yearbook: "One day I woke up and I was famous."

In June 1927 Johnny Goodman received his high school diploma. His determination to graduate was of a piece with his disciplined approach to the links. At a time when completing four years of secondary education was a significant achievement, he managed the feat while simultaneously supporting himself.

His accomplishment didn't go without recognition. At the South High graduation ceremonies, Johnny was named "the outstanding scholar of character." The award included a two-hundred-dollar scholarship.

Shortly afterward, Johnny's supporters at the Lakewood Country Club where he had been playing — membership fees were lower there than at the elite Field Club — got together and bought him a ticket to Colorado Springs for the 1927 Trans-Mississippi Tournament at the Broadmoor Country Club. They wanted to give Johnny a second crack at the big time.

Since his first appearance at the Trans, Johnny had won medalist honors in the Nebraska State Championship, but had gone down to a bitter defeat against Foye Porter in the semifinals. The *World-Herald* remarked on how hard he took his loss after his brilliant stroke-play performance in the qualifying rounds. "He [Goodman] cannot take his golf lightly. Some wondered at the anger and disappointment he manifested when he made strokes that cost him the state championship. Outwardly, he didn't put on the 'I don't care' attitude that is supposed to mark the true sportsman. For Johnny, an error isn't just a bit of bad luck, but a blunder in his business, something that mustn't happen again."

The criticism rankled, but Johnny also believed it was true. In the manner of Bobby Jones, amateurs were supposed to veil their drive to win behind "gracious" gestures. Johnny knew that. But he also wondered why the *World-Herald* had made such a big deal out of his visible disappointment. After all, Bobby Jones had thrown more than a few clubs when he was growing up. Why had the papers been so ready to forgive Bobby, but so eager to jump all over him? It didn't seem fair. Still, he swore he'd cover up his real feelings from now on. There was an art to losing too, a subtle, mysterious art he longed to master but feared he never would.

Only seventeen, Goodman was growing tournament-tough. Getting mad just hurt your game. Once you blew your stack, you started throwing strokes away, and he wasn't giving away a damned thing if he could help it.

Bobby Jones didn't give anything away. Johnny had tacked five different articles about Bobby on his bedroom wall, including three of the columns Jones had just started writing for the Bell Syndicate. Bobby had written a book, *Down the Fairway,* and Johnny was always pestering the local librarian to get it for him.

When he read Bobby Jones, he wasn't looking for little tips that would transform his game. He could always feel his way toward this or that shot. What he wanted from Bobby, and sometimes found, were his thoughts on how to analyze the percentages and how to win. Around the green Bobby was always asking, How much room is there? What's the right club? What's the safest route? Or as he put it in one column, "Ground, wind, slope, lie — everything must be accounted for and valued accurately."

Everybody loved talking about Bobby's gorgeous swing and how far he could hit a golf ball, but Johnny was interested in how orderly Bobby's thinking was, and how he paid attention to the golfer's psychology. Jones wrote things like "too much ambition is a bad thing to have in a bunker." Bobby wasn't talking about technical tricks there; he was talking about mental balance.

In trying to explain the temperament of the great golfer, Bobby also drew on what some of the best players in history had told him. Johnny read these quotes and took them as gospel. One of his favorites was the British master J. H. Taylor's remark that all great champions possessed "courageous timidity." You could spend days trying to figure out what that meant, but when you finally grasped it, it was like understanding the mystery of the Holy Trinity.

Then he remembered that Stanley Davies had studied with Taylor. From Taylor to Davies to him. Golf's history running straight through his veins. It was a heady feeling.

Johnny also loved to read how Bobby Jones handled himself, win or lose. Sure, he'd had his blowups as a kid, but as a grown man, Jones was so restrained, so smooth, so understated. Everything Johnny wasn't. He couldn't keep letting his guard down, giving galleries a glimpse of the fury that drove him, anger he so often turned on himself. He had to get control of himself. He wasn't a boy anymore. Everything was changing; his friends back in South High, the Lakewood Country Club, and the Field Club had high expectations for him. He had to give it everything he had, and keep a tight leash on himself, all at the same time.

With the *World-Herald*'s criticism ringing in his ears, Johnny made a point of wearing an impassive mask. The *St. Louis Post-Dispatch* made much of his calm demeanor, describing Johnny as "cool as the top of Pike's Peak." The reporter was particularly impressed by Johnny's disposition in his semifinal victory over Jimmy Manion, "one of the hardest amateurs west of the Mississippi to beat."

In the *Post*'s words, Manion was "a money player, but to John Goodman he looked like anybody else. John pursued the even tenor of his way. When he had a hard putt, he squatted down Indian fashion behind his ball, his slim body tied into a knot, and studied the situation. To John Goodman there is never any hurry. If Davey Crockett had not said 'Be sure you are right, then go ahead,' John Goodman would have said it. That is if he ever said anything, which he doesn't. He is a true son of silence, beside whom the Sphinx is a chatterbox."

Johnny had discovered a deep secret, one that transcended the trick of winning a golf match. If he said absolutely nothing, no words could be held against him.

Observers at Broadmoor compared his swing to the British ace Abe Mitchell's graceful stroke, also noting its resemblance to Harry Vardon's classic style. Against Manion, Johnny started with a rush, dropping a five-footer for a birdie on the second and exploiting Manion's shaky start to go three up after four. Nothing exemplified Goodman's play better, however, than his performance on the par-five sixth, when he completely missed his drive, the ball squirting through a trap and barely reaching the fairway. Without blinking, Johnny ripped a long iron, pitched on, and rolled a forty-footer dead to the pin to retrieve his par. Manion, who had split the fairway with a perfect drive, could do no better. Johnny's steady play against Manion vaulted him into the championship round.

In the finals against James Ward, Goodman's morning round was nearly flawless. He drove the ball well, he pitched brilliantly, and he sank several putts inside fifteen feet, including curling one around a near stymie that dropped into the back of the cup. He faltered on the short par-three sixteenth, making his only three-putt. Ward dropped a ten-footer for a birdie on the 528-yard seventeenth, but Johnny's par on the last hole put him back up by five, a formidable lead.

In the afternoon round of the match-play affair, Ward launched a furious comeback. The *St. Louis Post-Dispatch* piled on the superlatives. "Then the fireworks. Ward, who the day before had set an alltime tournament record with a dazzling 68, began to find his stride. Birdie followed birdie as the Kansas City ace relentlessly hacked into Goodman's advantage, and while Goodman was shooting par golf he came to the thirty-second hole with only a one-hole lead."

The reporters all agreed. The battle-tested Ward would swamp the inexperienced upstart now. Goodman was an appealing oddity who would soon fade back into obscurity.

In fact, after Johnny duck-hooked his drive, pushed his approach, and missed a two-footer on the thirty-second hole, a 428-yard par four, it looked as if he was handing the title to the veteran Ward. Johnny's putter was starting to desert him, too.

The next hole, a short par four, proved to be the turning point. Johnny nailed a drive straight down the right side, dropped a niblick ten feet from the pin, and banged the putt home for a birdie three. Ward could do no better than par.

Off the tee at the par-five, 528-yard thirty-fifth hole, Johnny's low drive raced down the center, a long roll putting it 250 yards out. After a perfect spoon, he chipped from the front edge, barely missing an eagle, and tapped in for his birdie. His nerveless performance in the crunch couldn't have been more decisive. As unlikely as it seemed, the scrawny seventeen-year-old was the new Trans-Mississippi champion.

For his efforts he took home an elaborate silver loving cup, which the modest Lakewood Club had the right to display until a new Trans-Mississippi winner was crowned. In the peculiar calculus of amateur golf, Johnny himself was rewarded with a sterling silver tea set, an expensive reward that somehow didn't compromise his amateur status.

The tournament organizers showered Goodman with praise, but none was sweeter than the wire service copy. "The new champion is a slender, clean-cut youth and a sportsman throughout. He neither smokes nor drinks. He is also an unusual golfer in that he doesn't swear at his club when he makes a poor shot."

A sportsman throughout. Goodman savored that one.

At least no one heard his swearing anymore, now that he'd put a lid on every steaming word.

Johnny was stunned by his reception back home.

Automobiles draped with banners tooted as they joined the parade. Led by a motorcycle-police escort, Father Flannagan's Boys Band and Frost's Battery Band, and trailed by a calliope, the procession snaked its way through knots of well-wishers on its way to the Lakewood Country Club, where members had organized a banquet. Mayor Dahlman announced the creation of a Johnny Goodman Education Fund, and before the event was over, the club's members and various dignitaries had pledged $1,565.

School Superintendent Beveridge explained that the community wanted Johnny to get a college education, which would keep him in Omaha and prevent him from being enticed into the ranks of golf professionals. Repeatedly, dignitaries compared Johnny to America's most revered hero, the pilot of the *Spirit of St. Louis,* Charles Lindbergh.

Still, there was a bittersweet undertone to the *World-Herald*-sponsored affair. In honor of the festivities, many of Goodman's brothers and sisters were reunited for the first time in nearly three years. The children, Tom, seven, Peter, nine, Mike, twelve, Mary, fourteen,

Anton, fifteen, Anna, seventeen, Will, nineteen, and Joe, twenty-one, were displayed in two Packard automobiles furnished by the J. H. Hansen Packard company. (Within three years, Pete and Tommy would be farmed out from the orphanage to the Montana beet fields. In his eighties Tom Goodman recalled that the grown men picking beets, sorting potatoes, and working on threshing crews next to him earned twenty-five cents an hour, while he was paid fifteen cents for the same work.)

At the end of the parade route, waiting for Johnny to arrive, Anna clutched Tom and Peter, who had been furnished with white suits by the orphanage. Mike was decked out in his Boy Scout uniform. The wait dragged on and on. The boys showed off a few golf balls they had gathered from some mysterious source. They squabbled about the last time they had seen Johnny. Had it been three or four months?

The *World-Herald* provided them with root beer. After this exciting distraction, the conversation turned back to Johnny. Would he ever show up? The family huddled together like any other pack of adoring fans.

When Johnny's face appeared behind the windshield of his touring car, he looked more bewildered than elated. Finally, he groped his way to Anna and his brothers, but his few, choked words were drowned out by the crowd. The boys thrust their golf balls in his hands. He smiled slightly. In a moment, parade officials hustled him away.

PART TWO

The Battle by the Sea

12

WHEN JOHNNY GOODMAN finally reached Monterey in late August 1929, he had more on his mind than the U.S. Amateur. He felt uncomfortable without his new sports jacket. Maybe there would be some sort of formal affair at Pebble Beach, and he'd be the only one without one. Then there were meals. They'd be sure to cost a fortune, and he'd be miles from the nearest cheap restaurant. Not to mention caddie fees. The bag haulers who were used to working the posh Del Monte clientele weren't about to loop for a measly fifty cents a round. Maybe they wouldn't be kids at all. Maybe they'd be tough, full-grown men who'd give him a hard time if they thought he was a cheapskate.

The hotels were jam-packed, and most were too expensive for him anyway. Wandering the streets, he noticed how different the buildings were from Omaha's. Some had iron grilles on their windows. Others had dusty white walls, some kind of plaster, he thought. Combing the back streets, he found a rundown but clean rooming house that offered stuffy quarters just off the kitchen. It was still too much, but he took it.

He dumped his things and headed for Pebble Beach. He had to see the course he'd been reading so much about. The links were miles away, but he hitchhiked the first part of the trip. Then he started walking. Along the way he noticed pine trees he'd never seen before, and then a strange, red-legged frog hopped across his path. Now he knew he was in California. He couldn't wait to see the ocean.

When he gave his name at the gate, there was a message for him. The USGA Amateur Status Committee wanted to see him. What for? His heart jumped in his chest. An officious marshal in a straw hat and white trousers led him to the clubhouse porch, where he was left to cool his heels.

A woman in a sleeveless jersey pushed open the clubhouse door and stepped out into the light. Another and then another followed, all long-legged and athletic-looking. Laughing softly at some private bit of gossip, they looked so bright, so healthy, so confident, they seemed unreal. Under their frank gaze, Johnny slid down into his chair. He watched them move across the lawn.

He waited, and then waited some more. He wanted to get a peek at the first hole, at least. What did the committee want from him?

Then the marshal, a malicious look on his self-satisfied face, returned and gave him the bad news.

It turned out that USGA officials had gotten wind of the fact that Johnny Dawson, his old Trans-Mississippi opponent, had been working in a Spalding sporting goods store, and they'd given him the boot. Now they wanted to talk to Goodman, who was also working for Spalding, and put him through the same third degree.

Johnny wondered how the USGA had even found out where he worked. The application for the U.S. Amateur didn't ask where a player was employed. Maybe they'd heard about it from some reporter, the regional association, or a former competitor. Whoever it was, he didn't have Johnny's best interests in mind.

The marshal told Johnny to stay put. The subcommittee would call him when it was ready. The slatted wooden chair grew harder. Were they going to make him wait forever?

Johnny had never thought much about his clerk's position. He was making all of eight bucks a week. Could they say he was exploiting his golfing reputation to the tune of eight measly dollars? He had more serious worries as well.

What if they found out his Lakewood supporters had bought him that train ticket? He squirmed. It wasn't fair. Johnny had heard that Chick Evans and some of the other top amateurs had sponsors, bosses who paid them good salaries and let them play in tournaments whenever they rolled around.

Compared to them, he'd stuck to the rules a lot closer. Sure, he could turn pro, but he'd never be able to play in the great amateur events again. Ever since he'd taken the Trans-Mississippi title, strangers had been pestering him about playing for pay, but the deal just wasn't worth it.

Losing his amateur status meant being barred from America's most significant tournaments, like the U.S. Amateur. What could be worse? And that's exactly what the USGA Amateur Status Committee was trying to do to him right now.

Johnny also had a very personal reason to cling to his amateur credentials. He didn't want to be banished from all those comfortable and relaxed country club lounges. Ever since his family had disintegrated, the Lakewood golf club, the only one in Omaha he could afford, had become his second home. He often grew tired of staring at the four walls of his furnished room. The modest Lakewood clubhouse, with its soft armchairs, its lamps, its framed pictures, its camaraderie, was the perfect living room. Sometimes, he never wanted to leave.

The Websters couldn't have been more accommodating, but at the club he wasn't the kid who stoked the furnace — he was the rising amateur golf star who deserved respect, even adulation.

How could Findlay Douglas and the rest of the USGA Executive Committee imagine what it would be like to be banished from his only refuge?

Whether a true simon-pure amateur existed was an open question. According to press accounts, Bobby Jones didn't have any qualms about capitalizing on his golfing fame. In April 1927 Bobby had signed a lucrative contract to write his syndicated golf column, a practice the USGA had historically allowed. The terms weren't disclosed; no doubt their generous nature would have embarrassed the immaculate amateur.

Although Francis Ouimet and Chick Evans had been paid to write columns long before Bobby got into the game, the *New York Times* expressed shock at Jones's move, noting that "news of his action was received here with surprise . . . as Jones is known to have declined many such offers to profit by his reputation." The paper pointed out that previously Bobby had said, "I am not a writer and I refuse to sell my name for $25,000. If I were not fairly well known as a golfer, anything I might write would not be worth $10."

~~Evidently, Bobby couldn't turn his back on the rich 1927~~ offer, however. Despite all his previous expressions of distaste, he took the money.

Selling sports equipment, however, was a different matter. As far back as 1916 the USGA had laid down the law, barring the popular 1913 U.S. Open and 1914 U.S. Amateur winner, Francis Ouimet, from the amateur ranks because he had opened a sporting goods store in Boston.

The twenty-one-year-old Ouimet, who had invested his life savings in the venture, was stunned. When as an amateur he had upset Harry Vardon in the 1913 U.S. Open, he had been clerking at Wright & Ditson's, a Boston sports equipment store, yet the USGA hadn't challenged his status.

Although trade in sticks and balls somehow sullied an amateur's character, USGA president Frank Woodward also ruled that writing columns or accepting "gifts" such as automobiles as prizes for winning didn't compromise a golfer's amateur standing. The public was outraged by the ruling against Ouimet, but the USGA stuck grimly to its supremely illogical decision. For years Ouimet, at the height of his powers, was shut out of amateur competition before he was finally reinstated after World War I. Of course, Ouimet had to give up his store to regain his amateur credentials.

The USGA's inconsistency dogged Walter J. Travis too. Two years before the Ouimet ruling, in 1914, Travis, a self-made businessman, proposed to foot the bill for an American "team" to travel to the British Amateur. Travis also offered to serve as coach for free. The USGA ruled against Walter J.'s plan shortly after allowing the Woodland Club of Massachusetts to cover expenses for another amateur's trip to England. The recipient of the club's largesse was none other than Francis Ouimet.

Later in his career, Travis ran afoul of the USGA again. In its 1916 ruling, the USGA barred golf course architects from playing competitively, effectively ending Travis's playing career. The ruling body used sweeping language in its decree, stating that "amateurs are prohibited from holding any position as agent or employee that includes as part of its duties the handling of golf supplies, or engaging in any business wherein one's usefulness or profits arise because of skill or prominence in the game of golf."

Policing amateurism in general struck Grantland Rice as a morally myopic exercise. After the Amateur Athletic Union stripped Jim Thorpe of his Olympic medals for playing a summer of professional baseball, Rice recoiled at the ruling body's hypocrisy: "We know of at least four star college athletes from the past seasons who toiled through the summer in about the same brand of bush scenery as that which enticed Thorpe off the trail. None of them played for any salary or received any coin for their services. But at the end of the season, two sold their suspenders to their manager for $800 each, and the other two bet their manager $900 in the last game played that neither would make nine errors in the lone battle left. Strangely enough both won their bets." In another column Rice remarked, "The best definition of amateur is one who can get away with it and not be nicked with the goods."

Although Bobby Jones carefully observed the letter of the USGA's laws, his lucrative syndication contract began to create resentment in the amateur ranks. George Von Elm, among others, felt that Jones was being allowed to operate under separate rules. Von Elm, a gifted California amateur many considered the second best in the country, had managed to stop Jones in the finals of the 1926 U.S. Amateur, and he expected fair treatment, if not a star's prerogatives.

The blond, narrow-eyed Von Elm handled Jones with frosty respect, but didn't hide his animus toward the Atlantan.

An experienced businessman, Von Elm also wondered why the USGA could make money by charging admission to tournaments, yet not share a single cent to cover the expenses of the athletes who created the wealth.

The Dawson ruling put Johnny Goodman in a quandary. Exactly what was he supposed to tell the USGA? He had worked on saying the right thing to reporters, politicians, and assorted bigwigs for years, but he had never studied the intricacies of USGA statutes. Unable to sit still, he bolted from his chair and paced nervously up and down the veranda, trying to formulate a plan, but before he could make sense of his muddled thoughts, he was whisked into the clubhouse.

Behind a long table, two middle-aged men fussed with papers while several other officials openly gaped at Johnny as if he were some newly discovered, exotic species. Wary, Johnny shifted his weight from foot to foot. He didn't quite know what to do with his hands. Finally, he clasped them behind his back.

One official didn't appear too threatening, however. Dressed in a tan, sleeveless V-neck, white shirt, and striped tie, he looked crisp but not overly formal. He had a weary look about him, his eyes puffy from lack of sleep. Sitting next to him was a man with unruly gray hair, incipient jowls, and a double chin. A private smile played on his lips, as if, Johnny thought, he were enjoying a secret joke. Was the man laughing at him? Johnny stiffened.

Then the questions came in a torrent. Was he a member of the Lakewood Country Club in Omaha? Had he been given an honorary membership? If so, why? Did he pay dues?

Johnny knew what they were getting at. He told the truth, at least most of it. He played at Lakewood because he couldn't afford the Omaha Field Club, and yes, he paid dues. He didn't say anything about the cash his supporters had advanced him for the Fast Mail ticket. That was his private business.

The officials exchanged knowing looks.

Did Johnny know if the Lakewood Country Club was in good standing with the USGA?

He did. It was. They'd always been on the up and up with him.

He saw right away that he'd put things the wrong way, but he couldn't for the life of him figure out how.

Now they wanted to know if he worked in a sporting goods store. He thought about denying it, but then figured they knew all about it. He said he was just a trainee.

Was he a partner also?

Johnny felt like laughing, but he kept a straight face. No, he didn't own the business, he was just on half-salary. Improvising, he added that he wasn't going to keep working there anyway. That would be news to his boss back in Omaha, but it seemed like the right thing to say.

Did he get any special deals from the management, say, on golf clubs?

The line of interrogators leaned forward as one. Goodman, who barely looked his nineteen years of age, fidgeted and gazed at his shoe tops. Prickles of sweat broke out on the back of his neck.

Did they know something about the discounts? He had no choice now. It was time for a white lie. He denied the committee's insinuations, hoping they wouldn't take a look at his shiny new clubs before they made their decision.

Nervous, he rattled on about how little he'd made at the store, and how he wouldn't make anything anymore. He could feel his face flushing as the words flew from his mouth in bunches. If he kept talking, maybe they wouldn't ask him where he got his train ticket. As he spoke, his mind cleared, and he hit on a closing argument. He explained that as a trainee on half-salary he wasn't a regular employee at all, at least not yet, adding that his salary was so low it didn't qualify as actual income at all.

Now he held his breath, hoping he had diverted discussion away from how he'd bought his clubs.

Luckily, the questioning veered in another direction. Had anybody ever handed him a gratuity for participating in a tournament? *Gratuity.* He knew that word. It meant money. Drained, he just shook his head.

When it was over, he slunk away, weak, drenched in sweat. He'd said something wrong, he knew it, but he couldn't quite put his finger on what it had been.

At first Goodman's case probably seemed clear to the USGA officials. His transgression was the same as Francis Ouimet's all those years ago. Ouimet had opened a sporting goods store, he'd been profiting from his golfing prowess, so by definition he was no longer an amateur. And the USGA had already dispensed with the unfortunate Dawson.

On the other hand, Goodman had argued, in a somewhat over-heated manner, that he no longer had any connection to trade, and that in fact, he was practically destitute. He appeared to be making the novel argument that since he had no resources he couldn't be exploiting his golfing prowess for monetary gain. His penury was his trump card. No one had quite put it that way before. It was all rather embarrassing.

Judging by the scanty record, some USGA officials wanted to give Johnny Goodman a chance. To say that he was exploiting his fame when he was drawing such a pitiful salary must have seemed like pushing the point. The opposing faction probably pointed out that applying the rules selectively would let the USGA in for the same old charge that had been leveled against it in the past: inconsistency. In addition, however little Goodman was making, was there any doubt that he was hired to lure trade into the store? And didn't that make him a professional, plain and simple?

Then there was all that grumbling about Bobby Jones and his columns. Despite the fact that Jones's syndicated writings fell well within established USGA guidelines, George Von Elm was constantly making snide remarks about how Bobby was raking it in, and now he was starting to complain about how much it cost him to pay his own way to the great amateur tournaments. Was it worth all that expense just to be announced as *Mister* Von Elm on the first tee, the Californian wanted to know.

The USGA officials wished that the Goodmans and the Von Elms would do what decent fellows like Walter Hagen and Jim Barnes had done since the beginning of time and simply become professionals. When all was said and done, some of the amateurs coming up practiced so much, and put on such grim expressions when they competed, they might as well have been playing to line their pockets.

There was also the popular press to consider. The USGA had been battered around the head over the Ouimet affair, and Goodman seemed so hell-bent on pushing his way in, who could imagine what tales he would tell if the officers summarily dismissed him? Was there any point in courting derisive headlines on the eve of the amateur game's finest show?

On the other hand, should the USGA compromise its principles and give in to this sort of pressure? With the old sporting ideals under siege, wasn't it the USGA's duty to protect them at all costs? It was hard to decide what to do. Some officials argued for a show of spine. Others thought the boy had a point. However disjointed, his argument had some merit, and he'd certainly shown his mettle against the odds.

On one sentiment, the feeling was unanimous. Johnny Goodman had put the officials in an uncomfortable position. If they kept him out of the tournament, the public might start howling for their scalps. If they let him in, the USGA's most fervent supporters would want to perform a similar operation.

After the interrogation, Johnny crept over to the first hole. A foursome was just teeing off, so he stood at a respectful distance. Once they hit their drives, he stepped out on the tee for a look down the dogleg right that narrowed down good and tight at the turn. He could see the green in the distance, slashes of sand guarding the putting surface. Not too long, less than four hundred, he guessed. He wished he had his clubs with him; he wished he could just jump out there.

The cliffs and the sea were hidden from view, but he watched a gull catch an updraft over the fairway, a foreign sight to a midwesterner, and he smelled the ocean. It was all so exhilarating, but he feared he'd never see the way the seventh hole jutted out into the bay, or walk up the eighteenth fairway after a solid niblick to the green. The committee was going to send him packing for sure.

The news that Dawson had been barred had already filtered out. Now it got around that the kid from Omaha was going to get the same treatment, but this rumor didn't make much of an impression. Among the elite players, Goodman's name barely drew a flicker of recognition. He was from somewhere out there, somewhere on the vast, undifferentiated plains.

13

THE CONTROVERSY OVER Johnny Goodman's amateur status wasn't the only issue bedeviling the USGA on the eve of the 1929 U.S. Amateur championship. Rogue state golfing associations were becoming as pugnacious as that perennial thorn in the USGA's side, the Western Golf Association. As far back as 1904 the WGA had protested the USGA's two-tier membership system, which gave the vote to a small number of eastern clubs while sidelining the rest of its members. At a meeting in Chicago's Grand Pacific Hotel in 1910, WGA secretary Albert Gates offered a radical resolution, proposing that the WGA expand its membership to "any properly organized club on the continents of North and South America." While this modest proposal failed, the WGA, in subsequent years, continued to defy the venerable governing body, especially regarding covering expenses for amateurs.

Now a rebellion had broken out in the very heart of the USGA's empire, Massachusetts. Evidently, the Massachusetts Amateur Golf Association intended to pay its team's expenses in upcoming tournaments, and the move, an obvious violation of USGA rules, was gaining support in other states. In other words, the same complaints George Von Elm had voiced against the amateur status rules were being voiced all over the country.

It was humiliating, but the USGA was finding the strongest support for its principled stand within the Professional Golf Association, which had passed a resolution demanding that "unless a golfer can pay his way, he should give up amateur competition and turn professional."

Willie Ogg, a pro golfer from Worcester, Massachusetts, didn't pull his punches. "The pros at least pay their way to the national tournament, and that's more than half the top-ranked amateurs attempt to do. The whole complicated system with its Walker Cup exemptions and public links exceptions is a travesty of fair play."

Of course, Ogg had overstated the case, the USGA believed, but it did have to take quick and decisive action. Once again, the ruling body issued an explicit threat. Any amateur accepting expense money to play in a tournament would lose his amateur status. Period.

In this charged atmosphere, the Goodman matter, with all its ambiguities, needed to be dealt with expeditiously. At a recent meeting of the Executive Committee, USGA officials had wrestled with defining amateurism yet again, concluding, "It has not been possible to draft a rule describing an amateur that clearly defines the subject so anyone could apply it, but the rules and regulations as they now stand have been reasonably satisfactory when strictly administered with proper regard to the spirit of the underlying rule."

In other words, despite their inability to fashion a coherent explanation of amateurism, officials relied on their exquisite instincts. They knew an amateur when they saw one.

Take the case of the ace golfer Mrs. Biddle, of Philadelphia's Main Line. She had received payment to appear in a cigarette ad, but was she capitalizing on her golfing prowess? Clearly not, the USGA decided. Rather, she was trading on her good looks and social position, an entirely different affair. No reason to ban Mrs. Biddle from amateur competition.

Goodman was a more vexing case. If the boy had accepted expense money, the USGA would have had a cut-and-dried case against him, but what were they supposed to do? Send detectives to Omaha? Unable to define precisely what the midwesterner had done wrong — his impassioned plea had sufficiently muddied the waters — the board considered what might happen if Goodman were actually allowed into the qualifying rounds. Wouldn't Pebble Beach eat him alive? And then wouldn't he simply slink away, never to be heard from again?

USGA officials had more important business to deal with than Johnny Goodman's fate. With thousands of fans pouring in to witness their premier event, they were concerned about crowd control. Would the army of marshals they'd put together be sufficient? They were anxious about press relations. Had the right stories been put out to the right reporters? They worried about how knowledgeable a few of the referees were. Above all, they were keeping their eye on gate receipts. Would dragging the tournament halfway across the world really translate into the bonanza that Pebble Beach's impresario Samuel F. B. Morse had promised?

While the Executive Committee debated his case, Johnny Goodman waited on the porch. At first he folded his slender frame into a rocking chair at the far corner of the veranda. He wanted to make himself inconspicuous. From his vantage point he could watch the genial husbands in their summer sports jackets, knickers, and argyle socks, and their wives in their painted cloches and printed silks, but it was the younger men and women who really struck him. They smiled and laughed and exuded such relentless good cheer they made him suspicious. If you acted that way in the Midwest, people would say you were a phony.

As time dragged on, he stood up and stretched, trying his best not to attract notice. Then he sat down again and curled in on himself. He had dragged himself over a thousand miles and squandered every dime he'd saved, just to be turned away at the last moment, he brooded. Finally, he couldn't take it anymore, and he wandered back to the first tee. Eyeing the way the fairway bottlenecked when it bent right, he calculated the line he would play if he ever got the chance.

He was aching to hit just one solid drive. He'd been reining in his sweeping hook lately, going for a tight draw instead. If he caught it right, he still got the same overspin and the ball still ran those extra few yards.

Then he hurried back to his corner of the veranda. He couldn't risk staying away long. He had the distinct feeling that if the officials couldn't locate him, they'd give his place away quick as a flash. Swallowing his anger, he adopted a neutral expression and set himself down on the same rocking chair. He wished some of his own people had traveled out to the Coast with him. At least Bert Waddington, from Lakewood, was supposed to show up. Bert had plenty of experience on the board at Lakewood; he was a professional, an engineer, and a former football coach too. He'd know what to say to these people.

Then again, Burt could have gotten tied up back in Omaha. Johnny's heart sank. He wished his local rooting section was around. Stanley Davies. Mary Levings. Sam Reynolds. Omaha was his whole world, and now he was cut off from all those familiar faces. Although he hated to admit it, he felt lonely to the bone.

He'd been waiting on the porch so long he was certain people were starting to stare at him. He was glad he was wearing his dressy V-neck and clean white shirt. Nice clothes helped you blend in at a place like this. How many hours had it been? Two? Three? He'd lost all sense of time.

Finally, the same self-important marshal came out and offered a single sentence. "The board says to check for your tee time."

However reluctantly, the USGA was letting him slip into medal play. His heart skittered up into his throat. Containing his excitement, Johnny shrugged as if he'd been expecting the news all along. Don't show a damn thing. That was his motto.

14

O N THE EVE OF THE 1929 U.S. Amateur, East Coast writers began speculating about the tournament's little-known setting. "What about this Pebble Beach course?" John Kiernan of the *New York Times* asked. "Explorers who have returned from the Coast report that it is laid out along the shores of Carmel Bay, an arm of the Pacific Ocean."

Once the establishment scribes took a look at the layout, they were charmed — and relieved that they didn't have to play the challenging course themselves. "Temptation beckons on all sides at Pebble Beach, and danger lurks everywhere," William D. Richardson of the *New York Times* observed, adding that the course was created by "a conspiracy of nature and man."

Taking in the entire landscape, the reigning British Amateur champion, Cyril Tolley, remarked, "Words cannot describe the beauty of Pebble Beach, Del Monte, or for that matter the entire Monterey Peninsula."

What struck Tolley and the sportswriters new to the Pebble Beach links was its juxtaposition of dramatic elements, the sea, the dunes, the pine forests, the mountains, and the stunning views of Point Lobos across the bay. Monterrey pine, cypress, and live oak ran alongside the links, with stands of trees scattered about the coastal meadow. Fog rolled in off the sea, but in the morning it also rose in plumes from the dense forest that formed the border of the course. At times the waves hissed in, low and quiet, but when the tide was up, breakers crashed against the rocky shore. Sea lions basked on water-slick boulders; white gulls banked over snaking fairways. If you were lucky, you might even see the disappearing tail of a gray fox.

Cyril Tolley wasn't the only one at a loss for words.

Pebble Beach had come into being like many of California's wonders, as a by-product of a real estate deal gone sour. When Charles Crocker, the Southern Pacific Railroad baron, started putting up Monterey's Del Monte hotel in 1879, wags called it "Crocker's folly." There was good reason. Since the United States had seized California from Mexico in 1846, Monterey had shown little sign of life.

In the same year that Crocker began construction, Robert Louis Stevenson wrote that Monterey was "a place of two or three streets, economically paved with sea sand, and two or three lanes, which were watercourses in the rainy season . . . There were no street lights. Short sections of wooden sidewalk only added to the dangers of the night . . . There is no activity but in and around the saloons, where people sat almost all day long playing cards."

Crocker, who, along with major Southern Pacific stockholders Collis Huntington, Leland Stanford, and Mark Hopkins, owned great swaths of land along the Southern Pacific route, believed his venture would succeed because the property's marvelous setting, and California's mild climate, would attract the leisure class.

In fact, the California climate proved irresistible, and the Del Monte flourished. During the early years the hotel offered billiards, bowling, and a race track for sporting entertainment, and by 1897, a golf course as well. Expanded to eighteen holes in 1903, the layout was good enough to become the site of the 1912 California State Amateur championship. However, by 1915, land sales, the heart of Crocker's Pacific Improvement Company, were languishing, particularly in Pebble Beach, and the hotel's glamour was fading.

A young property manager, Samuel F. B. Morse, one-time captain of the Yale football team, was hired to liquidate the Pacific Improvement Company's Monterey holdings.

After looking over the Del Monte property, Morse decided that before he put it on the block it needed to be refurbished. A first-class golf tournament would add to its appeal and drive up the price, he believed, and one was already scheduled for the Del Monte course: the 1916 Western Amateur. While the California Golf Association was hoping to enhance its prestige by holding an important tournament in the state for the first time, Morse had other things on his mind: the well-off golfers who would make a perfect audience for his freshly appointed resort.

Morse's hopes were soon realized. The tournament went off smoothly, but more important, eastern papers praised the course and the stunning landscape.

Now Morse turned his attention to the unsalable Pebble Beach properties, where he saw an opportunity. Instead of pushing seaside lots, the company could develop a golf course with holes that ran along the cliffs. In Morse's new vision, prospective inland homes would gain spectacular views across the links to the ocean. By adding a championship test of golf, he could create a California version of Pinehurst.

"There were two outstanding golf architects in those days — Charlie Macdonald, a wealthy man and first U.S. Amateur Champion, and American; and Donald Ross in England," Morse wrote in his memoirs. "Mr. Macdonald couldn't be persuaded to do the job at Pebble Beach, and Donald Ross was in the English army, so I decided to take the chance on two amateurs and have never regretted it."

For the job he chose Jack Neville, a Pacific Improvement salesman and top amateur, and Douglas Grant, who had topped Neville for the 1916 Del Monte Mid-Winter championship.

Looking back at his handiwork, Neville remarked, "It was all there in plain sight, little change was needed."

Actually, the original Seventeen Mile Drive had to be completely rerouted, a major job. A few of the scattered sand dunes were incorporated into the design, but many had to be plowed under. Still, the original plan stuck close to the natural topography.

Morse maintained the fiction that the course hewed close to Neville and Grant's original conception, but in fact, it went through many revisions. While there was something charming about a creation myth giving so much credit to two amateurs, and to the landscape itself, eventually experienced hands shaped a far more demanding track.

Morse dearly wanted to lure the United States Amateur to Pebble Beach, but he had to overcome the USGA's hidebound resistance. The USGA's conception of the West didn't extend farther than Chicago. From the eastern establishment's point of view, California was a thousand miles from civilization.

Morse began his campaign by developing the Pebble Beach Open for professionals. The course proved quite difficult for the pros. Harry "Light Horse" Cooper took first place with a five over 293. Most of the players praised the layout, but some criticized the eighth green for not being properly canted. However, when the USGA visited and tested the course in December 1927, the organization's potentates were favorably impressed. Morse's fondest dream had come true. The battle for the 1929 U.S. Amateur crown would take place at Pebble Beach.

Despite the USGA's blessings, Morse brought in H. Chandler Egan to rework the links yet again. When American golf was still getting its footing, way back in 1904, Egan, then a strapping Harvard undergraduate, had won the United States Amateur. Now in his forties, he was a pipe-smoking veteran of every aspect of the game. He tore into his task with relish.

In an essay titled "What We Have Done at Pebble Beach," Egan wrote: "The front nine needed stiffening and, if possible, greater length, and secondly, sixteen of the eighteen greens needed returfing, reshaping and retrapping. Some of the old greens were rather old-fashioned, unattractive and dull, and some were a bit unfair in their slopes and lack of visibility, and almost none of them offered a real target for an iron shot."

Morse didn't shrink from Egan's sweeping indictment. Instead, he granted the thoughtful and precise Egan a free hand.

Out of respect for the indigenous landscape, Egan created new "imitation dune" traps around the fourth, sixth, seventh, eighth, and seventeenth holes. In fact, his mock dunes were so well done that they often fooled visitors, who mistook them for the real thing.

A careful look at Egan's work reveals just how extensive and, in some instances, how radical it was. He transformed the sixth hole, moving the green farther right, adding a fairway that ran along the ocean's edge, and creating a new championship tee well back of the original. As Egan put it, "To get safely 'home' in two demands some ocean risk from the tee and considerable ocean risk on the second, including a carry over a short bay in the ocean faced with a bold rocky cliff."

"Ocean risk" is a dry way to describe the sickening sight of a golf ball rattling off the rocks and into the sea.

The former collegiate golf star also reconceived the ninth completely, obliterating almost the entire old fairway except a sliver on the right, and lengthening the hole a good fifty yards. Now the hole offered players two distinct routes, the shorter bringing the ocean into play yet again. Egan also transformed the seventeenth green, turning it into an island in a sea of sand.

By reconfiguring and rebuilding almost every green on the course, Egan left a strong personal stamp on Pebble Beach. Now the putting surfaces could "accept" fine iron shots instead of allowing them to roll off the greens for no good reason. Golfers who hit well-placed tee shots were also rewarded with more "good looks" at their targets, a number of which were now more distant.

Many hands had shaped Pebble Beach, but it still reflected the spirit of the landscape Neville and Grant respected so deeply. Still, when the links were unveiled at the 1929 U.S. Amateur, they had been refined into an altogether more striking and difficult test of nerve and skill.

15

THE 1920S WERE ALMOST SPENT. The country had survived its obsession with crossword puzzles and Rudolph Valentino's sexy sideburns. Radio, by now an all-pervasive medium, had lost its novelty. Flappers with skirts up to their knees and rolled-down stockings no longer shocked, and the illicit thrill had gone out of the speakeasy. Prohibitionists had surrendered much of their zeal, but no one knew quite what to do about the wide-open warfare, fought with machine guns in broad daylight, over distilled spirits.

Jack Dempsey had retired and Gene Tunney after him. The outrage over Sacco and Vanzetti's execution was a memory. Lindbergh mania was fading. Even the writers and intellectuals had grown weary of revealing the secrets of sex and the shallowness of Main Street businessmen. A certain nervous exhaustion had set in.

Curiously, one of the few manias left was the American public's passion for miniature golf. Evidently, putting a ball over mashed cottonseeds and into a tin clown's mouth lifted the spirits of an enervated public.

Wall Street reflected the nervous national temper. Although Coolidge prosperity had so much momentum it hadn't noticed that Herbert Hoover had taken up residence in the White House, the stock market had trembled a bit in December 1928, and quivered again in February 1929 after the Federal Reserve spoke out against the "extension of speculative credit." Each time it had recovered and surged higher. In March the averages took a precipitous plunge when call rates shot up, but with an optimism bordering on hysteria, the public bought on the dip, and the party rattled on.

Just as the 1929 U.S. Amateur was about to kick off play at Pebble Beach, the Dow Jones average reached its dizzying peak.

After spending time in Hollywood with Douglas Fairbanks, and sampling the star's private, Donald Ross–designed course, Bobby Jones made his entrance at Pebble Beach. Not long after his appearance, rumors started to fly that he had signed a lucrative deal to star in motion pictures. The *Chicago Tribune* reported that in declining the proposition Jones had concluded that "it was not his speaking voice, his figure, his gifts for mimicry or his manly beauty or even his legal learning which prompted the proposal, but rather his renown as a golfer."

The USGA breathed a conspicuous sigh of relief. At least its star attraction, who had won four out of the last five U.S. Amateurs and who had just tucked another U.S. Open in his pocket, understood the rules. There had never been a golfer as dominant or as charismatic as Bobby Jones. Losing Bobby Jones, the USGA feared, would deliver a fatal blow to its coffers.

Bobby Jones had more-personal concerns. Although he liked having his wife, Mary, along for the ride, she was also a reminder that he was a family man now. He couldn't pretend that he was on the road with O. B. Keeler one more time, and that things weren't all that different from the day he'd broken in as a kid at Merion.

And unlike the newspapermen who seemed to think he was invulnerable, Bobby was all too aware that his swing was a delicate instrument that, inexplicably, drifted off-plane from time to time. Take the recent U.S. Open. To an outsider, Jones had put on a magisterial performance, burying Al Espinosa by twenty-three strokes in their thirty-six-hole playoff.

In fact, Espinosa was only able to force the playoff because Bobby had lost his stroke in the last round. He had barely escaped posting an ignominious 80 by sinking a downhill, sidehill, wide-breaking twelve-footer on the eighteenth. The putt had hung on the lip for a lifetime before dropping in. One-half a turn of the golf ball had saved him. Later, Jones described his misadventures as "an agony of anxiety."

Then there had been that damned thunderstorm at East Lake in July. Bobby had been playing a practice round with some friends when a bolt of lightning struck the fairway so close to him he felt a tingling sensation running right up through his spikes. Suddenly, one blast of light after another flashed around the foursome, and they took off for the clubhouse. On the verge of reaching safety, Bobby heard an explosion just above him. A powerful bolt of lightning had shattered the clubhouse's twin chimneys, sharp bits of brick and masonry raining down.

Inside, Bobby's friends were shocked to see a deep gash running from his shoulder to his spine. A shard of brick had sheared off the back of his shirt. Making light of the incident, Bobby headed for his locker, where he secreted his stash of corn liquor, but the incident preyed on his mind.

Perhaps the lightning strike was a warning. He felt far older than his twenty-seven years, and he had promised Mary that he would retire soon. Still, he loved the game so much, and he was playing so well, tearing himself away would constitute its own form of agony.

During his practice rounds at Pebble Beach, Bobby didn't disappoint his worshipers. On August 28, he went around in record-low fashion, shooting a two under par 70. To grasp how fine a score this was at the time, consider his partners' performances.

The other members of Jones's foursome, the British Amateur champion Cyril Tolley, and the fine amateurs Phillips Finlay and Francis Brown, of Honolulu, posted 79, 80, and 82, respectively.

A few days later, Jones proceeded to break his own record, shooting an eye-popping 67, which included seven straight birdies. In three days of practice on a rigorous links he'd never seen before, he had shattered the course record twice, lowering it by an extraordinary five strokes. The spectators who took in Jones's brilliant performance could never have imagined how Bobby felt on the eve of the championship, how he always felt before going into battle.

Bobby Jones was nervous. He knew how to ride the sensation, how to channel his racing pulse into his languid swing; he knew how to live with the quivering energy that ran through his muscles to his very fingertips. He had long since accepted the fact that these attacks would blow through him before he could settle down to the grind of round after round. But he never got used to them.

Once medal play began, Pebble Beach showed its teeth. Chick Evans failed to qualify for the first time in years, following an opening 81 with an 80. His playing partner, the little-known Lawson Little, representing the Presidio in San Francisco, slipped in just under the cut, but former Western Amateur champion Ben Stein fell by the wayside, as did Ross Somerville, the Canadian champion.

Jones posted a brilliant 70 for his first medal round, but then in the afternoon he ran into a blustery wind, almost a gale, and struggled in with a 75. Actually, in conditions that drove scores sky-high, Bobby had put on a fine performance. Although he hadn't quite repeated his blistering practice rounds, no one bested his 145.

Francis Ouimet squeaked in, as did Jess Sweetser. Fighting the wild wind, Johnny Goodman qualified, too, but just barely, following an 80 with a slightly better 78. None of the national newspapers offered a single line on the Omahan's rounds.

After Johnny checked the board and found out he had qualified, he made his way out to the covered porch, bursting with excitement. Bert Waddington was waiting for him. At the sight of Waddington's long, weathered face, he exclaimed, "I got in, Bert! They let me in!"

Over dinner he described his interrogation before the Amateur Status Committee. Bert Waddington shook his head, indignant. "Wouldn't treat you like that if you came from some hotsy-totsy club back East," he observed. "Now you've got to calm down, though. Get your head screwed on straight."

Waddington spoke with the authority of the old football man that he was. He knew how green Johnny was, but he admired the skinny kid's determination. "You see the pairings yet?"

Johnny told him they hadn't been posted. He didn't want to haunt the clubhouse waiting for the board to go up either. The last man on earth he wanted to run into was USGA president Findlay Douglas. At the same time, he was itching to see who he'd face in the first round.

"I'll wait around and check for you," Waddington suggested. "Why don't you go and rest. You looked all washed out."

"Can't rest," Johnny said, bolting out of his chair.

Waddington took him by the shoulder. "Pretend then," he counseled. "Go back to your room. I'll find out what's up."

In the early evening USGA officials passed the word to Waddington. When he heard the name Bobby Jones, he was stunned. Shouldn't they have matched Johnny with some other no-name, somebody on his level?

How would the kid react when he heard who his opponent was? Johnny was a walking, talking Bobby Jones encyclopedia. He could recite Bobby's winning margins in the U.S. Amateur — he'd been particularly impressed when Bobby crushed Britian's best player, Phil Perkins, 10 and 9 in the 1928 U.S. Amateur, and he knew all the details of Bobby's back-to-back victories in the British Open.

He was full of Bobby's maxims, especially the one about ignoring your opponent and just playing Old Man Par. If you make one par after another, your competitor will sooner or later crumble under the steady onslaught. Bert had heard Johnny repeat this principle over and over, as if he were reciting the rosary.

Johnny would probably jump out of his skin if he heard the news. Waddington took a slow walk back to the rooming house to think things over. Finally, he decided that the best bet would be to keep his lips sealed. Why give the kid a case of the heebie-jeebies the night before the match of his life?

When Johnny asked him if there had been an announcement, Waddington offered a consoling lie: not yet.

Thrilled that he'd squeaked into match play, Johnny fell into an exhausted sleep, the middle-aged Waddington watching over him.

On the eve of the first round of match play, the sportswriter Frank Getty evoked the scene: "Pebble Beach's far-flung fairways were deserted at sunset, left to the querulous white gulls swooping along the rocky shores of the Pacific. The most picturesque course ever tramped in a national tournament is groomed and ready for the morrow's campaign."

In closing, Getty added, "Standing astride the scene like a young colossus is the chunky figure of the defending champion, Robert Tyre Jones Jr."

Few observers disagreed. Jones hadn't lost an eighteen-hole match in a national championship in years. Still, some experts noted that despite the Atlantan's extraordinary practice scores he might falter in one of the early rounds. Later in the competition, when the golfers were scheduled to play thirty-six-hole affairs, Jones had a greater chance to assert his dominance.

O. B. Keeler had already expressed similar sentiments, and Grantland Rice, while pegging Bobby as the overwhelming favorite, hedged his bets on the eighteen-holers, too.

Waddington wanted to hope, but he was a grown man, and he didn't put much stock in fairy tales. If Johnny went out and gave a decent account of himself, if he managed to push the match against Jones to fifteen or sixteen holes, what a victory that would be. Back in Omaha, they'd treat the kid like a hero if he didn't go to pieces. For the rest of his life he'd be able to say, I went toe-to-toe with Bobby Jones.

Waddington was up bright and early, waiting for his nineteen-year-old charge to open his eyes. Finally, Johnny stirred, stretching his lean frame. Still half-asleep, he muttered, "You hear yet?"

Waddington, who had considered holding back the news until they reached the golf course, decided Johnny would need time to collect his wits. "Yeah. It's Bobby Jones. Get up and eat an orange." Bert was a stickler for a decent breakfast.

"C'mon, Bert, who is it?" Johnny sat up, eager to get going.

"Yeah, the big cheese himself. You got a date. Can't be late. Let's go, kiddo. Chop, chop." Waddington rushed Johnny into his outfit and rushed him to the breakfast table, hoping to keep him from dwelling on the news.

The strategy almost worked as Johnny hurried to button his shirt, tie his shoes, and bolt down some oatmeal, a slice of ham, and a fat orange. Then, just as Bert was pushing him out the door, he felt the revelation in all its force. Settling into Bert's car, Johnny Goodman grew quiet. Very quiet.

16

A CHILL MIST SWEPT off the ocean, but the fog didn't deter a gallery numbering in the thousands. West Coast fans had been waiting years for a glimpse of Bobby Jones, who now, smiling shyly, materialized before them. Not much more than five feet eight, the solidly built Jones moved with an easy grace. With a slight nod to his admirers, he strode toward the first tee, casually drawing on a cigarette.

As always, Jones was the picture of fashion in a long-sleeved beige V-neck and matching plus fours. His long, dark socks tapered down to a pair of perfectly shined, two-toned golf shoes.

His opponent, a skinny young man who weighed no more than 125 pounds soaking wet, was all but invisible in the crush at the first tee, but those who caught sight of Johnny Goodman saw a sober-looking youth whose bony, handsome features appeared pinched with strain. Though blond-haired and blue-eyed in classic American fashion, his face bore a trace of his Baltic heritage. When a smile flickered across his lips, his eyes disappeared in slits.

Johnny was wearing his best, a canary yellow sleeveless sweater-vest that buttoned down the front. The pointy collar of his white shirt was slightly askew. His floppy brown knickers hung down as if they were empty.

By 1929 Johnny had weathered more than one tough tournament, but nothing could have prepared him for the crush at Pebble Beach's first tee. Packed tight, the onlookers were as quiet as possible, but he could hear shuffling feet, whispers, suppressed coughs. There was too much color. Too many beautiful women. Were they all actresses out here?

He felt hemmed in, smothered in the open air. Craning his neck, he tried to catch a glimpse of Bobby Jones, but the onlookers blocked his view. His head had been so full of Bobby Jones for so long, he had acted out this very scene in Mrs. Webster's kitchen so many times, he didn't quite believe the Georgian was about to show up in the flesh. Over and over he told himself, "Don't act like a fan. Don't stare. Don't gape like some stupid rube."

Goodman kept on his stolid mask. His stomach fluttered, but it was a distant sensation. Otherwise, he felt an otherworldly calm. Surreptitiously, he gripped his driver, setting his hands the way Vardon prescribed in his book.

Waggling the club, he could feel the strength flowing to his hands. He knew what he had to do. He had to *narrow down*. Make his swing the whole world. There was nothing but turning back, his body coiling, his stroke cutting through the air.

Just to distract himself, Johnny checked the distance with his caddie. Happily, most of the bag haulers bore a distinct resemblance to his friends from Golden Hill, just skinny boys in flat caps who knew a bit about the course, but not too much about golf.

Johnny's caddie, who sported a muddy-colored checked jacket, looked a bit different. He wore a smaller version of a Hoot Gibson cowboy hat and a neckerchief around his throat.

As a matter of fact, Hoot was in Monterey shooting his latest horse opera, *The Long, Long Trail.* The press release promised "Hoot riding his wildest, fighting his hardest and loving his grandest."

"Call me Kito," the caddie told Johnny.

"What's your real name?"

The boy looked down at the ground. "Sylvester."

"Kito it is," Johnny agreed. He quizzed the kid rapidly. The caddie did seem to know the names of the clubs. Paying him wouldn't break the bank either.

Strands of fog obscured the fairway just where it bent right. They'd be playing the first hole half-blind.

Then Jones sailed into view. Bobby didn't look like his pictures. He seemed more imposing, an experienced, older man. Johnny could see where the razor had missed a clump of dark beard around Jones's chin. The familiar, round face, so pleasant in all those pictures, was devoid of mercy.

Kito did his best to pay attention to Johnny, but he couldn't help gawking at Bobby Jones. He wished he was carrying Bobby's bag, instead of that know-it-all Charlie Castro, but he had to do his job for whatever-his-name-was.

Bobby Jones gazed at his first-round opponent. Goodman looked undernourished, virtually hungry, strangely out of place. He'd won some midwestern tournament, Bobby recalled. Not much else. Jones had never seen a less prepossessing specimen, but Willie Hunter hadn't looked like much, nor had Bobby Cruickshank, for that matter. Overconfidence. That was the greatest danger.

Jones took a few practice swings. All timing and rhythm, the famous stroke whooshed through the dense atmosphere, a rapier in motion, invisible to the eye.

In the Atlantan's presence, Johnny felt an odd sensation take hold. It was hard to describe. His bones felt soft, ripe.

Mechanically, he shook the champion's hand. He told himself to take in every detail — he might never get this close to Bobby Jones the rest of his life. Then he found himself grinning like an organ grinder's monkey, baring his teeth to the crowd. Quickly, he wiped the expression from his face.

Then Johnny turned away. He had to *narrow down*. Grip the club, turn, and find the slot. That's the way it felt when he was on. He twisted back, the club dropped into a preordained plane, and he unleashed it with a whipping motion. He had to discover that elusive angle, he had to get that rubbery feeling in his wrists, he had to swing the club like a wand. Hadn't he won the Trans-Mississippi? Hadn't that sportswriter said he was as cool as Pike's Peak?

How could they know what his frozen features hid? What reporters thought was coolness under fire was a trick, a strategy. To play at all he *narrowed down*, focused on the sliver of ground at his feet. Then one, two, three, he would *clip* the ball right off the grass.

Some old guy he'd beat for a dollar once told him, *You got the dead nerve, kid.*

He didn't know if that's what he had. It was hard to put it into words. When a match started, he felt far away, far away from his opponent and the spectators and far away from himself.

His dark brow furrowed with concentration, Jones took a half swing, loosening his wrists. His shoulders were broader than Johnny had imagined, his frame stockier, rooted to the ground. He seemed to swell into the air around him.

Johnny hoped he still had the dead nerve.

Then the starter announced the match, and he heard his own name, Mr. Goodman, paired with Mr. Jones. Johnny suppressed a laugh. Mr. Goodman and Mr. Jones. He'd pretended this was happening so many times he barely knew how to react. He shook his head in wonder.

Johnny gathered his thoughts. The first hole was a par-four 385. Tight bottleneck where it doglegged right.

On the eve of every tournament, Bobby Jones always worried. Would his swing drift out of line? Would his touch, that mysterious sense, suddenly desert him? Would he yank his first drive into the undergrowth, embarrassing himself right out of the box? In short, Bobby Jones was afflicted with all the same fears that plague every fifteen handicapper at every club championship. Jones knew of only one way to exorcise these terrors. He stepped up quickly and whistled one out of sight.

Johnny watched. How could he stand up to that kind of ball striking? Then again, no one expected him to. Wasn't that an advantage?

In a dream he lined up his shot. Cut it just a bit, but don't fan the face open. He'd rather draw the ball any day, but the fade was the right shot. Someone else's hands drew the club back, someone else's weight shifted, someone else hit the ball flush and sent it rising into the fog, a white bullet that disappeared in the blink of an eye. Had it faded around the dogleg? It felt like a solid hit — that was all he could tell.

Walking helped immensely. Nobody expected much from him. He'd already ripped one good and hard, albeit thirty yards short of

Jones's drive. The flag fluttered, barely visible in the mist, but he could see the nest of traps around the green.

"A little extra club," Kito whispered. This green fell away at the back, Johnny recalled. He didn't want to muscle it over, but he wanted to carry the sand. The kid was right on this call. Nodding, Johnny grabbed the hickory stick and nailed one over the traps and onto the rain-slick putting surface. *One, two, three, and clip it.* He knew how to do that.

That shot woke Kito up. His man could play the game.

Goodman had no way of knowing that Jones's ball lay in a muddy divot, so he was stunned to see the Georgian's second shot pop up weakly and land thirty yards short of the green. Was it possible? He might win one hole. A surge of hope, an emotion more dangerous than fear, rushed through him. Get up and down in two. Let Jones take care of his own game.

Play Old Man Par, just the way Bobby did.

He took a deep breath and a couple of practice putting strokes. Drenched, the grass would slow the ball down, but the slope would send it running.

Stepping away from his ball, Johnny waited for Bobby to hit his approach. Jones pitched up, the ball skidding and running twenty feet past the hole.

Now Johnny had his chance. One more practice stroke and then a smooth swing through the ball. There it was, exactly as he'd envisioned, the ball sliding into a controlled roll to the hole, leaving just a tap-in. And just like that he was one up on Bobby Jones.

He was playing golf. It felt like home.

Now that Bobby was in motion, his nerves quieted down. Losing the first hole was a mild irritation. There was a lifetime of golf left. If the Goodman kid could play a bit, all the better. With a little competition, the game swelled to fill his mind, forcing out extraneous thoughts. With all those Hollywood producers swarming around him, hinting and winking and chattering about wild sums of money, who wouldn't be distracted?

On the second hole, a 480-yard par five, diagonal traps ran across the fairway, threatening to swallow errant tee shots. Johnny proceeded to fade one right at the beckoning sand. Was he in? He couldn't quite tell, but his heart sank. As Jones addressed the ball, Goodman examined his shoelaces. Why watch that gorgeous swing? What good would that do? A moment later he heard a single word.

"Bunkered?" Jones asked.

"Missed it. On the edge," his caddie replied softly.

To Johnny's relief, his own ball had skirted danger, too. It rested near the lip of the trap, a mere three feet from Jones's tee shot. Both players left their long approaches considerably short of the green. On his third, Johnny misjudged the distance and barely got over the cross-bunker guarding the putting surface, the ball trickling to the fringe.

Just skittering onto the putting surface, Jones's chip wasn't much better. Bobby lagged his long putt four feet from the cup. Johnny measured his backswing once, twice, and then nipped a chip tight to the hole. He'd laid Bobby a dead stymie.

Jones was forced to eat a second bogey. Now he was more than irritated. He sensed his old rage blossoming. He had long since driven his demons deep inside himself. Still, especially after a stymie, the anger boiled up, almost to the surface. He'd simply accepted the fact that he would battle it until the end of his days.

Before Johnny had time to absorb the shock, he was leading two to nothing. The crowd became uneasy. They hadn't come out to see their idol lose to a nobody from some midwestern cow town.

"Oughta play thirty-six," an onlooker muttered.

"That's the real test," his pal agreed.

But they weren't playing thirty-six holes as the rules dictated for later rounds. And Bobby Jones was digging himself an early grave. Then it got worse for the favorite.

Goodman drew his tee shot just right on the 355-yard, par-four third. Although Jones had outdriven him by thirty yards, Johnny marched up to his ball and popped a midiron twelve feet from the stick. After Jones's lag putt came to a stop a couple of feet from the hole, Goodman stood right up to his putt and without hesitation knocked it in the heart. Quick, crisp, and clean. Nothing to it.

Three holes, three up on Bobby Jones! Was he back on the Websters' porch, lost in fantasy? His heart played a crazy fast beat in his skeletal rib cage. Hope had never been so perilous. *Narrow down.* Fifteen twisting, turning, devious holes lay ahead of them. His lead could evaporate just like the fog that, shred by shred, was dissolving in the morning light.

Bobby was furious with himself now, but it just made him concentrate more. He would have to go on a run now, as he'd done so many times before. Strangely enough, flat on his back, his confidence was surging back. He'd won seventeen out of eighteen first-rounders in the last five years against the best amateurs in the world. Why should this be any different?

The fourth hole, a short par four, required a two-hundred-yard shot over barrancas, or an alternate route to the left. Down below the fairway, the Pacific's muscular waves crashed against the rocks. Terns cawed and the air tasted of salt.

Deep in concentration, Johnny was only barely aware of the view across the water. The fog had burned away by now. In the clear light, a rocky promontory pointed out to the sea. It was funny, though. For late morning it was still cool. Back in Omaha, summer would be going full blast. A sea lion yawped on the rocks below. They weren't in the Midwest now. Surrounded by Chandler Egan's "imitation dunes," the small green didn't offer much of a target.

Holding steady, Johnny laced his drive into the fairway. His expression never changing, Jones ripped one that sailed past Goodman's ball on a fly. This time, Johnny faltered, chunking his approach into a greenside trap. Sensing an opening, Jones calmly stroked a short iron eight feet from the pin. Blasting out, Johnny pulled off a fine shot, the ball curling to a stop four feet from the flag, but Jones knocked his birdie putt in with a confident stroke. Bobby had snatched one hole back. Just two down after four.

"Nice one, Mr. Jones," Johnny said, barely audibly.

Bobby heard the polite words, but he also thought he sensed a bit of awe, a bit of weakness. He nodded imperceptibly. There was a time for fine manners, and there was a time to play the game.

Whether Jones heard him or not, Johnny couldn't tell. His back a shade straighter, the Georgian was already stalking to the fifth tee.

At 180 yards, the par three presented its own particular terrors. On the left ran a densely wooded ravine. On the right, out-of-bounds. A pair of traps guarded the front of the green, and another ran along the right. Most of the top players went at it with a long iron — or more depending on the wind.

It was still early, Bobby knew, but sometimes the breaking point could come early. In their U.S. Open playoff, Espinosa beat himself before he stepped onto the first tee. If he could take one more hole from Goodman, he'd change the flow of the match; he'd have the momentum.

Holding the honor, Jones flew one effortlessly onto the green, the ball feeding to the pin and stopping fifteen feet away. He was getting it going now.

It was a perfect time for Goodman, the skinny imposter, to crumble. Instead, to the gallery's astonishment, Johnny lashed at his tee shot, sent one out to the right and drew it back at the flag. Flying at a lower trajectory than Jones's shot, the ball struck short but kept rolling until it came to rest only ten feet from the hole.

That swing caught Bobby's attention. His eye took in the kid's mechanics, the left side set rock solid, the smooth weight shift. There were flaws there, however. Goodman's backswing was a few degrees too flat, and he kept the clubface shut a little too long, it seemed. Probably making last-second adjustments with his hands, Bobby speculated. The kid needed perfect timing to pull it off. Tough to sustain, though.

The onlookers began to stare at the stony-faced Goodman with greater interest. Didn't he understand that he had missed his opportunity to slice one out-of-bounds? Why not get the charade over with as soon as possible?

Jones looked over his line for a moment, and then he guided Calamity Jane through the putt. At first the ball looked as if it was shooting into the center of the cup, but at the last moment it veered ever so slightly.

Bobby felt a twinge of disgust, but he kept it to himself. He'd hit it solid. Just one of those things.

"Right over the edge," Johnny's caddie whispered, taking the liberty of breathing again.

Now Goodman could deliver a crushing blow, and he had the advantage of seeing Jones's putt first. Adjusting ever so slightly, he sent the ball on its way, but it tracked the high side, caught the edge of the hole, and spun out. No blood.

After five, Johnny was still two up.

Still holding the honor, Jones lined up and surveyed the par-five, 502-yard sixth. Hazards on the left demanded a tee shot that had to skirt the cliffs on the right. This time Bobby's greater power came into play. He seemed to barely exert himself, but he hit a towering, high draw that kept running long after it hit the ground. Two-seventy at least.

Goodman was a shade too quick, hitting a low screamer that, while finding the short grass, barely covered 220 yards. Worse still, the approach demanded a high shot over the bay. But he didn't have to reach the green, just get over the dunes. Johnny hit the spoon clean, his hopes soared, but the ball suddenly ran out of gas and dunked into the sand. Now it was Jones's turn. This sort of play was red meat to him, and he didn't disappoint his supporters.

Fully extending, he struck his three wood flush, his rapid footwork leaving him perfectly balanced at the end. The crowd gasped as the shot rose higher and higher, flying straight over the patchy dunes and onto the green. Five hundred and two yards in two swings.

Now Johnny understood why Jones had been intimidating the opposition for years. It wasn't how far he hit it. It was the complete lack of strain. What had Jones written? "You can't swing a golf club too slow." His lazy backswing looked effortless, but when he let fly, the blur of his swing was pure power, plain and simple.

A drawn expression on his face, Goodman stepped down into the hazard. With a quick chop he dislodged the ball, only to send it screeching into a greenside bunker. Jones waited patiently while his opponent quieted his nerves and blasted out onto the short grass. Then Bobby lagged one close and the match tightened up good and proper.

Only one down, Bobby Jones had all the time in the world to dissect the upstart from Omaha.

Head down, Goodman groped for his focus. How could he hope

to beat somebody so smooth, so relaxed, so talented? Every time he broke down and watched Jones waggle the club, he got chills. There had to be a way around it. He dug deeper, concentrated harder, and then the words rose from his memory again. Bobby Jones's words. Don't play your opponent. Just play Old Man Par.

Gazing out at the short par-three seventh, a mere 110 yards long, Johnny revised this prescription. *Don't even look at your opponent, especially if it's Bobby Jones.* He would pretend Jones wasn't there at all. He was just out for a stroll with Old Man Par.

Shaped like a ragged star, the seventh green floated in a sea of sand. One hundred feet long and about forty-five feet wide, it made a good target, but surrounded on all sides by dunes, which sprouted tufts of silvery grass, it grew smaller the longer Johnny gazed at it. Waves frothed on the boulders below. A light wind kicked up. While Jones stroked his shot, Johnny watched a gull bank over the bay.

"Back edge," a spectator said. Johnny couldn't ignore that piece of intelligence. Jones's tee shot had sailed long.

Just 110 yards to the heart of the green, but the target tilted right above the waves. A simple niblick, his favorite club. With his brisk, inside-out swing, Goodman nipped his tee shot onto the green. Not all that close, but on the dance floor.

His ball tangled up in the froghair, Jones hit a mediocre chip. A duffer's crime. Hit through the ball, he swore to himself. Hit through the ball. Bobby was still away. Against his will his hands jerked imperceptibly, pushing his approach putt wide of the mark.

All Johnny had to do was roll it close and knock it in. Easy as pie. Old Man Par took another one.

Just like that, Goodman had forged two holes ahead again. The two men trudged to the eighth hole, a 425-yard par four, a steep, uphill affair. Johnny knew what it would take, a high, arching drive and then, in order to cut the dogleg, a second shot over 180 yards of ocean to reach the well-trapped green. Precipitous banks plunged seventy-five feet down to the water.

Depending on which direction the sea breeze was blowing, the second shot demanded a full brassie, a midiron, or an easy mashie. A slight misjudgment and you were down on the rocks.

Johnny managed the chasm, but his midiron found the trap. To the gallery's disappointment, Jones followed suit.

Bobby blasted out neatly, but Goodman made a weak pass, barely swatting the ball out of the sand. When Jones's putt half-stymied the young Omahan's ball, Bobby took the hole, despite making bogey five.

Coming to H. Chandler Egan's redesigned ninth hole, Jones was only one down. He was making it a match now, despite his misadventures. Hagen had the right idea. Expect to butcher a few, and then knock in the ten-footers. Bobby wished he could get that chip from the froghair back, though. He did his best to push the dismal stroke out of his mind. He'd seized the momentum again. That was what mattered.

Running along the bluffs at the water's edge, the ninth threatened danger on the right, Chandler Egan's beloved "ocean risk." A pushed tee shot left the player a precarious approach over the cliffs and the bay. Leave it short, and the ball would find the deep ravine that ran in front of the green.

The 450-yard par four offered the long-hitting Jones a good opportunity to overtake his surprisingly adept antagonist, but after a solid drive, Goodman whipped a fairway wood twenty-five feet from the pin. Johnny was gaining confidence.

Jones came off his second shot, but he had a stroke of luck. Offline, his approach caromed off a steep bank, shot straight for the hole, and curled six feet from the pin. This was the break Bobby had been waiting for, but after Johnny lagged his close, Calamity Jane failed the Atlantan. He could not put down the simple six-footer, and Goodman held on to his slender lead.

Johnny was giving a good account of himself, but it seemed as if he was only postponing the inevitable. With nine holes to go, a one-hole cushion against Bobby Jones was no cushion at all.

17

CLINGING TO HIS SLIM LEAD, Johnny Goodman made his way to the tenth, a par-four 406-yarder whose fairway hugged the coastline. He didn't think of winning the match; in fact, he tried with every fiber of his being not to think of anything but the next shot.

A man in an argyle sweater elbowed his companion. "This could be it."

"Bobby's going to let loose now," his straw-hatted friend agreed.

A distant trap on the tenth bifurcated the fairway. Protected on the right and back by Egan's invented dunes, the green, perched close to the cliffs, was guarded in the back by sand as well. A jagged trap set in the front prevented players from running low irons onto the putting surface.

Bobby Jones felt loose now, his muscles limber from the battle, but in brief flashes his mind drifted from the task. It had been fascinating to spend so much time with Doug Fairbanks, though the pasteboard Hollywood life had a laughable quality about it. Still, fooling around with Doug on his private course had reminded him of how he had thoughtlessly chipped and putted afternoons away as a boy at East Lake. Pure play, pure pleasure. Of course, Mary wasn't comfortable with the movie crowd. She thought they were too full of themselves, and rather cheap.

Bobby dragged himself back to the task at hand. The Goodman kid was a tough nut. Bobby, who understood the crushing weight of championship play all too well, eyed his opponent warily.

Hitting their stride, Jones and Goodman both laced strong drives and followed with fine long irons, leaving them similar twenty-five footers. In quick succession, they got down in two, halving the hole. Johnny was holding on, still one up.

The tail of Johnny's laundered white shirt hung down now, but he was too lost in the match to notice. Then he recalled a single word Bobby had used in *Down the Fairway.* He'd *scraped* his scores together at St. Anne's when he won the British Open. Keep on scraping, he muttered to himself. Keep on scraping.

On the eleventh, golf flashed its perverse nature. Jones stopped his second shot on the sloping 380-yard par four a mere ten feet from the pin. On his approach, Goodman barely managed to get within forty feet of the flag. Crouching, he eyed the green's subtle undulations. The men in ties and sleeveless sweaters, and the slender women in straight skirts and saddle shoes, seemed to stop breathing at once. It would be easy for Goodman to three-putt from that distance and Bobby was sitting pretty, ten feet away. It seemed like the right time for the pretender from Omaha to give up the charade.

Johnny told himself one thing: give yourself a chance. Don't come up short. Then with one long, resolute stroke he sent a hot one toward the distant target. A double-breaker, the putt curled a bit left, then bent a little right, rolling hell-bent for the hole, where it rattled into the back of the cup.

Bobby watched Goodman's putt duck into the hole with a sense of disbelief. There was an element of luck when you sank a long one like that, but also an element of courage. Taken aback, he shook his head ever so slightly, a smile flickering in the corner of his mouth.

At first, when Goodman's snaky putt found the heart of the hole, the crowd let go a collective groan. A ball stroked that hard could have raced right off the green. It almost seemed unfair to Bobby. Then, as if in penance, a few spectators offered tepid applause.

A moment later, silence descended as Jones drew back Calamity Jane and nudged his ten-footer home. The tying birdie brought only nervous relief to his supporters.

Jones had lost a big opportunity. It was disturbing. He couldn't quite seem to catch this nobody. It wasn't as if he were playing Francis or Jess or some other accomplished player. There was no shame in losing once in a while to the top dogs, who were, after all, also his friends. Losing to this grim character, though, would surely be an embarrassment.

Some of the onlookers felt a bit indignant. Others took a second, frank look at the boy from Omaha.

As the gaunt Goodman made his way to the twelfth tee, the whispering grew. The kid had some nerve, didn't he? Look at the way he kept a straight face. Not a sliver of a smile. It was just possible . . . But no, Bobby would let loose now and wipe the floor with him.

Before Jones stepped onto the next tee, he cupped his hands around a match and lit a cigarette.

Jones didn't disappoint his acolytes. Hard by the water, the twelfth hole, a 185-yard par three, required a spoon or a two iron, not an easy shot to stop on a treacherous green. Jones drew his iron shot right on, but Goodman uncorked a wild wood to the right and then butchered his chip shot. With an aura of inevitability, Jones made an easy par.

This was the moment everyone had been waiting for. The match was dead even now, and the imposter was coming apart at the seams. He'd looked like an ordinary hacker on that one.

Coming to the 380-yard thirteenth, Bobby sensed he could get the upper hand. Out-of-bounds beckoned on the right, forcing a shot down the left side, where a diagonal trap linked up with a sandy gully. Jones hitched up his beige knickers.

Taking care to avoid the trouble, Bobby came over the top and pulled his shot too far left. Concentrating assiduously on nothing at all, Goodman barely reacted, but he was all too aware of his big chance. With Bobby facing a tough angle, Johnny could forge into a one-hole lead with five to go.

Johnny put his hand out for his driver. Kito seemed about to say something, but sensing Johnny's complete absorption, he bit his lip. He couldn't help pulling for his man now. Imagine if he turned out to be the kid who carried the bag for the kid who beat Bobby Jones? He'd make better money too. The bigwigs would forget Charlie Castro and the rest of them. In his mind's eye, he saw a gentle storm of quarters and half-dollars raining down on him.

Keep it in the short grass, Johnny told himself. Put the pressure on Bobby now. Instead, Johnny came in too flat — it was amazing how he could sense his backswing drifting a few degrees offline, how ~~he could feel his right shoulder coming in too strong as he tried to~~ compensate. Unable to control the deadly move, he yanked his drive left, too.

Head down, he stalked toward his ball, his mind focused on a single task. *The next shot and only the next shot.* His second was a bit off-line. So what? He'd make a good chip.

Bobby lined up his second shot. He had it in mind to drop it just over the lip of the trap and run it up to the flag. Hit through it, he told himself, but he lost the club at the top, decelerated, and dumped the ball into the trap. He stared at the result in disbelief. He was so weary of it all, the endless, tense matches, his peeled-white nerves, the way his stomach cramped into a hard ball. At moments like these, he wished he could shed his skin, escape for just a moment the suffocating knowledge that he was Bobby Jones.

Grim-faced, Bobby climbed into the sand and cut the ball out strong, leaving a long lag putt.

It looked as if Jones was the one coming apart at the seams, but Goodman, chipping weakly, couldn't capitalize. His approach putt was mediocre as well, but luckily, he stymied Bobby. The gallery murmured. Bobby could cough up a double bogey here, an unthinkable turn of events, and fall two behind yet again.

His face drawn, Jones set up for the only shot available — hit the ball a scant few feet up in the air and send it diving home. So close to the hole, the average golfer's instinct was to finesse the stroke, but the experienced player knew that in this case all the rules of logic were suspended. You had to hit the damn thing or it would die. Opening the clubface of his niblick, Bobby popped the delicate shot into the air. It felt right in his hands. Solid. Vaulting over Goodman's stymie, the ball dove into the cup. A brave, nerveless stroke. He'd saved his bogey. Never changing his expression, Bobby brushed a strand of hair off his forehead.

Now the pressure shifted onto Goodman's shoulders. He emptied his mind and surrendered to motion, as if speed of movement were his only protection. Crisp and clean, he knocked the four-footer into the back of the cup.

A pair of shaky bogies. Still tied, the competitors trudged toward the fourteenth tee.

"I'd go crazy," one spectator muttered.

"That's you," came the reply.

The gallery was full of weekend players who trembled and shook over four-footers worth a dime. It seemed incomprehensible that these two men, who at least resembled other human beings, could stand the heat.

Meanwhile, behind his carefully prepared game face, Bobby Jones was roundly cursing his performance. Johnny Goodman, on the other hand, felt detached from his body, dangerously calm.

The fourteenth, a 555-yard behemoth. A few sentimentalists had started pulling for Johnny, but their hearts sank when he opened his hips too fast and sliced his drive into the right rough.

In quick fashion, Jones lashed his tee shot, catching it flush. It was the sort of magisterial drive Bobby had been stroking for years. As the ball soared impossibly high and impossibly far, a satisfied sigh rose from the gallery. A sense of ease spread over the crowd. Bobby was settled safely in the fairway.

Lining up his shot, Goodman was careful not to disturb his lie. Nestled deep in the grass, the ball was barely peeking out. Just outside Johnny's line, a downed limb covered with an orange-tinged moss also presented a problem. Edging around the branch, Johnny found his footing. Then he tried to muscle the ball out of the thick undergrowth, the vegetation grabbed his clubhead, and the ball hooked into the left rough.

Out of this mess, gripping the club tighter and carefully keeping the face open, Johnny managed to catch a niblick square, lofting his pitch onto the green. He was facing a long putt, but he could get down in two. He was still alive.

After his second shot nestled in the fairway, Jones was in a perfect position. He had a straight, short iron right to the carpet, but once again Bobby let up. He cut it too fine, the ball smacking into the lip of the trap and trickling slowly, sickeningly, back into the sand.

Bobby wiped his brow, then dug in, blasting out onto the short grass a full fifteen feet from the cup.

For the first time Johnny let himself hope. And a strange thought came to him. *Maybe Bobby Jones was human.* He'd spent the whole round trying to ignore Bobby's all-too-pervasive presence. Now he gave his adversary a single, frank look. Bobby Jones had two arms and two legs. He had a husky, compact body. Maybe a bit too much weight in the gut. A dark, handsome face, a bit soft around the cheeks. A nice-looking man, but Johnny had defeated more formidable-looking specimens. Jones was a well-put-together fellow, but a man nevertheless.

His inspection complete, Johnny turned back to his long putt; squinting, he feathered practice strokes to sense the distance. As he probed the air with his putter, his hands spoke to him, telling him how far away he was, how hard to hit it. Then Goodman lagged his putt close, and, with Jones's permission, knocked the next one in for a par five.

Now it was Bobby's turn. Uncertain of the line, he pushed the ball too far right; it headed for the corner of the cup, did a 360-degree tour, and spun out. Bogey six. Goodman had taken a slim lead yet again. One up with three to go.

The two players halved the sixteenth and seventeenth holes with pars, though Jones rimmed the cup on the seventeenth on his birdie attempt. Yet again. He looked askance at Calamity Jane, fingering the putter's heavily taped shaft. She had saved him so many times before. Would she be the instrument of his undoing?

The two competitors came to the brutal par-five, 540-yard eighteenth. Jones had to win the hole to keep the match alive.

By this point, Johnny was barely conscious. His muscles good and stretched out, he took such a long backswing he caught sight of the clubhead through the corner of his eye. Swinging from the heels, he sent a low, sweeping hook far out to the right, but he'd judged it just right. With wicked overspin, the ball darted twenty-five yards on the ground and came to rest dead center. His longest drive of the day.

As he fought through the swarming gallery, Johnny had the sensation that he was deep underwater, the weight of the sea pressing him down. Now for the brassie. He took one brief practice swing and almost in the same motion let fly — he hated to freeze over the ball — striking yet another right-to-left shot pure.

"Every golf tournament has its dramatic moments," William E. Richardson wrote, "but there has never been a tenser climax than when the Omaha boy and Jones came up to the last green. Having had the honor all the way from the fourteenth hole — the turning point in the match — Goodman hit two tremendous shots almost to the chalk line which is the stopping point for the galleries."

In fact, it was Jones who wavered, not Goodman. Slicing his second shot, Jones caught a break when the ball, sailing straight out-of-bounds, smacked into a tree branch and dropped down safely on the fairway.

Johnny shook his head. What did that old judge at the Field Club say? *Luckier than a two-peckered dog.*

Bobby had a wide-open shot now. He had to stiff one and get down for his bird, but instead he hit his pitch a shade fat. The shot trickled to a stop, way short of the hole.

Goodman set up for his third, a long chip. The entire match hung in the balance, but by now Johnny understood that Jones was fallible. One thing he had to avoid: tightening up and dumping the ball short. Anything but that.

Johnny followed his swift routine and clipped the ball off the grass. Solid, too solid. The ball darted straight for the pin, all too hot, flashed by the hole, and ran all the way to the back edge of the green. Damn. He'd have been better off dumping it short. Now he'd left himself a slippery, downhill putt.

From his perch above the hole, Goodman could easily three-putt, but Jones's best chance was to sink one for a birdie and send the match into sudden death. Bobby was away and had to putt first. The sprawling gallery fell into an unnatural silence. He'd drained that fifteen-footer against Espinosa on the last stroke of the last regulation hole, but this putt was much longer.

Bobby struck the ball, and it veered right for the hole. Would it get there? At first it seemed as if he hadn't nudged it quite hard enough, but the ball kept turning over and over, heading straight for the heart of the cup. Six inches from the hole, though, it ran out of steam, curled off to the side, and came to a dead stop. Bobby Jones had left his fate in Johnny Goodman's hands.

Goodman read the treacherous downhiller, trying to sense the speed. It could run away and easily slide five or six feet past. But he couldn't baby it either. Softening his hands ever so slightly, he tapped the ball, starting it in the right direction. But he'd barely touched it. Would it keep sliding down the slope or die, leaving him another wicked challenge? Defying gravity, the ball almost stopped, but then it rolled over once more, and once more again. Had it started to get away from him?

Finally, the putt lost all velocity, wobbling and falling off-line before halting a foot from the cup. In a daze Johnny tapped the ball in to halve the last hole.

He'd beaten the greatest player in the world. How did he feel? He couldn't have put it into words. It wasn't wild elation — he'd been numbing his emotions too long to lose his head. He felt happy, sure, but his pleasure was tinged with some other emotion. The excitement was there, it came in waves, but the sensation fluttered and died out all too soon. Maybe it was because the world looked the same as it had a few minutes before. The faces around him, the trees, the sky, hadn't been altered one jot.

He felt slightly off-kilter, a bit unhinged, and very, very quiet inside. The cheering was all so distant.

Then he realized that his victory in the Omaha City Championship had elicited a louder applause. The clapping was scattered, and there was an undercurrent of something else he couldn't put his finger on.

The *San Francisco Chronicle* correspondent cast the gallery's reaction in apocalyptic terms, but it was an apocalypse marked by nervous silence. "If an earthquake had suddenly rocked the peninsula, the shock could hardly have been greater . . . There was as much gloom around the home green at the finish as there was enthusiastic appreciation for the astonishing feat of Goodman."

In defeat, Bobby Jones couldn't have been more gracious. After shaking Johnny's hand, he made a point of smiling and complimenting his young antagonist. He also apologized for his lucky break on eighteen. "I got all the luck," Bobby said, "and I still couldn't beat you."

In turn, Johnny insisted he'd had some luck out there, too. The lines came out of his mouth as if they'd been written in advance. Then he shook Bobby's hand in turn. He felt a grin split his face, but everything seemed muffled, swathed in cotton.

The gallery, the mass of reporters, the tournament officials, all assumed Jones was doing an elegant job of covering up his disappointment.

In truth, Bobby was flooded with relief. As soon as Goodman had rolled his lag putt close, his whole body had relaxed, and he'd realized that he wouldn't have to drag himself through another endless series of public displays. He'd come to loathe the omnipresent attention as much as match play's killing pressure. Give him a friendly Nassau back at East Lake, or nine holes horsing around with Doug Fairbanks any day.

With Bobby Jones's hand in his, Johnny's excitement broke through his emotional retaining wall. It seemed as if he'd been admiring pictures of Bobby his whole life, he'd been reading his words with such reverence, he'd been play-acting their mythical encounter so long that only the touch of Jones's hand had the power to make their match real.

Johnny also felt a certain regret. Bobby, for all his fine clothes and handsome face, looked faintly worn and bedraggled. In a fleeting way, Johnny realized that by beating the greatest player in the world, he had diminished him.

Then a single, powerful thought ran through Johnny's mind, and he barely felt the ground under him — *he had beaten the greatest player in the world.*

PART THREE

The Pullman Days

18

THE STORM OF QUESTIONS swirled around him. No, he never imagined he would beat Mr. Jones. Yes, his opponent was a wonderful gentleman. "His congratulations, I could feel, were right from the heart," Johnny told the reporters. "It made a lump come in my throat. 'Johnny,' he said, 'I just couldn't beat that kind of golf.'"

Johnny's real feelings were too complicated, and too unformed, to share with a bunch of strangers. By conquering Jones, he had reduced his idol to human proportions. Yet Bobby's ease and grace in defeat had reaffirmed Johnny's admiration for the man, and made him want to emulate his style more than ever. Even after spending an afternoon in intimate combat with Jones, Johnny still saw the Georgian as an otherworldly figure.

He had a better chance of playing golf like Bobby Jones than *being* like Bobby Jones. Yet, as much as he looked up to Jones, he resented the aura the press had created around Bobby, all the while dreaming it might someday be his own. These feelings confused and disturbed him. They were so hard to sort out.

The reporters had more meat-and-potatoes questions. They wanted to know when Johnny thought the match was turning in his favor.

The turning point? Johnny wasn't sure. He'd been too busy playing. He concentrated as hard on giving the proper, modest answers as he had over his crucial brassie on eighteen. "My game was the best I had in me. The course is one of the toughest in the country. I was as cautious as possible, and kept my head, but you have to take long chances when you're playing someone like Jones," Johnny explained.

Finally, the press drifted away, but then came the crush of fans, waving their programs. He signed and signed, edging through the crowd with the help of a phalanx of marshals.

As he fought his way to the clubhouse, his thoughts came in bright, disconnected flashes. He was telling the truth. He'd never quite believed he could beat Bobby Jones, but he had, hadn't he? His face ached from smiling.

The rapid-fire questions, the cries of the golf fanatics, the officials breaking a path for him through the waves of humanity were all evidence of his feat — solid reality he could see and hear. Belief and disbelief coursed through him in alternating currents.

He ate lunch mechanically. A stranger came over to his table and asked to shake the hand of the man who had beaten Bobby Jones. Johnny shook. He chewed. He was aware of the eyes on him. He signed a few more programs, all too aware of the whispers, the smiles, the appraising glances. The same people who had looked straight through him when he'd been cooling his heels on the veranda, waiting for the USGA to pronounce his fate, now stared straight at him with newfound interest.

The realization was setting in now. If nothing else, from now on he'd be the Man Who Beat Bobby Jones. They'd be all over him back in Omaha. Would it be easier to comprehend what he'd done when he returned to the Great Plains, where the ground was flat and firm under his feet? He could talk to his friends at the Field Club and Lakewood and to his girlfriend, Josephine. She'd be on cloud nine. With her excitement washing over him, he'd go over every shot, and he'd experience the match all over again. He couldn't quite grasp it here. California made him dizzy.

A golf tournament is a relentless affair. A couple of hours after pulling off one of the most startling upsets in twentieth-century golf, Johnny Goodman had to go out and play another eighteen-hole match, this one against a nineteen-year-old as obscure as Jones was famous, the brawny Lawson Little.

Strangely enough, he was far more nervous against Little than when he faced Jones. All the fears he had savagely suppressed against Bobby finally broke through. Still, his game held up well under the strain, though in the end he lost the hard-fought match, 2 and 1.

The newspapers were painfully ambivalent about Johnny Goodman's upset of Bobby Jones. Praise rained down from the Omaha papers, of course. The *World-Herald,* straining to evoke the match's dramatic close, resorted to a mixed metaphor. "It ended and in the twinkling of a split second history had been rewritten, a great champion had been unfrocked and a game little fighting golfer had reached the goal of his heart's desire."

George Trevor, the *New York Sun*'s golf writer, admired Goodman's solid swing and his fortitude. The *New York Times* allowed that there was "no wavering on Goodman's part," also noting that on the fifteenth, "Goodman hung on grimly."

But by the next day it seemed as if, instead of pulling off a remarkable upset, Johnny had committed some nameless crime. Ring Lardner put his finger on the nature of Johnny's offense. "The ancient Scottish pastime in this age is a one-man sport, and the one man is public property, like Lindbergh, or Charlie Chaplin, or Babe Ruth. If you're giving a show, don't kill the star in the prologue."

The *New York Times* concurred, calling Jones's defeat "nothing short of a calamity." Certainly, USGA officials, noting the precipitous drop in attendance and the proceeds after Jones had been ousted, shared this view.

William E. Richardson went so far as to disparage Goodman's achievement. "It is doing the winner no injustice to state that he was lucky in a way to meet Jones in an eighteen-hole round and on a day when Bobby's putter, Calamity Jane, was not obeying her master."

Yet to argue that a man was the better player except for his poor putting is to negate golf's cruel logic. The better player is almost *always* the better putter — at least for one day. And a cursory look at the match shows that Jones had the luckiest break of all when his second shot on eighteen careened back in-bounds after hitting a happily positioned tree limb.

In fact, experienced players had been disintegrating for years when they came face-to-face with Bobby Jones, yet nineteen-year-old Johnny Goodman had managed to control his nerves — and keep his profound concentration — despite the extraordinary pressure.

Over and over, descriptions of Goodman's game go back to his ability to focus, to descend into an almost eerie hypnotic state. For golf's mind game — the whole game, some would say — he had a singular gift.

Despite the fact that Johnny Goodman had slain the star in the opening scene, the 1929 U.S. Amateur came to a far more dramatic close than all of those mourning Jones's demise could have hoped for. On the eighteenth hole of the final match, Harrison "Jimmy" Johnston found his second shot on the beach, waves nuzzling his ball. With the championship on the line, Johnston waited calmly for the tide to recede. Setting up rapidly before the next wave floated his ball out to sea, he pulled off a miraculous recovery shot, parred the hole, and claimed the amateur crown.

Patriots of Pebble Beach couldn't have wished for a better final act, with their dramatic links taking center stage at the penultimate moment. From the USGA's perspective, however, Johnston's performance was anticlimactic. An understudy stood in the star attraction's place.

The Del Monte hosted a lavish dinner for the competitors and USGA officials after the tournament was over. Although Johnny Goodman found himself seated in a place of honor on the dais, he sensed that the same brass hats who had grilled him about his ties to the sporting goods trade were distinctly standoffish. He thought he knew the reason. Despite wearing a tie and his dressy sweater, he looked too casual in the formal assembly. There were one or two other golfers who weren't wearing jackets, but they went around slapping backs and telling jokes, and no one seemed to mind. Johnny was sure he stood out like a sore thumb.

Or maybe the bigwigs were nursing a grudge against him for knocking off Bobby Jones. He'd heard that attendance had gone down the drain once he'd eliminated the Georgian, but it wasn't his damn fault that Jones had made a hash of the first three holes. What was he supposed to do after that, roll over and play dead? Was he getting the cold shoulder for playing his heart out? It burned him up to get treated that way.

Still, the roast beef was the best he'd ever tasted, so tender you barely had to chew it, and there were so many fancy desserts, his head was spinning.

He'd spent more money than he'd expected on room and board, much more, but there was no need to panic. He'd been down on his luck plenty of times, and something always turned up. Now that he'd beaten Bobby Jones, he'd get offers, wouldn't he? His name had to be worth something for the first time. Not to worry. He'd pack away a few slices of pie so he wouldn't get too hungry later on. Maybe have a couple of drinks too. Without a nip or two, he always felt tongue-tied in front of rich people.

Sipping his drink, he listened to the chatter around him. Everybody was talking about Jimmy Johnston's incredible recovery from the beach on eighteen. But Johnny also picked up a few stray remarks about stocks, the same thing he'd heard all week. From what he could tell, the bull market was shooting straight up to the moon.

When the man with the silky baritone voice slid in next to him and started chatting, he felt grateful. There was something different about him. Maybe it was the brown houndstooth suit, or the gold-flecked silk handkerchief in his pocket. Johnny could barely spit out a word, but he grinned and nodded, and the guy didn't seem to mind. He wasn't one of those stuffed shirts.

He said he was some sort of singer, Bing Crosby, and then Johnny placed him.

"Paul Whiteman, the *Old Gold Hour,* right?"

"Found me out," Bing admitted. The favorite of Whiteman's more-advanced jazz players like Bix Beiderbecke, Bing had also struck up a friendship with Louis Armstrong, who admired the young singer's style. Recalling Bing in his early days, Armstrong remarked, "There were just as many colored people 'buying air,' raving over Bing's recordings, as much as anybody else. The chicks were justa swooning and screaming when Bing would sing."

"Your band gave a concert in Omaha," Johnny recalled.

"Yeah," Bing allowed. On Whiteman's tour out to the West Coast, Bing sang with his trio, the Rhythm Boys. "I suppose we did. You played some game, kiddo," Crosby said, laughing easily. "You see the headlines?"

"Yeah, a few."

"Ten feet tall. All the big papers. No one thought it was possible. They thought Bobby was invincible."

"Yeah, thanks."

"So, what're your plans?"

Maybe it was the drinks, maybe he just felt relaxed with the entertainer. The man had the damndest speaking voice, just like syrup. "My friend Bert, we're driving up for a look at the Northwest," he said.

"I heard a rumor you were taking a cattle car back home," Crosby said with a wry smile.

"We've got a car," Johnny replied, stiffening. "Don't believe everything they write. Bert's got a car."

"When do you leave?"

"Day after tomorrow."

"I'll tell you what," Bing went on in a confidential tone. "Tomorrow, you and me, we'll play for, what? Say, a hundred dollars a hole?"

A chill ran through Johnny. Where would he ever get that kind of dough? Was this joker making fun of him? He just stared at that thin, grinning mug of Crosby's in wonder.

"Just give me a shot," Crosby added. "I want to lick the man who licked the Emperor Jones."

Crosby had begun playing golf with his Rhythm Boys partner, Al Rinker, in his late teens, and since he'd hit the Coast he'd been getting in quite a few rounds with Hollywood golf fanatics Oliver Hardy and Johnny Weissmuller.

While he waited impatiently to see the script for his upcoming film, *King of Jazz,* Paul Whiteman was paying Crosby a generous two hundred a week for doing nothing at all, giving Bing even more time than usual to slip out onto the links. The singer picked up even more cash performing at the Montmarte with the Rhythm

Boys at night. He was flush, and if he wasn't drinking up the proceeds, he was more than happy to spread some around on the fairway.

Johnny wanted to say, "Forget it, bud. I don't have that kind of scratch," but the words stuck in his throat. He didn't say yes, but he didn't say no.

"Good, it's fixed. See you at the clubhouse about seven. We'll sneak out for nine, at least."

All night, thinking of his match with Crosby, Johnny tossed and turned.

For relief, he directed his thoughts to the match against Jones. Lovingly, he went over his drive on eighteen and the brassie he'd crushed almost all the way to the distant green. What had he thought at that moment? Nothing at all; that was the beauty of it. He'd turned into a single, flowing muscle, his swing an extension of his heart and hands.

His mind darted from the slippery downhiller on eighteen to that first drive into the fog. Yet despite recalling every stroke, his own and Bobby's, too, in his memory the match seemed soft around the edges, as if the mist that had pressed down on the first fairway had never lifted.

Then he was jolted from his dreamy state.

What if Crosby turned out to be a hustler? Maybe he made his living on the golf course. Maybe he'd suggest complicated bets, or ask for a handicap. Make it all sound sporting.

How in the world, Johnny wondered, could he come up with a hundred bucks, much less four or five hundred, if Crosby spanked him good and proper?

Johnny showed up at the clubhouse early, his eyes dry and red, his head throbbing. He tried to flash a grin, but he didn't think he convinced anybody. He knew he looked sick as a dog because he felt sick as a dog.

Crosby had top-of-the-line sticks in his bag, the latest Wilsons. In a canary yellow V-neck sweater and spotless white ducks, he could have been on the deck of a sailboat. Johnny noticed how Bing bantered with the old starter, and how everybody in the small gallery seemed to like him. Evidently, word of their match had gotten around.

Wouldn't it be swell to be so relaxed, to be able to tell jokes and get people to laugh?

Johnny had only one refuge, the club in his hands. When he gave his driver a quick waggle, he started to feel like himself. Balanced and smooth and self-contained. Without thinking, he lashed one down the fairway.

Crosby didn't have a bad swing, but the second Johnny saw the entertainer slap his first shot off the tee, not more than 190, he forgot all his worries. He could beat Bing with one hand behind his back.

All he had to do was put his head down and play his game like he always did. Crosby didn't do all that bad, posting a succession of bogeys, but Johnny cranked out one par after another.

Walking off the fifth, Bing laughed, as if the money leaking out of his pocket didn't mean a thing. "Like a hot knife through butter, huh, kid?"

"What?"

"Your game. I was wondering what it was like."

"I don't know . . ."

"Okay, gimme a couple more chances. Maybe I can whip you on one hole."

Crosby managed a few halves, but there was too much dough at stake, so Johnny closed out the singer by taking the eighth and ninth. Five hundred dollars. More scratch than he'd ever seen anywhere but in a bank. This character Crosby must be rolling in dough.

Back at the clubhouse, Bing disappeared into the locker room, then emerged and put his arm around Johnny's bony shoulder. "C'mon, I'll buy you a drink. You look like you could use one."

What Johnny really wanted was lunch, but he was too shy to say so. At the bar, a pair of fresh beers were set before them, and Crosby discreetly pulled out his bankroll. "Straight from my sock," he deadpanned, counting the bills out of the barkeep's sight. "Now keep this under your hat. And stay out of the boxcars this time."

Johnny wanted to correct Bing and point out that he'd ridden to California on the Fast Mail, but he couldn't bring himself to contradict his benefactor. He even thought, fleetingly, about forgetting the trip to the Northwest with Bert and taking an honest-to-goodness Pullman all the way back to Omaha. But five hundred dollars, which seemed like a small fortune now, would last only so long.

19

JOHNNY GOODMAN WAS SUPPOSED to arrive back in Omaha in the early afternoon, but as one line of coaches after another failed to produce the young star, the mayor, who had prepared a formal welcoming speech, finally wearied of waiting. The rest of the town fathers deserted the station as well. Only Johnny's adoptive family, the Websters, remained stubbornly rooted to the platform until the last train pulled in, but Johnny still didn't show. Mrs. Webster returned early the next morning, and not long after dawn Johnny descended into the quiet morning.

He was relieved that he didn't have to face a mob. They always asked him so many questions, and he liked to think things over before he said anything in public. If he had a chance to weigh his words, he could come up with the right phrase, but he was always nervous that he'd blurt out some expression that had South Omaha written all over it. Then they'd say, What do you expect from a Porkopolis kid?

When a reporter asked him a question, he made sure to skip the slang and sound as formal as possible. It was as if he spoke two languages. What he thought of as his real voice, the one that came natural during a game of pinochle or pitch, he kept that under his hat.

Johnny was happy not to see any reporters. Only Mrs. Webster was waiting on the platform. The coast was clear. Hoisting his clubs over one shoulder and gripping his bag, he made his way toward her. "Hi, Mom," he said shyly. "I'm back."

She gave him a long hug. "We're so proud of you, Johnny."

Now he wriggled out of her grasp. "Hey, did my jacket turn up anyplace?"

"Your jacket?"

"I must've had my head screwed on backwards when I got on the train . . ."

"I'm not sure what you're talking about, Johnny."

"The jacket I bought just before I left!"

Understanding dawned on her face. "I'm sure it will turn up," she said doubtfully.

"I think I left it on the ledge over there, near the ticket counter."

"Why didn't Bert drive you all the way back?" Mrs. Webster asked.

"I don't know. He had some business in Minneapolis. That's where he dropped me off."

Close by, a *World-Herald* reporter Johnny hadn't noticed recorded the conversation with a sense of disbelief. *The kid conquers the great Bobby Jones, and all he can think about is a measly suit jacket?*

Now Johnny spied the newspaperman. He groped for his name . . . Al Wolf. Sighing, he surrendered to the usual interrogation. Before he knew it, one more scribe materialized, then another. Gathering his resources, he evoked all the phrases he'd been thinking up on the long ride back from the Coast.

"Beating Bobby Jones is the one thing I never dreamed of. Mr. Jones is a wonderful gentleman, and I'm sure he didn't blame me for winning those first three holes."

That didn't sound bad, he thought, and he breathed a little easier. "I was playing the best golf of my life, but when Bobby caught up to me, I thought I was a goner."

"How'd you keep your head, Johnny?" Wolf asked.

Now he drew on his precise recall. "After Bobby hit into that trap on fourteen, for the first time I realized even Bobby Jones is human."

A reporter laughed. "I don't know if the rest of the golfers in the world believe that, kiddo. I heard you've got Bobby's picture pasted up on your walls."

"Pictures and articles. I've looked up to Mr. Jones for years."

"How'd you like the Coast?" the *Omaha Bee* man asked.

"Well, I played a round with Mr. Bing Crosby. The *Old Gold Hour* singer. That was swell, but if you ask me," he added expansively, "movies are a flop."

The reporters exchanged glances. The kid was loosening up now. "Wadda you mean by that?"

"Well, there are all these girls out there, they're trying to get into the Hollywood game, they all think they're going to be stars, and they end up out on the street. And California's full of foreigners too."

That line's worth a laugh, Wolf decided. Wasn't this kid some kind of Polack or Lithuanian? He'd need some polishing before he was ready for those sharks from the big eastern rags. In Omaha, though, he was a big hero now, so they'd have to play down that remark.

"You going back to school soon?"

Johnny didn't want to let this cat out of the bag, but he was sick and tired of pretending to hit the books at the University of Nebraska. He explained that he had to miss the fall semester, adding, "I've got to work and earn a little money meanwhile. Amateur golf doesn't mean anything in dollars and cents."

"Why don't you just turn pro?"

Johnny had been bedeviled by this question ever since he took the Trans-Mississippi. Reporters either didn't believe his standard answer or they just didn't understand him. "I could make six or eight thousand dollars for a couple of years, but I could never play in amateur events again, and it isn't worth it."

He couldn't quite get his real feelings out. All those years growing up and reading every word Bobby Jones ever wrote, following his every move in the papers, and dreaming about becoming just like him . . . It would probably sound nuts if he came out with the truth. He wanted to be the next Bobby Jones. Maybe it was better to keep that stuff to yourself.

"What do you mean not worth it?"

"I want to have a successful career in business," Johnny insisted, as if he were trying to convince himself. Maybe he was right. All those politicians and executives would be after him to play a few rounds. That couldn't hurt his chances in business. "An amateur plays the game just because he loves it. There's no money to get in the way." He had his own twist on this standard argument, though, especially after his brush with the USGA in Pebble Beach. Who were they to keep him out of the amateur game? Who said he wasn't as clean as the next guy?

Now they turned to his adoptive mother. "Are you proud of Johnny, Mrs. Webster?" Wolf asked.

The matronly Webster didn't hesitate. "Of course I am, but not because he can play golf, but because he has a beautiful character."

Johnny wished she hadn't come out with that one. He could feel his face burning red.

The next morning Johnny carefully pasted the whole front page of the *Omaha Herald* into his burgeoning scrapbook. After reading the articles over again he decided he didn't sound like too much of a lunkhead, but he wished he could take back a few of his remarks, particularly the one about foreigners. That wouldn't go down too smoothly on Golden Hill.

For the first time, beating Bobby Jones started feeling thoroughly real. Alone, he read over the articles again and again, envisioning his best strokes. When he made contact with that last drive, it felt so smooth, so sweet. He felt that one all the way down to his toes.

Out of the blue, he burst out laughing. He'd beaten Bobby Jones. Didn't that mean he was a great player? Didn't that mean he was going places? Suddenly, he felt giddy. It was as if he'd been sleepwalking, and now it hit him full force. A warm glow rushed through him.

He had to see Josephine. They'd been dating for six months now, and he hadn't seen her since his return.

Jo lived in South Omaha, a few blocks away from where Johnny grew up. Her mother, Helen, was in the parlor, parked on the horsehair sofa. She gave him the fish eye.

"Hi, Mrs. Kersigo," he said. "Jo around?" Johnny knew the woman disapproved of him, but today, he didn't care.

"In the kitchen," she said grudgingly.

In a plain housedress and slippers, Josephine was scouring a pot.

She was always busy. She didn't have a bit of makeup on, and her clothes were worth about a dime, but with her dark eyes and her dark hair and her generous mouth, she looked as good as any of those California girls. Only Jo was different, very different.

And he could talk to her. Shifting from one foot to another, he poured out everything in a torrent of words. The sunrise he saw in Wyoming through the window of the Fast Mail train. The sun was blood red and huge. The brassie he hit on that par five. What the women were wearing on the first tee. Bing Crosby. Did Jo know who he was?

Josephine looked at him in wonder. "Who wound you up?" she asked, laughing.

"I guess I'm running off at the mouth," he said, embarrassed. He was quiet for a while. Then he said, "I can't explain it . . . what I did . . . I feel so good . . ." That was it. It was that simple. No one in the entire world felt as good as he did at that moment.

Josephine looked through the archway and caught her mother's eye, but she took Johnny's hand anyway, and squeezed it hard.

When he got home, he closed the door to his room and read the front pages he'd pasted in his scrapbook again, for the fifth time. He wondered what he would think when he was an old man and looked over the same articles. There was one about a woman named Mrs. Alice Wall, who'd been kidnapped, drugged, and left in a cornfield. Malta fever was sweeping through the local dairy herds, and a McGrew, Nebraska, bank had gone belly-up because of some crooked vice president named Charles J. Burke.

Johnny wondered if it was safe to deposit the five hundred big ones he'd taken off Bing Crosby. It was a huge sum, almost a third of what his brothers took home at Armour in a whole year. With a bank account he could get some interest, but look what that banker in McGrew had done with other people's money. He decided to wait and see.

Over the next week, the *Herald* was full of confusing stories. Stocks were sliding, but the financial wizards said it was because the market was dealing with "undigested securities," whatever the hell

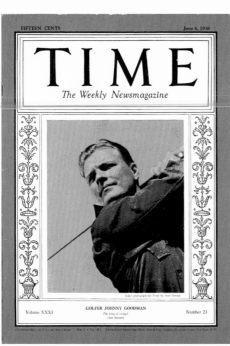

TIME

The Weekly Newsmagazine

GOLFER JOHNNY GOODMAN
The king of swing?
(See Sport)

Volume XXXI   Number 23

In 1938, *Time* magazine asks, "Is Johnny Goodman the King of Swing?"

Goodman (left) with his opponent and idol, Bobby Jones, at the 1929 U.S. Amateur.

Goodman in his
early twenties.
As his fortunes
improved, so did
his wardrobe.

Josephine Kersigo,
Goodman's wife.

Goodman spent countless
hours honing his swing.

Vanquished, the gracious
Francis Ouimet (right)
shakes Goodman's hand
at the 1932 U.S. Amateur.

The mercurial columnist
Westbrook Pegler.

Joe Kirkwood's willing
victim is in no danger.

Goodman (second from right) in his element at the Field Club.

Goodman (second from left) at an Omaha watering hole.

Prickly antagonists Gene Sarazen (left) and Walter Hagen give the Ryder Cup trophy a once-over.

1933 U.S. Open winner Goodman (left) matches smiles with runner-up Ralph Guldahl.

A military cordon protects Goodman from his adoring
fans at the 1933 U.S. Open.

Goodman (left) and the actress Loretta Young. Goodman
turned down every contract that Hollywood offered.

Goodman (front right) played number one on the 1934 Walker Cup team.

Jack Atkins, Goodman's nephew, at Goodman's obscure grave.

that meant. Finally, he decided to keep his money in his dresser drawer.

When he thought about the Del Monte Hotel, the lavish spreads and the way you could sink into the lounge chairs in the lobby, it all seemed like a dream. The Omaha papers were saying he had a brilliant future, that he was the city's most famous son, but meanwhile he didn't have his own place, or a job to keep body and soul together. The first thing he did was put himself on a strict budget.

Everybody wanted to play golf with him now. It was worse than ever. When he set a tee time with one foursome, he had to turn down three others, and he saw the way their eyes narrowed and heard the way their voices tightened when he promised to fit them in at a later date. Only weeks after he'd bested Jones, a guy he'd never seen before asked if he worried about being a flash in the pan. He could taste the resentment in the air.

He heard some businessman at the Field Club call him a golf bum under his breath. Where the hell did he get off? Other cracks got back to him, too. They were saying Johnny Goodman needed a new hat size, and Johnny Goodman had a chip on his shoulder, and Johnny Goodman was too cocky for his own good. All that jealousy, it got his back up. Why shouldn't he think a little more of himself, anyway? Jo was always saying that.

Things were looking up, though. When he appeared at a new Ford showroom, the head salesman slipped him ten dollars. Then Pete Lyck, a Field Club stalwart, started talking about a job that might turn up for him peddling insurance. Maybe, just maybe, amateur golf would give him a lift. Francis Ouimet's father dug ditches, and look at what golf had done for the Bostonian now. With his glasses, and his conservative suits, you couldn't tell him from a hundred other successful executives.

Every older man he played a round with told him the same thing. Stay in Omaha, you're a big name here. There'll be plenty of opportunities. You go someplace else, they won't know you from Adam. As far as Johnny could tell, their advice made sense.

In late October, just before it got too cold to play, he was eating lunch with a foursome at the Field Club when the older men started talking about the losses they were taking in the market. Johnny's ears pricked up. He didn't need to go back to college. The Field Club, with its successful packinghouse executives, beer distributors, doctors, lawyers, and politicians, was his university. And he read the papers, religiously.

All during October, trading on the stock market had fluctuated nervously, sometimes wildly, but shares held at historic highs. The Standard Trade and Securities Service suggested its investors follow "an ultra-conservative policy," and *Poor's Weekly* inveighed against "the great stock delusion," but most economists and market analysts agreed with Professor Irving Fisher, who contended that stocks had climbed to "what looks like a permanently high plateau."

Evangeline Adams, the famous mystic, declared that "the Dow Jones could climb to heaven." On October 22, 1929, Thomas J. Lamont, a senior partner at J. P. Morgan, fired off a memo to President Hoover, asserting, "The future appears brilliant . . . we have the greatest and soundest prosperity of any country in the world."

Panic seized the market the next day. Piers Brendon evoked the frightening scene. "A tidal wave of selling overwhelmed Wall Street. Chaotic scenes took place on the floor of the stock exchange. Hysterical traders ran, bellowed, cursed, gesticulated . . . sweat pouring down their faces and their collars and shirts in tatters."

On Monday, the rout picked up steam again, and the next day — Black Tuesday — the stock market succumbed to full-blown terror. On the floor of the exchange, Brendon went on, "Dealers besieged the 17 horseshoe-shaped trading posts, waving, scrambling, clawing and screaming . . . The roar conveyed a palpable sense of horror, as if in response to some monstrous natural calamity." One reporter wrote that the panic had "an eerie quality, like chords from a primitive requiem."

In Omaha, newspaper editors kept the catastrophe off the front pages. It all seemed to be happening far away, and the businessmen who influenced public opinion believed it wasn't all that significant. The grain harvest was reaching record levels, and the weather on the plains was holding up. True, some banks were under strain, but if fear-mongering stayed in the closet where it belonged, there would be no bank runs.

All through the 1920s, Coolidge prosperity had been uneven in the plains state. Farm prices had declined, and over six hundred banks had closed temporarily, or permanently, but Nebraska, strong and self-sufficient, had survived.

Josephine's mother wanted to know how Johnny expected to make a living, and he had a ready answer. He was going to get into the insurance business any day now. That seemed to pacify her. Insurance was a respectable occupation. As time went on, though, Johnny wondered whether Pete Lyck was going to come through with the job at his agency, or whether he just wanted to keep Johnny as a four-ball partner, but he kept his hopes up, and kept playing golf.

He wished Josephine's old lady would get off his back, but Jo said her mother had had a hard time back in Pennsylvania. Johnny understood, without it being spelled out, that the trouble had been about Jo's father and booze. Evidently, Old Man Kersigo got rough if he had one too many.

South Omaha wasn't the biggest place in the world. People talked. That's how Jo's mother found out about Johnny's father, and about the fact that the older Goodman boys liked to drink and play cards. She thought Johnny seemed to like drinking a little too much himself, and he always wanted to take Josephine out to those roadhouses. He wasn't a steady man, she warned her daughter. Why not find a Polish boy who had a good job with Armour?

Josephine tried explaining that Johnny was famous, and that he had a lot of opportunities, but her mother always asked the same question. "So where's his paycheck?"

To reassure the anxious woman, Johnny started attending Sunday Mass with the Kersigos. He'd always gone with his mother, but he also wanted to make the right impression. Still, the old lady never relaxed her vigilance. Josephine had to get home on time and not go running in the streets at all hours.

Winter drifted by, and the money he'd taken off Bing Crosby was dwindling to nothing. Josephine's mother was still asking a lot of questions about him, and he was getting antsy himself. Where were all the business deals Omaha's bigwigs had been promising?

Still, when the weather warmed up, and he could get out and hit a few, golf started filling his imagination again. After all those dinners over the winter with blowhard politicians and assorted Omaha dignitaries, he'd packed on some pounds, and he wondered if he could crank out a few extra yards off the tee.

Then Bert Waddington, his good angel from Lakewood Country Club, showed up at the Websters with the strangest damned thing he'd ever seen, a house on wheels. It was just like Bert, who was an engineer, after all, to discover the latest invention. He could take apart any engine under the sun, and build a radio out of parts. Inside the boxy vehicle it was a tight squeeze, but Bert showed him the bunks, the electric stove, and the utility sink. The trailer had everything a man needed to live on the road.

"Free transportation and free room and board," the hawk-faced Waddington explained. Then he poked Johnny in the ribs. "How 'bout a ride to the U.S. Open, kiddo?"

20

WHEN JOHNNY GOODMAN and Bert Waddington showed up in Bert's jerry-rigged trailer for the 1930 U.S. Open in early July at the Interlachen Country Club in Minneapolis, Johnny attracted plenty of attention. The *New York Sun*'s George Trevor wrote: "Goodman has color. He knows the value of publicity as witness his arrival at Interlachen in a modernized version of the 'covered wagon.' With several kindred spirits, Johnny traveled to Minneapolis in a motor-trailer, a sort of 'houseboat' on wheels, rigged up with a kitchenette, radio, and sleeping bunks."

One photograph pictured Goodman cooking breakfast in the trailer, dressed incongruously in a suit and tie. Since his showing at Pebble Beach he had worked hard to develop a more adult appearance. He had been feted by Omaha's Mayor Dahlman, County Attorney General Beale, and an array of Omaha's top businessmen. Although he hadn't yet found a position, he was growing more comfortable around the successful packinghouse executives, the doctors, dentists, and lawyers who golfed at the Omaha Field Club.

And he was working assiduously to make himself more amenable to Josephine's mother. Johnny was only twenty, but constantly in the limelight, he was growing up fast.

Goodman was also turning into a strikingly handsome young man. He took meticulous care of his clothes, preferring shades of gray in sweaters, dark, pressed knickers, and white shirts. When a single hair fell out of place, he would whip out a comb from his back pocket and slick it back tight to his skull. Goodman made as fine a photograph as he did a human-interest story.

Of course, Johnny wasn't pulling a publicity stunt by traveling in Bert Waddington's "modernized covered wagon." He was simply saving money. In fact, his scrambling to keep his head above water was part of his appeal. Johnny excited the hero worship of newspaper readers whose circumstances were much closer to his than to Robert Tyre Jones's.

In fact, more and more readers were getting the opportunity to identify with Goodman's inventive survival techniques. Gallows humor about the Wall Street debacle circulated widely, although Hoover's Treasury secretary, Andrew Mellon, thought the best medicine for the economic downturn was to let the disaster run its course. Mellon, "a passionate advocate of inaction," according to the economist John Kenneth Galbraith, believed in the old-time economic medicine: "Liquidate labor, liquidate stocks, liquidate the farmers, liquidate real estate."

Mellon's own corporations followed this prescription, and he continued to thrive, but the liquidated had other concerns. One in four factory workers were unemployed in 1930, and the situation was becoming worse. Heavily indebted farmers, who had suffered all through the supposedly flush Roaring Twenties, were facing falling commodity prices and a drought that was searing the eastern seaboard. States as far west as Missouri and Arkansas were burning up, too.

Liquidated farmers had a decided distaste for being reduced to nothing, as it meant surrendering the land that their families had worked for years, sometimes for generations.

The days when businessmen were held up as paragons of virtue were fading fast. As one 1930 letter writer to the Hoover administration put it: "Oh why is it that it is allways [sic] a bunch of overly rich, selfish, dumb ignorant money hogs that persist in being Senitors, legislatures, representatives[.] Where would they be without the Common Soldier, the common laborer that is compelled to work for a starvation wage."

The Depression, just picking up steam, was still being referred to as a downturn, another minor glitch in the business cycle, even a salutary tonic for a system that needed a bit of a purge, but the public's taste in heroes was changing, and Johnny Goodman's struggle to succeed in the tony world of amateur golf had just the right appeal.

Of course, like every other golfer at the 1930 U.S. Open, amateur or professional, Goodman was little more than a sidelight. Once again, the main story was Bobby Jones and his quest to win what had been called "the impregnable quadrilateral," the British Open, the British Amateur, the U.S. Open, and the U.S. Amateur, all in a single year. With his ear for American English, O. B. Keeler labeled this seemingly impossible feat the grand slam.

Jones had turned his defeat at the hands of Johnny Goodman to his own advantage. Now that he had lost an early-round eighteen-holer, and survived the embarrassment of going down to defeat against an unknown, his fears of the single-round encounters receded. He became more determined to seize the initiative in these quick confrontations, and never to fall far behind in the early going again.

If Jones was to realize his greatest ambition and pull off the grand slam, he had to play every hole of every match to the utmost. The 1930 British Amateur at St. Andrews provided the perfect test. The format demanded five eighteen-hole matches in a row, the highlight of which was Bobby's sudden-death victory over the long-hitting, talented Cyril Tolley. After taking the British Amateur final 6 and 5 from Roger Wethered, Bobby had gone on to sweep the British Open at Hoylake after surviving a final-round double-bogey meltdown on the eighth hole, where he carelessly swatted at a putt of a mere few inches and missed.

When he arrived at Interlachen with both British titles in his pocket, Bobby Jones had reached the halfway point in his quest for the grand slam.

Walter Hagen marveled at the way Jones was dominating the game. He told Grandland Rice, "The remarkable thing about this championship is just this. Here is the greatest field ever assembled on any golf course. Here you have the survivors of 1,200 entries, and yet it is one field against one man — Bobby Jones. Nothing like this has ever happened in golf from the days of Vardon and Taylor to the present moment. It is almost unbelievable, but it is true." This coming from a man who had won a pair of U.S. Opens, four British Opens, and four PGA titles in a row in the 1920s. Walter Hagen, the greatest competitor of his time, sounded like a starstruck reporter from the sticks.

After the first day of practice, Johnny Goodman became more than a human-interest story. Showing little reverence for Donald Ross's long Interlachen course, he shattered par for only the second time in the Minnesota layout's history, posting a one under 71 that included thirteen pars and three birdies. Only Bobby Jones and Leo Diegel did better on their first spin around Interlachen, shooting a pair of 70s.

Johnny had tried to keep his goals for the Open within reason. First, he simply wanted to make the cut, and second, he wanted to break into the top thirty finishers. After his effortless practice round, though, he couldn't keep his fantasies at bay. If he could break par once, why not twice or three times? Forget about the cut. The way he was driving, hitting every fairway and sinking every putt from ten feet in, didn't he have a chance to win? Why should he sell himself short? How could he help getting a little cocky?

In his second practice round, Johnny ballooned to a 78, but it didn't shake his confidence. "If my wood shots don't go bad," he told the *World-Herald*'s Al Wolf, "I'll be right in there tomorrow." In fact, Johnny had had trouble keeping his brassie shots out of the rough in his second Interlachen tour, and his driving had been anemic.

No matter. His expectations were soaring, and he wasn't about to put a lid on them. Why not give the reporters what they were begging for? "Even though I took a 78 today, I feel a 73 coming up Thursday morning and that ought to be good enough to keep up with the leaders," he promised.

Veteran observers shook their heads. Didn't Goodman understand the difference between practice rounds and tournament golf? In the recent British Open, the third-round leader, the Englishman Archie Compson, had missed an eighteen-inch putt on the opening hole of his last round and gone to pieces. The huge Englishman, who had taken the lead with a brilliant 68 just hours earlier, skied to an 80 before a horrified gallery of his countrymen. All because an eighteen-incher had hung on the lip. The Goodman kid was setting himself up for a fall.

John Kiernan may have been charmed by Johnny's "little lodging house on wheels," but when Goodman appeared on the first tee, the gallery simmered with thinly veiled hostility. After the announcer introduced Johnny as "the young man who beat Bobby Jones at Pebble Beach last year," the fans reacted with stony silence. It was as if in toppling Jones he had committed an unconscionable breach of taste. Only a handful of Omaha boosters straggled down the fairway after Goodman.

Still, Johnny didn't disappoint. On the second, a 370-yard par four, he dropped a forty-footer for a birdie. That loosened him up. He was really getting through the ball, driving it straight and to his outside limit, a good 250. His solid irons hit one green after another. The pars piled up.

Giddy, he had to force himself to slow down. Set up to putt the way Walter J. Travis recommended in *American Golfer*, his heels almost touching, he let his stroke flow. It was like feeling the history of the game run through his fingers.

The day was turning hot and soupy, but Johnny didn't pay much attention.

On six, a 343-yard par four, he stroked a niblick into the heart of the green and dropped a twenty-five-footer for a birdie three. On seven, another short par four, he nudged a fifteen-footer into the cup for his third bird.

Bands of heat reflected off the hard fairways. When Johnny blinked, sunspots shimmered before his eyes. His throat parched, he gulped some water and marched to the next tee.

On the eighth, a 379-yard par four, his chip from the fringe hung on the rim of the cup and refused to drop for yet another birdie, but still he made the turn in a searing 33, and he was willing to bet any of those sourpusses on the first tee that he'd just shot the best front nine of the day.

Word of his hot start had spread, and now a gallery of several hundred pressed in on him. Lightheaded, he kept up his onslaught. On the dogleg five eleventh, after hitting the drive of his life around the corner, he dropped in a five-footer for a birdie four.

That's when he started to calculate. All he needed was a string of pars for a 68. That would be enough for the lead . . . easy. He tried to make his mind go blank, but an inner voice kept repeating the seductive numbers, inflaming his imagination.

Dimly, he wondered if the heat was keeping him from thinking straight. His head buzzed. Playing without a hat, he could feel his hair pomade oozing down his forehead. He poured more water down his parched throat, but it didn't seem to help.

Walter Hagen was having the same problem, but under contract to Brylcream and duty-bound to display his stiff, shiny hair, Sir Walter eschewed a hat despite the blazing heat. The dye from the Reddy Tees melting in his pocket streaked his cream-colored trousers.

By noon, temperatures soared to 103 in the shade. The heat was so intense, Grantland Rice began calling Interlachen "Dante's Inferno."

After a bout of dizziness, Chick Evans almost quit the field. The Red Cross was on hand to treat many of the ten thousand spectators who had succumbed to the scorching atmosphere. The tightly packed galleries made conditions even more intolerable. "It wasn't so much the heat as the humanity," Herbert Warren Wind quipped.

News of Goodman's hot start drew fans from all over the course. After a perfect drive on the par-five twelfth, Johnny reached for his brassie. His hands dripping with perspiration, he sliced the shot straight into the tangled rough. Now the worm of doubt came alive. The fairway wood had let him down time and again in practice, but what was he supposed to hit when he was a full 250 yards from the green?

He felt logy. Had he gulped too much water? He wiped his hands and then wiped them again. He couldn't seem to get his fingers dry.

His ball barely visible in the thick grass, he took a hard swing, but the clubhead snagged in the weeds, closing the face. The short iron dunked into a greenside bunker. He was working now, working hard. He had a lousy lie, but he slipped his iron right through the sand and blasted out to four feet. He'd been making longer putts all day, but this one rimmed out. His first bogey of the day.

It was funny how you could hit every club in the bag except one sometimes. You tightened up a little, you peeked a little, and you butchered it yet again.

On the thirteenth, a par three, he tried to muscle his tee shot, but instead he pushed it into a greenside trap. His second bogey. He three-putted the fourteenth, his third bogey in a row.

It was hard to block out all the onlookers now. Hundreds of people were watching his every move. They cleared their throats. They whispered. They rattled their damn programs. They cheered and, wanting to do better, he pressed. His head throbbed in the stifling atmosphere. He drank more water, but it didn't bring any relief. His swing drifted a hair off-plane.

After struggling for par on fifteen, he promptly three-putted sixteen. On seventeen he missed a four-footer for par. By the time the sudden slide ended, he'd made 41 on the back nine. After 33 on the front.

Still, 74 didn't look too bad. Bobby Jones had shot a 71, along with some pro from a public course in Brooklyn, a former sailor named Wiffy Cox. Tommy Armour and Mac Smith were tied for the lead with 70. Even with his collapse, Johnny was only four shots off the pace. Making the cut would be a piece of cake.

Or maybe not. In the second round, his game deserted him. "Johnny's play was almost the reverse of that on Thursday," Al Wolf recounted. "He was wretched on the outside nine, which he negotiated in 41 . . . All his clubs seemed to trouble him. His tee shots had curves on the end of them, his irons sought and found trouble, his shots out of trouble usually found more tough going and his putting was just of the two-to-a-hole variety."

On the par-four eighth, Goodman's concentration fell apart, too. After driving into a trap and blasting his recovery shot clear across the fairway into the rough, Johnny faced a short double-bogey putt. Disgusted, he tried to backhand the ball into the cup, stubbing it instead. The ball trickled all of two inches, and he was forced to tap in for a triple bogey.

The moment for complete self-immolation had arrived, but Johnny somehow gathered his wits and birdied the ninth. Mixing a series of pars with several bogeys and a birdie on fifteen, he staggered through the back nine in slightly better fashion, posting a 39 for an inglorious 80. He'd shot his way out of the tournament.

While he was signing his card, Bert lit into him. "What the hell was that routine on the eighth? You think you're such a hotshot you can get careless?"

Johnny took it. Bert was right. And to quit trying in front of all those people who'd been pulling for him . . . He felt a wash of shame course through him.

"Well, you salvaged something with that bird on fifteen, though," the old football player said, softening.

"Yeah, what's that?"

"You made the cut."

Johnny blinked, uncomprehending. "With a lousy 154?"

"One fifty-six made it under the wire. Johnston had 161." Scores had soared in the blistering heat. "Tolley pulled out. You're tied with Sarazen and Von Elm. You're in, kiddo."

"Bobby on top?"

"Horton Smith. I don't know how he did it in this heat. Two under 70."

Grantland Rice was struck by Smith's unearthly performance. "Horton adopted a unique idea and put it into effect," Rice wrote. "This idea consisted in hitting his drive smack down the middle and then rapping an iron shot six or eight feet from the pin. It is a system that seldom fails, even if you are putting with a broom."

Finishing with a solid 73, Bobby Jones trailed Smith by only two strokes. Hagen was still in the hunt, but fading, after shooting a typically erratic 75.

It was clear now that Johnny Goodman simply lacked the experience to play consistent golf in a major tournament. It remained to be seen if he also lacked the heart.

Before the third round, Johnny decided to leave his brassie in the bag. He'd hit his driver off the deck if he had to, anything to avoid his nemesis. His second decision was to stop thinking. No adding his score. No figuring out how high he might finish. Block out the world and crawl back into his bubble.

The heat abated a bit, though it stayed in the nineties. Still, he wasn't seeing sunspots anymore. He felt a bit stronger too.

In the morning round, he had his shaky moments, a dub on the first fairway and a miserable sand shot, but he willed himself to forget them immediately. Hagen always said he expected to hit four or five bad shots. Just keep your head down, recover, and drop a few.

He was driving it straight again, and sinking some putts too. After a pair of birdies on the front, and another pair on his way back in, he wrote a neat 72 on his scorecard. Now he had to keep from getting too high. Forget the good scores as fast as the bad ones. Faster.

In the afternoon, he almost blew sky-high again. Starting out with back-to-back double bogeys, he appeared headed for disaster once more. This time, though, instead of folding, he played his hottest streak of the whole tournament, going four under in the next nine. The club felt like a whip in his hand. Take it back, then a heartbeat's delay, then *wham-ditty!* He didn't know where the word came from, but it sounded right. On fire, he birdied the seventh, the eighth, and holed a chip on fifteen for an eagle three.

Only after the last putt dropped did he let go, flinging the ball into the crowd of Omaha loyalists. Stanley Davies, the pro at the Field Club, grabbed his hand. Bert patted him on the back. He'd never been so thirsty in his life.

"Beer's on me," Bert offered.

Drained, Johnny was ready for two or three.

His 75 vaulted him into eleventh place and a tie with George Von Elm for second-lowest amateur. In his wake were leading professionals: Gene Sarazen, Walter Hagen, Al Espinosa, Jim Barnes, and Willie MacFarlane.

In what seemed like a foregone conclusion, Bobby Jones's ragged 75 was good enough to hold off the dogged Mac Smith, who could pull no closer than two strokes. In a seven-week rush, Jones had seized the year's first three major titles, the British Open, the British Amateur, and the U.S. Open crowns. Only the U.S. Amateur at the Merion Cricket Club lay ahead.

In Jones's obliterating shadow, Von Elm and Goodman finished fourteen strokes back, tied at 301. For Von Elm it was a mediocre performance, but for the young Goodman it was another step forward. All through the late 1920s George Von Elm had been considered second only to Jones, and he had beaten Bobby once in the finals of the 1926 U.S. Amateur and captured the title. Now Johnny had bested every amateur in the country but Jones and Von Elm, and he had done it without his best game.

Jones mania reached its zenith in Atlanta, where a crowd of 125,000 turned out to welcome Bobby home. Determined to outdo New York's ticker-tape extravaganzas and Armistice Day itself, Bobby's hometown organized a fleet of planes, the 122nd Infantry, and a phalanx of motorcycle police to escort the Jones clan down Peachtree Street. Along with the American Legion and the Boy Scouts, local caddies lined the avenue, holding aloft signs that declared, "Welcome Home Mr. Bobby. You Sho' Brought Back the Bacon."

The Omaha papers didn't spare the ink in lauding Johnny Goodman's achievement. While Johnny's performance had barely registered in the national press, from the *World-Herald*'s perspective Goodman had moved front and center on the national stage.

Al Wolf even yoked Goodman's name to the Walker Cup team, amateur golf's elite. Acting as Johnny's self-appointed champion, he wrote, "If a Walker Cup team were being selected at this time, Goodman would be one of the first in line behind the incomparable Bobby."

Wolf had struck the opening bell of a long and bitter battle.

21

A L W O L F B U I L T his case for Johnny Goodman's Walker Cup credentials partly on Goodman's 1930 U.S. Open performance, but Johnny's play in the St. Paul Open shortly afterward opened some eyes as well. In the first round Johnny reeled off a 69, and held second behind Gene Sarazen, who fashioned a searing 67. Playing steadily, if not spectacularly, in the later rounds at St. Paul, Goodman finished seventh against the pros and eleven strokes ahead of his nearest amateur competitor.

St. Paul proved that Johnny had become a more experienced and mature competitor, Wolf argued. In addition, Johnny had also taken the Nebraska Amateur during his yearlong spree. Wolfe's claim that Johnny was now one of the top three amateurs in the country would probably have been met with indulgent smiles in the eastern golfing establishment had the game's barons ever turned a page of the *Omaha World-Herald*.

After his fine showing in St. Paul, Johnny had high hopes for the 1930 U.S. Amateur at the Merion Cricket Club. He planned to practice on the course for a week before the qualifying round, in which he would be paired with T. Suffren Tailor Jr. of Newport, the socially prominent amateur whose father hosted the yearly "gold mashie" tournament on his estate's private nine-hole course.

A year after riding the Fast Mail to Pebble Beach, Johnny Goodman arrived at the Burlington Depot at eight in the morning on September 14, 1930, and boarded the Ak-Sar-Ben Limited bound for

Chicago, the first leg of his journey to Merion. On the Limited the ride was smooth, the luxurious seats tilted back. Passengers might enjoy the observation car or take a fine meal in the gleaming dining car. Of course, the service was first rate.

Johnny had saved every dime possible from his on-again, off-again employment, but his Omaha supporters had helped him once again with traveling expenses. Johnny's backers had too much pride in their favorite son to allow him to travel third class anymore. Goodman, who had never accepted a penny in prize money, knew the USGA would frown on the small amounts he'd accepted to make the trip to Merion, but he believed he was committing the smallest — and most common — of offenses. Who could stick to the USGA's contradictory rules anyway? And why was taking a ticket and a little bit of pocket money from friends any different from digging into your well-heeled daddy's pockets?

Johnny couldn't help but be giddy. He had rocketed to amateur golf's upper echelons shockingly fast, and he had every reason to believe his game was getting better. After feeding on a steady diet of glowing press clippings, he had adopted a bit of a swagger, but he remained sensitive to slights — references to boxcars set his teeth on edge. His cockiness, a mask for his insecurities, put off some of his competitors, but he was also plagued by a sense that he would never belong in the affluent precincts of the amateur game.

His inability to find a position in business, despite the promises of Omaha's bigwigs, only fueled his fears. Although he was keeping his head above water with a series of part-time jobs, and he was managing to stay out of the packinghouses, he was still floating along, unsure of his next payday.

He quelled his anxiety by focusing on what he knew best, golf. But there was a danger in making golf his entire world. He was counting on the game to somehow lead him to a decent living, and more subtly, to a more respectable social position, but so far the disjunction between his success on the links and his failure to stand on his own two feet was all too glaring.

But once a tournament got under way, it was easy to take his mind off life's intractable problems. How could he miss when the country's most important sportswriters were making such a big deal about him?

Commenting on Goodman's chances, the pro Al Espinosa remarked, "Goodman has a real golf game. A golf game that is sound from tee to green. He is unusually long for such a little fellow, plays his irons keenly, and is a fine putter. The kid also has a dogged temperament that will carry the fight to anybody."

On Johnny's technique, the famous golf instructor Chester Horton commented, "I've never seen better action of feet, legs and hands."

Singling out Goodman and Dough Moe as the chief threats to Jones among the young players, the syndicated columnist Francis Powers insisted that Goodman was no flash in the pan. In an article headlined "Goodman Center of Golfing Eyes at National Meet," Powers made his point unequivocally. "No one is attracting more attention at the Merion Cricket Club where the National Amateur Golf championship begins Monday than Johnny Goodman, the tiny sharpshooter from Omaha . . . To this writer Goodman is not only a better golfer than last year, but also a more modest one."

Whether Johnny was more modest was certainly debatable, but when Powers asked Johnny if he would like to play against Bobby Jones again, the young midwesterner's awe of the great Atlantan was palpable. "Bobby Jones! Gee! I only hope I meet him again! You see, Bobby is so much of a greater golfer than I am that I would like to meet him again." When he let down his guard, Johnny Goodman's innocent enthusiasm was a reminder that he was barely out of his teens.

Powers also picked up the theme that Goodman was a great "showman." Johnny had recently lost his putter, and had been in a state of high anxiety until a greenskeeper recovered it, but Powers believed that the incident was staged, "like the theft of an actress's pearls." Like many reporters, Powers imagined that Johnny Goodman was waging a cagey public relations campaign. This was highly unlikely.

In fact, the twenty-year-old Goodman was far too unsophisticated to feed the press enticing anecdotes. The simple truth — that

Goodman's chief support consisted of Bert Waddington, the engineer's "covered wagon on wheels," and a handful of Omaha's country club golfers — seemed beyond the imagination of a cynical press grown weary of clever press agents.

The mood at Merion in 1930 was different than it had been the year before at Pebble Beach, when the stock market was shooting to the moon, but the contrast wasn't as stark as might be imagined. Although many of the USGA's elite had sustained heavy losses in the market, and insiders in the banking trade knew how fragile the system had become, few corporate executives had lost their jobs. Industrialists had pulled in their horns, but business was by no means frozen.

In the 1920s, fortunes had been made on Wall Street and in the runup in real estate values; the major industries had boomed and incomes in the upper echelons of society had grown exponentially. Despite the unsettled times, the better-off had retained much of their wealth; they had been insulated from the worst of the previous year's economic collapse.

The public was far more concerned with the breakdown of Prohibition, best exemplified by wide-open warfare between bootleggers and the shocking discovery of an operation that sold strong spirits in the Senate Office Building. Widespread unemployment created more opportunities to drink, and Americans seized more openly on the pleasures of bathtub gin. Observers noted a sharp rise in public drunkenness, particularly among women. In the sub rosa American war between Puritanism and hedonism, the old-time religion was losing ground.

Within the next two months, an avalanche of bank failures and chaotic runs would send America into a fresh paroxysm of fear, but for the moment the country was in a mood for distraction. Tree sitting had become the latest craze. During this curious mania, records for remaining stationary while squatting high on a limb were set and broken with numbing regularity. For variation, competing exhibitionists climbed flag poles and stayed put for days on end. Out of the blue, backgammon caught on, giving a boost to department store sales. One of the biggest stories of all, though, was Bobby Jones's quest for the last major golf title of the year, the 1930 U.S. Amateur.

As portrayed on the sports pages, Jones was a success story untainted by corruption, a throwback to a more affluent, less morally compromised time. While the public grew more and more outraged by the stories of Wall Street manipulators and self-dealing bankers who seemed to have caused, or even profited by, the economy's sudden contraction, Jones remained a symbol of a winner who had played by the rules. Bobby's battle was driven by the old values. He played for love of the game, for the art and glory of it all. He floated above the fears of economic collapse, and the public wanted to float with him.

To carry Jones's adoring fans along on his selfless quest, the modern media were arrayed to flash hole-by-hole accounts via telegraph and live national radio broadcasts. Major newsreel companies, including Grantland Rice Newsreel, sent in their most up-to-date equipment to catch all the intimate details.

Bobby was ready to make one more supreme effort, but he had also decided, privately, to leave the game. His wife, Mary, was pregnant with their third child, he was under enormous physical and emotional strain, and for an inherently shy man, the demands of constantly being on public display had grown unbearable. He also had to fend off rumors that he had been offered a lucrative movie deal. Astonishing sums were bandied about.

Years later, Chick Evans admitted to being the source of these allegations and may very well have been motivated by jealousy. As yet, Jones hadn't cut any movie deals. While he had profited handsomely from his syndicated columns, he had always been careful to respect the USGA's woolly guidelines.

In straightforward fashion, Bobby denied the rumors but added a typically frank comment. "I haven't got the offer, but I'm not turning down $200,000 contracts if they come along."

The USGA had its own economic interests to tend to and — like any entertainment company — it did its best to protect its greatest attraction. Having seen the gate at Pebble Beach nose-dive as soon as Johnny Goodman knocked Bobby Jones out of the competition, the USGA resorted to seeding the competitors for the first time. The idea was to organize the draw so that the best players wouldn't face each other until the third round, when thirty-six-hole matches would commence.

More pointedly, the move was instituted for the protection of one man, Robert Tyre Jones Jr. If he faced weaker competition in the early, eighteen-hole matches, officials reasoned, he would have a better chance of marching all the way to a popular victory, and the USGA would fill its coffers. A year after Johnny Goodman had pulled off his stunning upset at Pebble Beach, his feat was still disturbing golf's highest circles.

Johnny's medal play offered little comfort to the USGA officials who wished to forget him. In his first qualifying spin, he hit the ball beautifully and buttressed his performance with solid putting for a 73, only one shot behind Jones. Playing safe golf the second time around, Johnny tacked on an afternoon 76 and made it into match play with many strokes to spare.

Conventional wisdom held that the seeding system would protect Goodman and the other top players as much as Jones. In fact, Johnny drew a little-known San Francisco amateur, Johnny Mc-Hugh, as his first-round opponent.

Ironically, although the USGA had done everything possible to protect its main meal ticket, Bobby Jones drew a formidable first-round opponent, Sandy Somerville. Despite being seeded as a weak entry, Somerville was one of the greatest athletes ever to come out of Canada. He had starred in college football and hockey, and was a good enough center on the ice to draw offers to play for pay before he turned to golf and won three Canadian Open championships.

Jones played the first six holes in one under, but Somerville stayed right with him, only one hole behind. The turning point came on the seventh, when Bobby ran in a slippery eight-footer for a bird, and Somerville, a foot closer, shaved the cup with his birdie attempt. Jones caught fire then, birdieing the eighth and negotiating a partial stymie for another bird on the ninth. Despite firing par after par, Somerville succumbed on the fourteenth, 5 and 4. Bobby Jones was on his way.

Johnny Goodman was not as fortunate. All the happy predictions in the world couldn't swing the golf club for Goodman. After stumbling out of the gate, and falling three holes down after seven, however, Goodman staged a spirited recovery.

On the eighteenth tee Goodman stood only one down to McHugh, the California State champion, but he pushed his drive into some long grass. Safely on in two, the San Franciscan lagged one close, and after Goodman sank a desperation forty-footer to retrieve his four, he calmly putted out for the halve. Johnny had turned in a brilliant 32 on the back nine, but it hadn't been enough to catch McHugh. In a match whose ebb and flow bore an eerie resemblance to Johnny's win over Bobby Jones, the San Franciscan had pushed Goodman right off the U.S. Amateur's first rung.

After Johnny's excellent play in the medal rounds, and his high expectations, it was a bitter defeat. He knew all too well that his chances for the Walker Cup team had been diminished, and that a first-round loss at the U.S. Amateur represented a step backward. With little to fall back on but golf, Johnny was shaken and confused by this unexpected twist of fate. He excoriated himself for his mental errors; he brooded on his cloudy future. He felt embarrassed to be a mere spectator. Finally he could take it no longer; he fled back to Omaha.

Other favorites fell as well. Francis Ouimet was knocked out, along with O. F. Willig and Phil Perkins, the former British Open champion. Most significantly, George Von Elm lost his first-round match. Von Elm did not succumb easily. Deadlocked after eighteen holes with the stubborn Maurice McCarthy, Von Elm refused to give in to the New Yorker for nine playoff holes. In the gathering darkness, McCarthy finally struck the killing blow, a birdie on the twenty-eighth hole, sending Von Elm down to defeat.

Von Elm, who had long chafed under the USGA's inconsistent regimen, made a brief announcement right after the match. He told the press that he had decided to renounce his amateur status. In a remarkable statement released several days later, he summed up all his resentments against golf's ruling body. "I have retired from amateur golf because competing in the American and British Amateur and Walker Cup international match isn't worth the $10,000 a year it costs me. For ten years I've had the 'Mr.' stuck in front of my name, and that insignia of amateurism has required more than $50,000 of hard-earned money . . .

"It's nice to treat the subject of my amateur status in cold terms of dollars. The USGA's Amateur Championship is a highly organized commercial project, while the thirty-two performers play their hearts out for honor and glory. Not a penny of the money the USGA makes is contributed to the expenses of the players. Tournament golf today is show business in a big way. The finger of suspicion points to many players in amateur golf today, but the show must go on, and the USGA is busy a good part of the time straining at gnats and swallowing camels."

The thinly veiled reference to Bobby Jones only hints at Von Elm's long-suppressed rage. Von Elm, a gifted and fierce competitor, was deeply frustrated by his inability to best Jones. The rumors about Bobby's pending movie deal could not have helped his mood. But Jones aside, Von Elm was stating the bald facts quite accurately. Amateur golf had always been an expensive luxury.

Von Elm was a small-businessman with a Depression businessman's worries. Unlike the barons of Wall Street and industry, he was already feeling the pinch. If he could no longer make a decent living, the privilege of being called Mr. on the first tee hardly seemed worth it.

Von Elm didn't win all that much cash as a golf pro, but he did make a nice living skinning Howard Hughes at the Beverly Hills Country Club as often as possible. As a sideline, it had to be more satisfying than losing to Bobby Jones for nothing.

Bobby Jones benefited from the first-round carnage. With many of the game's top players out of the way, Jones faced an easier path to victory.

In fact, Bobby brushed aside the rest of the opposition at the 1930 U.S. Amateur, as most sportswriters had predicted. In the second round he crushed a rattled Fred Hoblitzel and on the following day he ran away from Faye Coleman, closing the match 6 and 5. Jess Sweetser, who had never recovered the edge to his game after his bout with tuberculosis, was unable to put up much of a fight, surrendering to his close friend 9 and 8. In the finals, Bobby faced Gene Homans, who had beaten the powerful nineteen-year-old Californian Charlie Seaver in the semifinals. (Seaver never quite realized his early promise, but his son, Tom, threw the high hard one well enough to raise an entire New York baseball team from the dead.)

Against Homans, Jones took the first hole and shot out to a spirit-breaking seven-hole lead by the end of the morning round. The afternoon offered little drama, with Jones cruising to an 8 and 7 victory. It all seemed effortless and preordained, at least to a public shielded from Jones's private torments.

In an uproarious celebration, Big Bob wept, O. B. Keeler wept, and Bobby Jones may have shed a few tears of his own in his discreet way. He had conquered the impregnable quadrilateral. There was nothing left to prove.

All three national radio networks carried Bobby's acceptance of the U.S. Amateur trophy. Media coverage was all-encompassing, and, as usual, unstinting in its praise of the "immaculate amateur." The USGA reaped record receipts. Playing it close to the vest, Jones denied the rumors about his impending retirement, but there was a valedictory quality to his triumph. Bobby Jones, the avatar of the old values, would soon shift his ground along with the times.

Back in Omaha, Johnny Goodman faced the creeping reality of the Depression and his own meager prospects. The economy was going into a fresh nosedive, but President Hoover stubbornly refused to offer direct aid to victims of the widening disaster. When New York senator Robert Wagner proposed to establish a federal employment service, Hoover withheld his support. For the drought-stricken farmers, however, he bent a little by offering federal funds to feed their livestock. As one bitter Arkansas congressman put it, the president preferred feeding "jackasses" to "starving babies."

While the Midwest did not yet feel the full force of the gathering collapse, the warning signs were beginning to show. Grain prices continued their steep decline. Banks found it harder and harder to collect on loans and mortgages. Farms began failing at a quickening rate. There was a nervousness in the air, and jobs were harder and harder to find. In this climate, Johnny Goodman had to somehow cobble together a living.

What was most alarming to Goodman was that the Depression was starting to affect the very middle class he was trying to penetrate. None of his golfing achievements could elevate him to a job that didn't exist. Now he saw dignified men who had once been executives standing on street corners peddling apples for five cents apiece.

The apple sellers became so ubiquitous, President Hoover was forced to comment on their sudden appearance. In a Depression-era version of political spin, Hoover claimed, "Many persons have left their jobs for the more profitable one of selling apples." Still, the apple sellers, the new icons of the Depression, multiplied.

The economic crisis dovetailed with a personal crisis for Johnny Goodman. He couldn't shake his fear that he would never quite be good enough to get to the top of the golf game, and his vaunting ambition would accept nothing less. It seemed as if Bobby Jones would dominate the sport forever, and like every other amateur, and every professional, for that matter, Goodman would be doomed to labor in the great Atlantan's shadow. For Johnny, losing faith in his golf game amounted to losing faith in himself.

Although his childhood had been full of harsh reverses, the twenty-year-old Goodman had shot to the top of amateur golf in a mere three years. His rapid success had led him to believe he would keep rising in the amateur ranks, and that winning one of the big tournaments was inevitable. Now his major refuge, golf, was turning out to be as full of obstacles as was his private life. Losing in the first round at Merion had shocked Johnny, and shaken his confidence. Serious men were scrambling desperately just to make ends meet. How could he justify spending so much time perfecting a game in return for so little?

When he reached Omaha after his first-round loss at Merion, Goodman sounded like a much older man. Echoing George Von Elm, he told the *World-Herald*, "Amateur golf is a rich man's game, and I am far from rich. I am forced to make a living, and find it impossible to combine competitive golf with business."

Johnny went on in this blunt vein. "I'd rather play golf than eat, but I'm so broke now after the National Open and National Amateur tournaments that I won't be able to go back to school at Nebraska." In a revealing remark, he added, "Golf has been a mother and father to me, but it's just come to the point where I have to earn a living."

Goodman's name had been splashed across front pages in New York, Chicago, and L.A., but Johnny Goodman was still tending the Webster's furnace and sweeping out their yard in exchange for meals and a place to sleep. Josephine was working for Mutual of Omaha, and even her secretary's check amounted to more than he was bringing in. His brothers were clinging to their jobs in the packing plants, and his sisters were working as maids, but he still couldn't afford the price of a furnished room.

It was funny. He was on top of the world and at the bottom at the same time. He had to face facts. Golf wasn't putting one red cent in his pocket. In the fall of 1930, it looked as if his brief but stunning career had come to an end.

22

A T TWENTY-EIGHT YEARS of age Bobby Jones had been competing in national tournaments for fourteen years. His body ached like an older man's. His nerves were rubbed raw and his energy was spent. There wasn't anything left for him to achieve in amateur golf, and Jones had the law, his family, and a rich life to pursue. In the locker room after his victory at Merion, Jones confessed to Jimmy Johnston that golf was "wrecking" his health and frustrating his "business ambitions." The time had come to trade amateur stardom for Hollywood gold.

Jones was not exaggerating his physical ailments. He was still assailed by stomach problems. Since 1926 he had suffered from muscle stiffness and pain in his neck and back. In middle age this most graceful of athletes would be struck down by a rare spinal disease, syringomyelia, a congenital disorder that attacks the nervous system. The disorder may have already been plaguing Jones in his twenties. By middle age, he was confined to a wheelchair.

The USGA may have been hypocritical, but Bobby Jones had never pretended he was too pure to pursue his self-interest. He'd said he wasn't going to turn down $200,000 contracts, so there was no reason to back away from Warner Brothers Pictures' actual offer, a reported $250,000. (Since the deal included a percentage of the gross receipts, it may have come to more.) The contract called for twelve instructional shorts featuring Bobby tutoring such unlikely pupils as W. C. Fields, Walter Huston, James Cagney, and Loretta Young.

Bobby Jones had turned pro. There was no denying that the purportedly immaculate amateur was exploiting the fame he had won in a game whose values were diametrically opposed to profiting from that same renown.

Although Bobby Jones abandoned his amateur status for personal motives, his decision marked a shift in the culture at large. The public, which had previously identified with Bobby's selfless struggles, could now share the thrill of his glorious payday. Golf as an exercise in moral uplift had had its day.

When Bobby Jones broke the taboo against cashing in on his amateur golf exploits, he undermined, however unintentionally, the amateur ideal itself. In a single transaction, he would garner more money than most golf professionals could hope to make in a lifetime. Typically, the press reacted to Jones's hard-nosed decision by denying its implications. The *New York Times,* which had expressed horror when Bobby began his lucrative golf columns several years earlier, now observed that Bobby had "done the right thing." The rest of the American press sang similar hosannas. Jones, the papers claimed, had not only made the correct choice, he had done so with the dignity of a champion.

The British papers outdid their American counterparts. The *London Times* compared Jones to George Washington. Not to be outdone, the *London News-Chronicle* called Bobby "an invaluable traveling advertisement of the finer and rarer qualities of the human race." Evidently, Jones could serve his self-interest and the wider interests of humanity simultaneously.

Meanwhile, Jones went about the business of making as much money as possible. He signed a deal to endorse a line of A. G. Spalding golf clubs, and another to do radio broadcasts sponsored by the Lambert Pharmaceutical Company, whose accompanying spots promised Americans that Listerine Shaving Cream would prove "as valuable to your shaving comfort as Bobby's advice is to your game."

Some of Jones's statements at the time reflected the tension between his commercial pursuits and his attachment to the amateur ideal. While renouncing his amateur status, he insisted that he would never become a professional golfer. Then he turned around and praised professional golfers who made an "honest living at golf." Without professional golf, he contended, "there would be a great many 'crooks' falsely pretending to be amateurs." Untroubled by these contradictions, the USGA found Jones's decision to abandon the amateur game in the best tradition of amateurism itself.

Now the field was clear for a new champion to take Bobby Jones's place, and the press inaugurated a feverish search. Johnny Goodman's name was on every list except the USGA's.

Goodman, who had just sworn he could not afford the amateur game, faced a dilemma. His financial crisis was real, and so was his family's. His older brothers, who worked for Armour and Cudahy, were worried about keeping their jobs. His sisters, who cleaned the houses of Omaha's better-off families, feared for their livelihood. Two of his youngest brothers, still out in Montana, were picking beets for pennies and happy to have a roof over their heads.

One day as Johnny was walking past the Park Theatre, he watched as a man in a Stetson hat tossed free rabbits off the back of a truck to a mob of hungry men. That got to him.

Professional golf was not a viable option. At a time when the "tour" bore no resemblance to today's sleek, corporate-driven affair, the golf pro was usually an obscure character driving a jalopy along a pitch-dark country road, a fellow who kept body and soul together with tobacco juice and baling wire. Hands buzzing on the wheel, the Depression-era pro looped endlessly from coast to coast. It was no picnic.

Sam Parks, the 1935 U.S. Open champion, recalled the decidedly mixed thrill of the open highway. "It was always so dark at night, which was when we did a lot of driving. It might be as much as a hundred miles between gas stations or towns, but no signs to tell you how far you had to go. To get an idea, I'd look at my gas gauge, and then turn off my headlights so I could see better in the distance the lights of the next place I could gas up."

As Byron Nelson remembered, "We would drive on Sunday night, Monday and Tuesdays sometimes. Once you got to the tournament it took two days before you got rid of the shakes in your hands and the golf clubs quit feeling like the steering wheel. It's a wonder anybody could putt at all."

The car served multiple purposes for the early golf pro. You could sleep in it if you didn't have the price of a room, or get out of town fast if you caught the duck hooks and didn't make the cut. Ky Lafoon liked to tie his balky putter to the bumper and drag it a few hundred miles, just to give the damn thing a taste of its own medicine.

Sitting in a nest of rubber rings, insurance against the next pileup, these gypsy golfers drove Pierce-Arrows, the Nash Advanced Six, La Salles, and Packards through the Florida circuit and then out to California, with stops in Texas along the way. They looped thousands of miles every few months, scrambling over courses that bore little resemblance to today's primped pastures.

Take the Hazard Open, a Kentucky affair backed by a coal-mining family and one "Ma" Hibler, the proprietor of the only habitable hotel in town. The players chowed down at Alice Kennedy's Yellow Lantern Tearoom and fought for the Hazard title on a course carved out of the mountain. Its fairways meandered around slag heaps and the gallery consisted of miners whose familiarity with the game was such that once, when Charlie Danner made a hole in one, a coaldigger shouted, "Home run!"

Some courses with fine reputations, such as Pinehurst, had sand greens; others featured greens composed of oiled cottonseed hulls. A high arching shot onto this inky surface produced a miniature gusher, a fine oil spray that stained golf balls and white flannel trousers with abandon. Corpus Christi offered putting surfaces made of crushed seashells.

Earning a living stroking a golf ball that might be knocked offline by a stray piece of coral was not necessarily a rational undertaking.

It made even less sense for Goodman to pursue amateur golf stardom. The money it took to travel from tournament to tournament had even overwhelmed a successful businessman like George Von Elm. Keeping a golf game tournament-sharp consumed a tremendous amount of time as well.

Moreover, Johnny's dreams and ideals had been forged in the 1920s, when the U.S. Amateur was the most revered tournament of them all. As a teenager at the Field Club he had come to believe that playing for the pure love of the game was a higher calling than competing for a few shabby dollars week after week. His fixation on Bobby Jones cemented these beliefs, and now, with Jones's retirement, he had a chance to replace his idol. Just as American values were shifting under the pressure of the Depression, Johnny Goodman hung on to the old ideals. He also believed he could win the big ones.

When word reached Johnny that Bobby Jones had hung up his clubs, he quickly reassessed his chances of rising to the top. "I didn't think Bobby Jones ever would retire from amateur golf," he told the *World-Herald*. "Now that Von Elm is gone, too, it will be a real battle for the No. 1 position on the Walker Cup team and in the national rankings," he added, implying that he was in the running himself.

Goodman's quick response revealed key elements in his psychology. Apparently, spending years in Jones's shadow, even holding down a top-ten place in the amateur rankings, wouldn't have satisfied him. Now that Jones had stepped aside, the lure of making it to the top of the amateur game was too strong for him to resist — despite what it cost him.

He was resilient too. His missteps at Merion were already fading from his mind. A few bad holes and a hot round by Johnny McHugh, a player who would probably never be heard from again, had sunk him. Otherwise he'd played damn well, he thought, going low in medal play and turning in that brilliant back nine in his abortive first-round comeback.

The Walker Cup was also on Johnny's mind. He told the *World-Herald*, "We lost a great personality in Bobby. Now with both Jones and George Von Elm gone, the United States must attempt to find others to uphold the prestige of the nation."

Time and again Goodman defined his ambitions in terms of the Walker Cup, the ultimate amateur all-star team he had venerated as a teenager in the 1920s, and a flood of articles in the local papers boosting his Walker Cup credentials only fueled his expectations. Clearly, he had never lost his boyhood fascination with the battle for national golfing pride.

Despite Johnny's tenuous circumstances, the smartest businessmen in town kept extolling his prospects. If Johnny gave up amateur golf, the reason Omaha's most prominent citizens even gave him the time of day, what would he have left? If he played it safe and took some mundane office job, he might find himself trapped for the rest of his life. In a paradoxical way, staying in amateur golf seemed like a practical thing to do, even if it paid off in nothing but prestige. There was an element of calculation in Johnny's idealism, but it was idealism nevertheless.

Goodman's "retirement" from golf, which lasted only a few weeks, may have been the briefest in history. Once again he put all his eggs in the amateur golf basket. Then he hung on through the icy months of 1931, fretting that he'd made an all-too-quixotic decision.

Despite a brief uptick in business activity, the winter also brought a fresh wave of bank failures, which quickly undermined confidence. Unemployment rose; prices plunged; industrial production continued its slide. Riots rocked Boston and other cities. In Chicago, Al Capone shelled out three hundred dollars a day for a soup kitchen, but President Hoover, believing in the panacea of individual initiative, requisitioned Rudy Vallee to write an upbeat song. The famously humorless Hoover also called for one good joke to get America laughing again. None was forthcoming.

The country was stunned but not yet on the verge of revolt. The novelist Sherwood Anderson said that when he picked up hitchhikers, they apologized for their sorry state. *The New Yorker* observed that "people are in a sad, but not rebellious mood."

Like the rest of America, Johnny Goodman kept scratching to find a job, and when he failed, he was seized by the dread that he might never find one at all.

Finally, in the spring, Pete Lyck engineered an insurance agent job for Johnny. It was a seminal moment in his life. In the midst of the worst economic collapse in American history, Goodman was moving up. Always a quick study, Johnny learned the business rapidly, but he also found it somewhat less stimulating than a double-breaking twenty-footer.

In return for Lyck's help, Johnny agreed to become his official four-ball partner, and the two turned into a formidable team in local competition. Snagging Johnny was a coup for Lyck, who could do plenty of business on the links while Johnny, the ultimate Omaha social magnet, gave out tips to grateful customers.

Overnight, pictures of Goodman posing as an insurance agent in a suit and striped tie and with pen in hand appeared in the newspapers. His family was all aglow at his achievement. Josephine was proud, but more important, her mother was placated. The old lady had to admit that insurance was a clean, respectable occupation. For Johnny, his new job eased the anxiety he always felt at the posh clubs, and the papers could print "insurance agent" next to his name, solidifying his freshly minted identity.

"Boxcar Johnny," he hoped, would fade from memory. Forever. It irked him whenever he read another retelling of his freight train trip to that first Trans-Mississippi. Reporters always got the details wrong — he had ridden in a renovated caboose, not a cattle car, after all — and he wished they wouldn't dwell on all that now that he was a grown man with a decent profession.

At the exclusive Golden Valley Country Club in Minneapolis, where he hoped to win another Trans-Mississippi title, he passed out a few of his new cards, hot off the press. His name was emblazoned in capital letters dead center. JOHNNY GOODMAN. Underneath it, in a kind of type that looked like script, were the words *Insurance Agent*.

Then there was the patter. Small talk didn't come naturally to Johnny, but he reveled in his new identity. He'd heard successful men doing business at the Omaha Field Club since he was a kid. Now it was his turn. He tried out certain phrases in the Golden Valley clubhouse. *Oh, that's right. I'm in insurance now.* He trotted out, *What line did you say you're in? Is that right? I'm in insurance these days.* Or Pete's pitch: *In tough times you need insurance more than ever. We can protect your business with the right policy.*

Johnny was sure his new occupation would help tamp down any objections the USGA Executive Committee had to his background when it came time to pick the 1932 Walker Cup team. More than one Walker Cupper sold securities. Insurance was just as respectable. Didn't Sweetser peddle stocks on Wall Street? Or was it McCarthy?

Johnny was willing to bet there was a USGA brass hat who was tied up with some big New York insurance company, too.

Golden Valley, an A. W. Tillinghast–designed track, featured narrow fairways, dense woods, deep traps, and small greens that sometimes accepted an accurate shot and sometimes declined. No longer the obscure caddie from Omaha, Johnny returned to the Trans-Mississippi as one of the favorites. Older, more experienced, and a flat-out better player, Goodman decimated a strong, midwestern field, displaying an unearthly accuracy with his irons. First he took medal honors, and then he brushed aside one opponent after another in match play.

In the semifinals against Fred Dold, he played nine holes in which he rarely had a putt of more than a few feet. Up to this point in his career, Johnny had played dogged, highly competitive golf. Now his rare talent in the short game burst into full flower. His formerly streaky putter was steadier, and his niblick, always his best club, had turned into a potent instrument. Chipping and putting like a demon, he simply overwhelmed Dold, 11 and 10, to sail into the title round.

Playing with the cautious care of a veteran, he leaned on his steady flat stick to dominate Lester Bolstad, the former public links national champion, 5 and 4. At the ripe old age of twenty-one, Johnny had become a two-time Trans-Mississippi champion.

During a match, whether he'd just dropped a forty-footer or topped a drive into the rough, Goodman maintained a stony expression. His chilly lack of emotion rattled more than one of his opponents. But on the country club veranda, at the bar over drinks, at the awards ceremony on the grass, he felt more relaxed. After all, he was in the insurance game now, and for the moment, he felt as if he belonged.

23

B Y THE SPRING OF 1932 Johnny Goodman had compiled compelling Walker Cup credentials. The stars of the 1920s were fading, although George Voigt, Maurice McCarthy, and Francis Ouimet were still playing formidable golf. In fact, the venerable Ouimet, who first swept the U.S. Amateur way back in 1914, had pulled off a popular comeback in 1931 when he'd snatched the amateur crown for the second time. Otherwise, the Walker Cup team would have to be salted with up-and-coming golfers. No other young amateur, even those who had bested Johnny Goodman at the U.S. Amateur, had made such a long, steady run. In addition, Faye Coleman, another strong contender, had followed George Von Elm into the pro ranks.

Johnny had more than local support. Many of the country's leading golf writers, including the *New York Times*'s John Kiernan, the *New York Sun*'s George Trevor, and the Chicago-based wire service man, Francis Powers, had written extensively, and admiringly, about Goodman's nerve and talent.

In April, the *New York Sun* noted that "Goodman is definitely on the list of Walker Cup possibilities," adding that "the pros should heave a sigh of relief that Goodman has not joined their company. For the young Nebraskan has the shots and one of the greatest competitive temperaments in the country."

Leo Diegel, who was about to launch a tour with Gene Sarazen, added fuel to the fire when he declared Goodman one of the top three amateurs in the country. Asked about Johnny's chances for the Walker Cup, Diegel replied, "They can't keep him off the team. He should rank at least No. 3." If Goodman wasn't a Walker Cup shoo-in, he was certainly a plausible contender.

In June, Johnny improved his Walker Cup case by qualifying for the 1932 U.S. Open from his region while many of the best amateurs, including Doug Moe, Gus Moreland, George Voigt, Maurice McCarthy, Gene Homans, and Jesse Guilford, failed to make the grade. In fact, only ten amateurs played their way into the field, which included 106 top professionals.

When Johnny took the train from Burlington station on his way to the 1932 U.S. Open at Fresh Meadow Country Club in Flushing, Long Island, plush seats and dining cars still hadn't lost their novelty for him. Still, he couldn't help noticing that the gleaming Pullman was running fewer cars this time, and half of them were empty.

Johnny was also discovering that making it in the insurance game when businesses were doing nosedives left and right wasn't exactly a cakewalk. Supposedly, he had a good job with Pete Lyck's company, but who wanted to sell life insurance policies to golfing buddies who were afraid they couldn't make their mortgage payments? Johnny felt awkward badgering friends who might soon have to padlock their office doors if business got much worse.

High-pressure golf, he figured, was a hell of a lot easier. You played on manicured lawns; you ate and drank in clubhouses whose fine appointments hadn't changed in decades. To chatter on about uncomfortable subjects like paralyzed production lines and dead smokestacks was considered in poor taste. You were supposed to pretend that the U.S. of A. was still flush, and it was your duty to have a fine time.

Johnny knew the rules governing country club manners like the back of his hand, but as his venture into the insurance profession faltered, his old insecurities returned. He sensed that he was only playing the part of a successful businessman and that his pretense was all too transparent. Weren't the same old bigwigs giving him the same old fish eye? He still had a box of business cards, but he no longer passed them out. He'd have to answer too many questions and tell too many facile half-truths. He was no actor, and, he feared, not much of an insurance man either.

And he couldn't quite get all the bad news out of his mind. Just across the river from Omaha, Iowa farmers were blockading roads because corn prices had plunged to nothing at all — a bushel was worth less than a packet of chewing gum. Putting corn in the ground was just like throwing money away. Bread lines snaked around whole blocks while grain elevators stood stuffed with wheat. The South Omaha rail yards were half-dead. According to the *World-Herald,* Kentucky miners were eating weeds. Not so far away in Kansas, they were burning worthless grain to keep warm. All over Nebraska, farmers were fueling their kitchen stoves with corn. It was cheaper than coal, and travelers through the region said the blue smoke smelled pretty good, something like coffee roasting.

Up in the Dakotas farmers were feeding their cattle and horses Russian thistle, a plant of so little value, it was usually allowed to roll across the prairie like spools of barbed wire. Now, some farm wives were serving Russian thistle soup to their children.

In Chicago well over half a million men were looking for work, and the mayor warned Congress that the government could either send aid or federal troops. In Pennsylvania some steel mills had stopped producing altogether.

Charles M. Schwab of Bethlehem Steel seemed bewildered. "I'm afraid, everyone's afraid. I don't know, we don't know, whether the values we have are going to be real next month or not," he announced at an executive luncheon. Everywhere businessmen railed at "the lack of confidence," but not even the financial world's titans seemed to know how to manufacture the mysterious substance.

Of course, there was always some mass-media diversion to be had. When the body of a beautiful young woman, the improbably named Starr Faithfull, turned up on Long Beach in New York, newspapers enjoyed a brief lift in circulation, but tales of well-shaped corpses could do little to stave off the downward spiral of failing companies and failing banks.

Johnny's small defeats in the insurance game seemed almost ridiculous in the face of so much bad news. Down at Roseland the bands played "Life Is Just a Bowl of Cherries," a song that counseled:

> Don't make it serious
> ~~Life's too mysterious~~

Sometimes Josephine acted that way — too serious. If you kept thinking about how everything was falling apart every minute of the day, it could drive you crackers. Johnny liked playing a round with pals who could tell a good joke. He'd memorize the punch lines and, if they were clean enough, tell them to Jo, hoping to get her to crack a smile.

Johnny kept his darker thoughts to himself. The last time he'd gone to his sister Anna's for the family's weekly card game, she'd shown him the way she was laying in extra flour and tinned meat in case there were shortages. George said he was only working half-days now that the flow of cattle and hogs had slowed down so much, but he figured he was lucky to be working at all. Johnny got a kick out of his dark-haired, wiry brother Tony, who was wrapping groceries for a living. Tony was always peppering him with questions about golf, and Johnny promised to take him out to Lakewood and give him some pointers. Johnny knew his brothers and sisters were proud of him, but they didn't seem to believe him when he said he wasn't rolling in dough.

The next day he'd go and play a round at the Field Club, and he'd hear the usual from the Armour and Cudahy executives. According to them, the packinghouse workers were living the life of Riley. They'd squeal if wages were cut, but they didn't understand business. Some of them were starting to listen to the Wobblies, who were talking wild about general strikes and all kinds of mayhem. These radicals weren't even from Omaha. They'd ride the rails, slip into town, spread their poison, and then crawl into their rat holes, but Omaha was an open-shop town, and if it took the business end of a gun to keep it that way, so be it.

More confusing for Johnny, these golfing executives were the same people who had helped him time and again, who had shown him so much kindness since he was a boy. Johnny felt as if he lived right on a fault line. His brothers and sisters were on one side, his country club buddies on the other. If an earthquake came, he wouldn't know which way to jump.

Golf was his only refuge. Once he descended into the flow of a game, he couldn't think about desperate farmers and jobless slaughterhouse workers packed tight against the plant gate. He didn't have to block out his worries. Golf did it for him. It surrounded him, sucked him in, and he surrendered to its undertow. Once he found himself navigating another twisting fairway, another buried lie, another crucial ten-footer, he was lost in the struggle.

Johnny had said golf was his mother and father, but the game was also his only real home.

Some sportswriters were skeptical of Johnny Goodman's chances on the long and difficult 1932 U.S. Open Fresh Meadow course. Though Goodman was putting on weight, Francis Powers kept calling him "tiny." Others described him as "slender," lacking the brawn to take on the demanding par fours. The track ran 6,815 yards, a stiff distance for the time, and the consensus among the best players was that the winning total would run high. "It is far too tough for scores under 290," Olin Dutra predicted, and Dutra was known for his hefty drives.

But Goodman turned some heads when he posted a practice round of 72, the best among the amateurs and far better than notable pros like Al Watrous, Denny Shute, Leo Diegel, and the fading Sir Walter Hagen.

Then high winds struck Flushing Meadows, wrecking the opening rounds of some of the best players in the field. Fresh off a second-place finish in the British Open, Mac Smith blew up to an 80. Runner-up in the 1931 U.S. Open, George Von Elm, managed a 79. Six of the first twelve seeds shot themselves completely out of contention, including the great Tommy Armour, who toured the front nine in a humiliating forty-four strokes.

Olin Dutra was the only man to master the wind, turning in a brilliant 69. The reigning British Open champion, Gene Sarazen, was five shots back, one behind the second-place finisher, Leo Diegel.

Johnny Goodman barely survived the capricious elements, crawling in with a 79. Actually, despite the unsettled weather, he had played steadily until the last three holes, which had mystified half the field. Butchering this difficult trio, Johnny ruined what might have been a highly competitive performance.

Playing with stubborn concentration, but wielding a balky putter, Goodman managed to limp in with a second-round 78. Still, in the wild conditions, he'd done just well enough to make the cut. Better still, after the first two rounds, he was the only amateur left standing.

In the closing round, top professional Gene Sarazen threw caution to the wind. Tearing into the obstinate layout, he took dead aim at every pin. Now he was playing Sarazen golf. Ignoring all of Fresh Meadow's dangers, he banged every shot as hard as he could. Sarazen's swashbuckling strategy paid off. In the final round, he posted a gaudy 66, a new course record and more than good enough to take the championship.

The only other round at the 1932 U.S. Open that could be mentioned in the same breath with Sarazen's was Johnny Goodman's closing tour. In a scorching performance that helped him forget flailing away in the gale, Johnny parlayed two birdies and sixteen pars into a pair of 34s for a sparkling 68. His eighteen-hole score was the second best in the tournament, pushing him up the ladder into fourteenth place.

The only amateur to survive the cut, Johnny Goodman had also bested most of the professionals in the field. More important, he had fashioned an iron-clad case for making the Walker Cup squad. A USGA marshal supposedly in the know told Johnny that he was in for sure. Leo Diegel stopped by and remarked that the Executive Committee had to pick Johnny now. One fan swore the deal was a lead-pipe cinch. Even a few of the usual USGA pickle-pusses seemed friendlier. Calling Goodman "the outstanding amateur in the national open," Francis Powers said he had "practically assured himself a place on the American Walker Cup Team."

An ominous note came from an establishment corner, however. The *World-Herald*'s Frederick Ware reported that *Golf Illustrated*'s editor, A. C. Gregson, a "Fifth Avenue New Yorker," had strong feelings about Johnny Goodman. "Fellows like Goodman are a nuisance," Gregson fumed. "I haven't met Johnny Goodman, and he may be a fine fellow and all that, but he's a nuisance . . . Boys like Goodman belong on the public courses. They have no business going after the big tourney championships. They get in the habit of running from one major event to another when they should be out earning a living."

Gregson's unguarded rant couldn't have been more revealing, and he was certainly not alone. The USGA itself never used such raw language. Instead, it swathed its pronouncements in legalese, or killing silence, and if that didn't do the trick, it simply evaded unpleasant questions.

However, in a June 1930 *Golf Illustrated* editorial, Gregson spoke pointedly to the real standards the Walker Cup Committee adhered to: "It is more honorable to lose [the Walker Cup] because some members of the team cannot afford the trip, than to win with a team including some who are on the borderline of professionalism and who, in extreme cases, probably, except for the desire to win, might not be particularly welcome on the team."

In the last phrase, Gregson distilled the USGA's true policy, a policy it always avoided putting into words. Only the "right" people could qualify as amateurs, and the USGA was the final arbiter of exactly who made the social grade.

On June 28, the Walker Cup Committee named the new team — and blithely ignored Johnny Goodman's existence. Not only wasn't Goodman chosen as one of the ten participants, the committee didn't deign to pick him as an alternate either. Their final choices included veterans past their prime, in particular Jess Sweetser, who had been largely inactive for two years. George Dunlop's major claims to distinction were his two intercollegiate titles. Don Moe, a promising and talented player, had nowhere near Goodman's credentials.

Following its practice of covering its tracks, the USGA Executive Committee, in its minutes, blandly listed its choices without offering a single line referring to the rationales behind the decision.

If the USGA had decided not to put Goodman on the first team, the decision would have been suspect to begin with, but the committee might have named Johnny as an alternate to soothe public opinion. However, its deafening silence regarding the Omahan created more noise than A. C. Gregson's antediluvian roar.

The decision sparked a firestorm in the national press. Wire service writer Lawrence Perry commented, "The United States Golf Association pulled a funny one today. In naming the players for the Walker Cup team which meets the British next month in Brookline, Johnny Goodman, the young Omaha star, was ignored. Johnny has not done anything this season — except shoot a 68 in the national Open. Not only in Nebraska but elsewhere will rise a howling interrogation."

Perry's prediction was prescient. New York sportswriters rushed to Goodman's defense. The *Journal's* Nan O'Reilly argued that Johnny was the second-best amateur in the country, adding that he could certainly beat nine of the players named for the Walker Cup.

In the *Sun*, George T. Hammond observed, "In the absence of any statement and regarded in the light of his performance in the national open . . . the ignoring of the Omaha youngster is shocking." Hammond speculated that the USGA had been holding a grudge against Johnny since his refusal to drop out of the 1929 U.S. Amateur despite pressure from officials. Calling Goodman "a Horatio Alger type of celebrity who bludgeoned his way up the ladder in the face of hardships," Hammond added, "Publicly, Goodman's amateurism has never been questioned, partly because charges have never been pressed, and partly because the USGA prefers the formula of simply refusing entries or in similar ways expressing dissatisfaction."

As Hammond implied, the USGA's silence amounted to an accusation that Goodman had no right to call himself an amateur at all. As Frederick Ware put it, "Johnny probably sees now that he should have spent more time on country club verandas. He should have bootlicked the powers of amateur golf. He should have let them see that he held them in Great Awe — even if he felt a bit disgusted with their omnipotent pomposities."

Johnny Goodman had a choice now. He knew the unspoken rules. The USGA wanted him to show "good sportsmanship." It would be best to respond to the committee's slight with a shrug, a stiff upper lip, and a stoic comment such as, "I just play, the USGA picks the team," or better still, "I'm sure the committee acted on its best principles."

Johnny had studied country club language for years, and he understood the blueblood code of restraint, but instead of holding back, he spit out the unvarnished truth. "Well, that's too bad for me, isn't it? Everybody at the Open told me my performance practically cinched a place on the Walker Cup team," he told the press after the team had been named. "Officials, players, and sportswriters all thought my place on the team assured because I finished low amateur . . . One of my big hopes has been to represent the United States in these international matches, and I thought this would be my year because of my showing in the Open."

Frederick Ware speculated that regional prejudice played a part in blackballing Goodman. "My guess is that if young Goodman resided, say, in Chicago, Cleveland, New York City, Boston, or some other city east of the Mississippi River, then the United States Golf Association would have named the boy as a member of the Walker Cup team. Not as an alternate, either, but as a full-fledged member. 'Tis queer that a golfer like Goodman can't even get as much as honorable mention on the team."

Ware reminded readers that the USGA's animosity against Goodman went all the way back to Pebble Beach, recalling that after Johnny beat Bobby Jones there, his victory proved to be "a boomerang that hit the USGA right in the eyes. There was no gallery for the remainder of the tournament. All those Californians were climbing among the cypress trees to see Bobby; after that they went home. And the USGA's cashbox was as bare as Mother Hubbard's." From the USGA's perspective, Goodman had "stepped right on the gouty toes of those [he] was trying to impress."

The *World-Herald* also ran a telling cartoon. A policeman labeled "USGA" stops a driver named Goodman who has one bright headlight marked "Golfing Ability" and one dark one called "Social Rating." Floating in the background is the title "Walker Cup Team." The *New York Sun* predicted that the Goodman scandal would haunt Walker Cup play.

The USGA had hoped to maintain an Olympian silence about the Goodman affair, but the conflict refused to die down. *The Literary Digest,* not exactly a golf addict's favorite reading, ran an article headlined "Ten Good Men for the Walker Cup, but No Goodman." The controversy was bleeding off the sports pages now.

Against this avalanche of criticism, the USGA finally issued a statement. Offering a blanket rationale for ignoring Goodman's fine performance at Fresh Meadow, the selection committee explained that it had made its decision *before* the U.S. Open. But as Goodman's champions quickly pointed out, the selection committee hadn't made its choices public until three days *after* the U.S. Open was finished, giving it ample time to adjust its decisions in private.

Despite all the ink describing him as a "great showman," Johnny Goodman was a shy man who did his talking with his golf sticks. On the other hand, he had a gift for golf and an unbending will. Why should he roll over and play dead for the brass hats? He'd never taken a dime of prize money. He was as clean as the next character, as far as it went, and he wasn't floating on daddy's trust fund either.

The USGA had made a big mistake, he told his friends back in Omaha. Sure he was steaming over the way they'd snubbed him, but he'd already said enough. Now he was going to zip his lip. He wasn't going to make any predictions to the big-city reporters, but it was only a few months until the U.S. Amateur at Five Farms in Baltimore. He'd go back East, he'd smile, and he'd say all the right things.

It wasn't all that hard to act polite and tell reporters he had all the respect in the world for golf's governing body. Why make himself look bad? Why give A. H. Gregson and his pals the satisfaction? Then, when he rolled out onto the fairways at Five Farms, round by round he'd take down every one of the anointed, every single Walker Cup player they threw at him. Let Al Wolf and Fred Ware and that guy over at the *Sun,* Hammond, and the other one from Chicago, Francis Powers, let them do his talking for him.

The USGA would love it if he cracked and shot off his mouth again, but he wasn't going to play that game.

24

GOODMAN HAD ALWAYS loved the discipline of practice. He could lose himself hitting one short iron after another, cutting it just so, spinning the next one high, hitting a low one to bore into the wind. Every time he struck the ball, he probed for his own weaknesses and then tried to dream up a cure. Sometimes a new shot didn't come easy. He'd try a dozen different strokes, different ball positions, different stances, different angles of attack, groping for that elusive, clean feel. When he hit on it, he dug in, practicing the same shot over and over until he forgot who he was. It was enough to be a pair of hands on the grip, fingers alive to the blade.

In the run-up to the 1932 U.S. Amateur at Five Farms, he found a new pleasure, controlling his tongue the same way he controlled a short iron in the wind. There was pleasure in hiding his anger about being blackballed from the Walker Cup team, in masking his feelings, in tightening his jaw. He knew how Bobby Jones acted; he knew every gracious word the Atlantan had uttered, win or lose. At Pebble Beach Bobby had been a good loser, and the reporters had loved him more than ever.

Maybe he'd never sound as smooth as Bobby, maybe his Midwest accent wasn't syrupy sweet, but he could show his manners as well as the next guy. There was never a speck of dirt on his shirtsleeves, he always fixed his tie perfectly straight before he left the locker room, and he tucked his socks into his plus fours just so. Some of these college boys were too damn careless for his taste.

He used the same pomade Walter Hagen slicked on, and he always slipped a comb in his back pocket in case his hair got mussed. He picked every clot of mud out of his spikes. He polished his shoes until he could see his reflection in them, he cleaned every groove in every iron every day, and he kept himself that way, too. The papers, they were always sticking a camera in his face. He didn't want to look bad.

On his way out of town to Five Farms, Johnny stayed away from predictions. "I'm going to shoot the works," he told the local reporters. He didn't say a word about the USGA or the Walker Cup. He didn't have to.

The controversy might have died down if the press had let it. Shortly before the best amateurs gathered at Five Farms for the 1932 U.S. Amateur, the American Walker Cup team had swamped a weak British contingent. Still too dependent on the old-school tie, the British had assembled a weak crew that managed to win only a single match. With the American team performing well, whether Goodman had been chosen or not now seemed like a moot point.

But reporters kept hounding Johnny about the Walker Cup snub, and he finally admitted to Lester Rice — violating his promise to himself to keep quiet — that "he would like to meet and beat four of the Walker Cup squad and thus vindicate his faith in himself."

He was almost sorry he'd stated the case so baldly — how would he look if he didn't come through? — but he couldn't resist the satisfaction of plain words. If he didn't pull the trick off, he'd take all the ridicule he deserved. He'd lived through bad rounds and bad press before, and he'd found out that he could survive the worst of it and come back for more. He didn't know the source of his mysterious resilience; he just knew it was there, inside him, like some hidden, nameless organ.

The *Chicago Tribune*'s Westbrook Pegler fanned the flames of class resentment further when he claimed that Johnny was "fighting the social battle of the downtrodden," a statement more redolent of the times than of Goodman's own state of mind. Johnny, who was certainly miffed that he'd been passed over for the Walker Cup team, wasn't at Five Farms to foment a revolution. He was there to win the U.S. Amateur.

Pegler wasn't the only outraged scribe. Davis Walsh, a wire service man, pointed out that Goodman "had the questionable taste to be born poor and so had to get to these tournaments as best he could . . . This didn't go down well with striped umbrellas on the lawn and house parties at Newport."

In Omaha, a *World-Herald* headline blared, "New York Press Makes Johnny a Martyr." There was truth behind the sensational claim. The *World-Telegram,* the *Sun,* the *American,* and the *Daily News* all agreed. The brass hats had blackballed the kid from Omaha for no good reason.

Five Farms was long and hilly. The 6,622-yard, par-seventy track had been laid out over pastures formerly owned by silent-screen heart-throb Francis X. Bushman. The 590-yard sixth, a right-angle dogleg to a well-trapped green, and the fourteenth, a 600-yard monster, stood out for sheer, brute length. The course also featured several long par fours. But Johnny hit the ball long and unconscionably straight in his practice rounds, and he found the greens to his liking, not lightning fast, but not dead slow either. You could rap it in the back of the cup at Five Farms.

Sitting in a comfortable wing chair in the clubhouse, with a drink at hand, he wrote a pair of letters, addressing the one to Josephine as he always did: "To the most beautiful girl in the world." She liked to hear about the hotel, so he thought up a few lines about his room and the lobby. The bed was big as a boat, he told her. And the chandelier in the lobby had a million lights.

Then he dashed one off to his brother Tony, detailing his hot practice rounds. Looking around, he wondered how many of the players, or the members of the Five Farms Country Club, had brothers who wrapped fresh chickens in butcher paper for a living. He wouldn't have minded introducing Tony to USGA president A. H. Ramsey just to see the look on his face. *This is my brother Tony, Mr. Ramsey. He's a grocery clerk. Good man, too.*

In the first medal round at the 1932 U.S. Amateur, Johnny Fischer, the intercollegiate champion from the University of Michigan, broke the course record, shooting a brilliant 69. Right at his heels in second place stood Johnny Goodman. Johnny's confidence was sky-high. After his round he told Francis Powers that he'd seldom hit the ball straighter. Only a couple of botched putts had kept him from breaking par.

Fischer held on in the second qualifying round, posting a strong 73 to break the U.S. Amateur medal record, but only Goodman's misadventures in a sixteenth-hole trap had cost Johnny a tie for first place. Perhaps more striking, four Walker Cup players — Jess Sweetser, Harrison Johnston, Billy Howell, and Doug Moe — failed to qualify, and Francis Ouimet, the 1931 U.S. Amateur champion, had to shoot one under par over the last seven holes to squeak in at 151.

After disposing of the ageless H. Chandler Egan in the morning round, 3 and 2, Johnny faced a red-hot Charlie Seaver. The broad-shouldered Seaver had played halfback for Pop Warner at Stanford. A tall, powerful specimen, Seaver looked the part of a gridiron star.

Charlie had grown up in a twenty-three-room mansion on Wilshire Boulevard, but his father, after losing valuable beachfront property and taking a bath on Wall Street, cut the grand house in half and had one section moved to a new lot several blocks away. On the vacated land, he built an office building. The elder Seaver hadn't noticed that in the early 1930s there was a glut in office space. His new creation stayed empty, and the family's fortunes spiraled downward. But as Charlie Seaver recalled years later, he was unaware at the time that his father's wealth was evaporating. All he cared about was golf.

Charlie Seaver was the first of the Walker Cup elect in Johnny Goodman's path.

The Pacific Coast star hit a fabled long ball, but the slight Goodman, in a snappy, all-white ensemble, matched Seaver's 275-yard drives, and just as often outdrove the California strongman.

With the match dead even after nine, Goodman's rock-solid play began to wear Seaver down. Following Bobby Jones's philosophy, Johnny fired one par after another, picking up the tenth and twelfth when Seaver weakened. A long iron put Goodman on the fat part of the fourteenth green, and when Seaver went wide with his approach, Johnny took a commanding three-hole lead. Seaver shaved the margin by one, dropping an eight-foot birdie on the sixteenth, but Goodman closed out the match with yet another par on seventeen.

On the demanding Five Farms par fours, Goodman was forced to hit two- and three-iron approach shots, in stark contrast to the numbing parade of wedges we see in today's tournaments. Against Seaver, Johnny hit distant greens with one long iron after another, and eventually the Californian crumbled under Goodman's steady onslaught. Shrugging off his early-round jinx, Johnny had broken through to the quarterfinals for the first time.

Johnny was flashing the same consistency that had put him near the top in the medal rounds, but when he did stray into a tight spot, he kept pulling Houdini-like escapes. Brilliant recoveries had always been part of Goodman's arsenal, his most creative shots springing as much from his fighting spirit as from athletic ability.

A new Johnny Goodman was emerging now. He had a bit of a swagger, and he wasn't shy about saying he knew his own worth. In matches, he still featured his patented stony stare, and he rarely uttered more than a word or two over eighteen holes, but once he came off the course he turned into a veritable chatterbox. He could dissect every swing, and every twist and turn in a hard-fought match, and his sheer love of the game poured out. Reporters loved him, and many of their readers, after following the articles about the Walker Cup blowup, had swung over to Johnny's side.

But traditionalists, USGA officials among them, found Goodman's new persona entirely too brash. Here was the character they had always suspected was lurking beneath the grim, competitive mask. From their perspective, there was something overly manicured in the way he dressed, and there was more than a little of the corner drugstore in his manner. Look at how he whipped a comb from his back pocket at a moment's notice. Even when he said the right thing, there was something abrasive about his tone of voice. The boy simply tried too hard, and he would never get it right.

Now the USGA officials had to grit their teeth and hope that Maurice McCarthy, another Walker Cupper and a plausible amateur champion, would hold the line against Goodman's forced march.

Then there was good old Francis Ouimet, who was more than capable of staging a holding action against Goodman. Francis had struggled in medal play, but against George Voigt he'd played like a dream. Poor George posted a one under 34 over the first nine against Ouimet and found himself four down. Displaying a touch on the greens that was nothing short of magical, Ouimet had fashioned a front-nine 30, breaking the U.S. Amateur record. Francis wasn't about to give up his title without a fight. No question about it. Goodman faced the tougher half of the draw. It would be uphill sledding.

Several thousand spectators lined the first fairway when Johnny and Maurice McCarthy made their way to the first tee. Opting for comfort, Johnny appeared in a sleeveless sweater vest without a tie. The husky, dark-haired McCarthy also looked casual in a plain sweater and khaki knickers. The two men shook hands, but there was little small talk. These were two serious players about to play a serious match.

Reporters, photographers, marshals, and the referee marched in a quiet procession to the first tee. In the soupy atmosphere, the gallery, thousands strong, began to intrude on the short grass. The *Baltimore Sun* had been relating Johnny Goodman's rise from South Omaha's slaughterhouse district, and the fans craned their necks for a look at the "little giant." Oblivious, a Baltimore policeman strolled across the hilly fairway as if he were walking his beat.

Against McCarthy, the experienced New Yorker, Johnny got off to a shaky start in the morning round. He missed a six-footer for birdie on the second and had to settle for a halve. Then his par putt on the third rimmed the cup. Off the fourth tee, Johnny yanked a two iron into a trap, an atrocious shot, and found himself three down after a mere four holes.

The downcast gallery shuffled and muttered. Maurice McCarthy was a fine player, but his stolid demeanor couldn't inspire a crowd filled with Baltimore's public course golfers witnessing their first great tournament. The Pimlico touts, clerks, bus drivers, bureaucrats, and Baltimore Oriole bleacher bums couldn't help rooting for the kid from Omaha. He looked like he needed all the help he could get.

Where were the ungodly straight shots he'd been firing all week? Johnny wondered. There was nothing wrong with his mechanics. He just had to stay in there and keep on pitching. Shaking off his early-round staggers, he started firing pars, one after another, at his tournament-tough opponent. McCarthy didn't wilt, he didn't collapse, but he gave way ever so slowly in match play's dance of death.

First the New Yorker knocked his approach on six into a trap, and then on eight he came up short of the green. Taking both holes on McCarthy's miscues, Goodman clawed his way back to one down. But Johnny's swing was a hair off; he could feel it. One stroke would be smooth as silk, the next would be off-tempo. Timing, the golf swing's holy grail, was eluding him, but there were other ways to win. Keep your wits. Play smart. Imagine a new shot, transform a thought into a stroke you've never made before.

Johnny evened the match on twelve with another inexorable par, only to give it back on the next hole. After hooking into a trap, he hit a brilliant bunker shot, then promptly missed the simple putt for par. Now came the hardest part, blotting the blunder — and the sensation of his hands pushing the putt off-line — from his memory. If Johnny had a gift for the game it was this. When it mattered most, he could empty his mind and go on.

On the fifteenth, McCarthy dropped in a birdie putt, Goodman's just slid by the cup, and once again the Omahan was drifting toward the precipice. Two down with three to go in the morning round.

A low hum went through the gallery. Where was the Johnny Goodman they'd been reading about in Westbrook Pegler's columns? This little guy was staggering all over the place.

But McCarthy was unable to deliver the killing blow. He bogeyed the sixteenth, giving one back. Johnny was only one down now. The electricity of hope stirred again. At the long par-three seventeenth, Johnny finally found the swing that had been eluding him. Catching a one iron pure, he sent a low, boring shot right at the flag, where it came to rest twelve feet from the pin. Barely eyeing the line, he smoothly stroked the birdie putt into the heart. Dead even again. After halving eighteen, the two men remained in lockstep.

In the afternoon round, they kept trading blows, racing neck and neck through the first five holes. At the dogleg sixth, Goodman, attempting to draw his tee shot around a barn at the corner, snap-hooked his drive out-of-bounds. Briefly unnerved, he three-putted the seventh, digging himself into a deeper hole, two down. Once again McCarthy had a chance to put his tormentor away, but Johnny steadied and stopped the bleeding for the next five holes.

On the eleventh, under the steady drip drip drip of Goodman's pars, McCarthy slipped up once more, slicing his drive into a trap. Then his irons began to desert him, and when he failed to reach the next green in regulation, Goodman knocked in another par and drew even.

Neither man could gain the advantage on thirteen and fourteen. After thirty-two holes of head-to-head competition, they were tied yet again. To the dismay of the marshals, the restive gallery started spilling out onto the fairways and swarming around the tee boxes. Now the game was living up to expectations. Maybe Grantland Rice, Gould, and Powers were right all along. A tight golf match was like a big race in slow motion. Every shot was agony now.

Then at the fifteenth, McCarthy caught a break. Just as Goodman was driving, the tense crowd broke free and flooded onto the fairway. Marshals shouted, to no avail. The spectators ran over a Baltimore cop and raced around militiamen from the 110th Field Artillery, narrowing the landing area down to nothing. Johnny's perfect drive struck a spectator flush on the arm and careened into a fairway trap. Officials ruled that Goodman had to play it where it lay. His bad luck was simply the rub of the green.

Shrugging, Johnny climbed into the trap and squinted at the distant green. He would have to pick the ball clean. Even a shred of sand would deaden the shot and leave him forty or fifty yards short. Wielding a mashie, he clipped the ball without brushing a grain of sand, his recovery shot flying to the front edge of the green. Calmly stroking his long chip tight to the pin, he made off with his par — and fended off disaster yet again.

Bad breaks inspired Johnny Goodman and they inspired his boosters too. The fans whistled; they punched each other on the shoulder. A flat white cap sailed from the depths of the crowd and landed on the manicured seventeenth tee. Scowling, a marshal retrieved it. Another stepped forward, and gesturing palms-downward, tried to still the crowd. Five Farms had turned into Johnny Goodman's home court.

The valiant McCarthy lost his swing on the next tee, cutting his drive into a trap, and Goodman seized the opening with a regulation par. One up on the par-three seventeenth, Johnny's nemesis, the hook, seized him yet again. Closing the face on his mashie, he knocked his tee shot straight into a greenside bunker, giving McCarthy yet another chance. The New Yorker stroked a perfect shot onto the heart of the green.

Stolid as ever, Goodman surveyed his miserable lie. Limp with expectation, the gallery fell silent. Would the grim confrontation overflow into sudden death? Digging in, the wispy Goodman took one more look, measured his stroke, and blasted out in a shower of sand. The ball arced over the lip of the trap, bit into the turf, then released, dribbling a scant few feet from the cup.

Still in danger of falling back into a tie, Johnny moved swiftly. Don't wait, don't tighten up. The first look is always the best look. After lining up the make-or-break putt with a quick glance, he sent it on its way. The ball rolled firm and true. Never a doubt.

He'd done it again, pulled another rabbit of a recovery out of his hat. Sensing that this was the deciding blow, the gallery burst into applause.

When McCarthy's approach putt failed to go down, the crowd swarmed to the eighteenth tee. After grinding into the lead, Goodman simply would not let go. Parring the final hole in easy fashion, he slipped into the next round.

Commenting on the semifinalists, Grantland Rice wrote, "These four golfers fought their way through fire and brimstone. They left a big gallery with jumping pulses and frayed nerves before they crossed over the hill into the promised land beyond. I have never seen finer golf played on the way to the closing act."

Johnny had his mind on only one man, Francis Ouimet. The 1931 U.S. Amateur champion was waiting in the wings.

25

I F BOBBY JONES was America's most beloved golfer in 1932, Francis Ouimet, the reigning U.S. Amateur champion, was the most revered. American golf was in its infancy when he beat Harry Vardon in 1913 to win the U.S. Open. The next year the young Ouimet, whose angular face was winged by a pair of jug ears, took the U.S. Amateur, beating two former champions, Bob Gardner and Bill Fownes, before sweeping the best match player in the country, Jerry Travers, 6 and 5 in the finals.

The son of a French Canadian laborer who was openly hostile to his boy's infatuation with golf, Francis grew up across from the seventeenth green at the Country Club in Brookline, Massachusetts. He caddied as a boy, and played Franklin Park, a public course, as a teenager, but his game really flowered when a member of the Country Club took him under his wing. Ouimet shot three over par for his first nine holes at Brookline, and from that point on the indulgent caddiemaster looked the other way when young Francis joined members for a round.

In some ways Ouimet's story was similar to Johnny Goodman's, down to the skirmishes with the USGA over amateur status. Both men rose from unlikely origins. Early in their lives, they became utterly absorbed in golf's mysterious arts. They taught themselves the game. They had great native talent, particularly around the green. And they both enjoyed quick success on the national stage as young men. They shared similar values too — eschewing the money game in favor of the amateur ideal. Naturally, they both craved one title above all others: the U.S. Amateur.

Yet their temperaments could not have been more different. From the beginning Francis had been modest and direct. Although he was intransigent as a competitor, he had a gentle character that expressed itself in his mild manner and his love of music. As he grew older, he found success in the business world. Later on, he needed spectacles, which gave him a professorial air. Sympathetic to his peers, reliable, judicious, he was a natural to captain the Walker Cup team. Despite the fact that he wasn't born into select circles, Ouimet eventually became an establishment figure who moved with ease in golf's most powerful circles.

Johnny Goodman had a rougher edge. He was by turns cocky, innocent, tight-lipped, and loquacious. More than once he was accused of having a chip on his shoulder. Though his taste in clothes was conventional, he had taken to wearing two-toned golf shoes. There was something just a bit flashy about Goodman. Fair-haired, he had slate blue eyes and classic, even features. He was good-looking, and he knew it. Always cast as the tough underdog, Goodman bridled at the way he'd been snubbed by the USGA. Instead of passively accepting the ruling body's highhanded treatment, he preferred to battle it out. An altogether knottier figure than Francis Ouimet.

But more than anything, Johnny knew the history of the game, and he had tremendous respect for Ouimet. He understood that Francis had broken barriers that made his own rise conceivable. For Goodman, Ouimet was a more plausible hero than either Walter Hagen or Bobby Jones, but Ouimet was already a figure from the past when Johnny was growing up and America was in the grip of Bobby Jones mania. He had always admired Francis from afar, and they had a nodding acquaintance, but Ouimet was usually buried deep in his Boston entourage, many of whom regarded Johnny with suspicion, if not outright hostility.

Johnny's prospects against Ouimet depended almost entirely on his putting. He couldn't afford to miss down the stretch because invariably the champion started canning them from all angles when the pressure was on.

Goodman had played off-and-on golf against McCarthy. Time and again, inspired recoveries had kept him in the game. Against Ouimet he would need every improvisation in his bag. Francis was anything but an antique. Not only was he the reigning U.S. Amateur champion, he was also riding the hottest streak of his long and brilliant career. Against the young Sidney Noyes, Ouimet had posted a front-nine 30, and sunk a birdie putt on the last hole to take the match against an opponent who was playing the best golf of his life.

Bobby Jones, who was covering the Amateur for his syndicated column, had followed his old opponent and close friend during his matches. He described Francis's play as "so unbelievable I had to see it with my own eyes to believe it was true."

It was clear where Bobby Jones's sympathies lay. As he stood waiting for the contestants to arrive at the first tee, Jones signed autographs and chatted with his intimates, O. B. Keeler and USGA president H. H. Ramsey. Even in retirement, the charismatic Jones dominated the scene.

Francis appeared on the first tee wearing a seedy cap he had yanked low over his eyes, his thin nose pointing out from beneath the crushed brim. His bony white wrists protruded from rolled-back sleeves. Both men wore knickers, but Johnny had donned a white mesh shirt with the texture of burlap, a garment whose loose weave would soon expose him to trouble.

Once or twice Johnny drew his pocket comb from his back pocket to tame his wavy hair. He was acutely aware that Bobby Jones was close by. It seemed impossible to shake the omnipresent Jones, but how could he draw the club back without wiping Bobby from his mind? Johnny concentrated, over and over again, on gripping the club.

Approaching the first tee, Ouimet was serenaded by his Boston entourage, who put a twist on "Ol' Man River" by inserting Ouimet's name into the song. Goodman was trailed by Omaha loyalists from Lakewood and the Field Club, chief among them Bert Waddington and Field Club pro Stanley Davies.

Baltimore fans swarmed around the competitors. Their sympathies were sharply divided. Ouimet, whose upset victory over Harry

Vardon at the 1913 U.S. Open had meant so much in the early days of American golf, appealed to the nostalgists in the gallery. Ouimet's simple manner suggested a less-cynical time before the war. There was about Francis a whiff of the Edwardian age. But Ouimet had for so long been part of the Boston golfing establishment that fans mistook him for his more-privileged supporters.

Johnny Goodman had beaten tough times. Fans who were new to golf liked that. Goodman seemed more like them than the accomplished and settled Ouimet. And they knew all about the snobs on the USGA Executive Committee who had barred Johnny at the Walker Cup door. Johnny Goodman was their boy. He was like some scrappy second baseman on their beloved Orioles.

Goodman, who barely came up to Ouimet's shoulder, appeared slight next to his tall, sinewy opponent. Ouimet leaned over to shake his young opponent's hand. The wind kicked up; the sky darkened.

Johnny got off to a weak start. Francis was outdriving him by twenty yards, and on the long par fours Goodman was forced to hit two irons that twice fell well short of the green. Still, he managed to keep even after five holes. On the sixth he faltered. At the 575-yard, par-five dogleg, Johnny topped his brassie and the ball skidded into a fairway trap. He could do no better than bogey, and fell one down. Overshooting the green on the par-four, 349-yard seventh hole, Goodman chipped back and two-putted for a bogey, leaving him two down.

Ouimet's loyalists chortled among themselves. Their numbers were strong, and they sensed that Francis would grind down the midwestern upstart now. Goodman, after all, had been playing over his head, and eventually he had to come down to earth.

Murmurs of sympathy rose from Johnny's backers, who feared the formidable Ouimet was about to crush their favorite. Stanley Davies exchanged dark looks with Bert Waddington, who had seen Johnny falter more than once. The Omaha favorite always seemed to find a way to lose at the U.S. Amateur, and perhaps his time had come again.

But Goodman's expression never changed. He was playing in his usual bubble of concentration. Both players reached the eighth, a short par four, in regulation. Johnny read his twenty-footer swiftly and struck it hard. It looked to be all too hard, but the ball hit the back of the cup, popped into the air, and plopped in. Birdie three. Johnny had one back. Uncharacteristically, Ouimet three-putted the 179-yard, par-three ninth, and Johnny took another one. They made the turn dead even.

On the tenth, a 378-yard par four, both players stuck their approaches ten feet from the hole. Ouimet, away by a hair, knocked his birdie putt in. Johnny calmly rolled his into the cup for a birdie, too.

A burst of applause and a few unseemly whoops of joy rose from the gallery, which then raced to line the next hole. Ropes had yet to be introduced for tournament play, and the raucous fans began mounting every rise in the ground, perching themselves on the edges of fairway traps, oblivious to the line between fairway and rough.

Strolling along next to Johnny, Francis complimented him on his pressure putt. "Fine play, Johnny," the gentle Bostonian said. Francis sounded so sincere, Johnny began wondering if Ouimet was half on his side. There was little chance of that. In his own understated way, Francis Ouimet burned to win.

Neck and neck, both players parred the eleventh. On the twelfth, a 488-yard par four, Johnny drove just short of a sharp bend in the fairway but still managed to draw a solid spoon onto the green. When Ouimet's approach sailed long, Johnny capitalized, taking the hole with a four. He had inched into the lead, one up.

On the thirteenth tee, the wind gusted behind the players. Eyeing the elements, Francis squinted behind his glasses. Johnny tossed a bit of grass and watched it blow, weightless, down the fairway. The 171-yard par three would be easy to reach, but what to hit? Goodman took his mashie, clipped the ball perfectly, and watched it sail right for the heart of the green — and clear over into a thicket of spiny blackberry bushes.

Johnny gazed with a sense of disbelief as his ball disappeared into oblivion. When he came face-to-face with the impenetrable wall of vegetation, he gave way, briefly, to despair. In that jungle, there could be nothing but unplayable lies. Still, he had to see how deep his ball was buried, if only to make a show of resistance.

With a USGA marshal at his side, Johnny plunged into the tangled, thorned nest. The ball was nowhere to be found. Ducking his head, he crawled deeper into the shadows, his eyes probing the gloom. Just when he was about to declare a lost ball, he saw a sliver of white, like a slice of a new moon, nestled in the brambles.

Spiky branches surrounded Johnny's lie. Ducking his head to keep from being lacerated, he burrowed deep into the thicket, managing finally to settle over the ball. Niblick in hand, he measured his backswing. A bare few inches. The shot would have to be all wrist, and thorns be damned. Again Johnny drew his club back, but this time his loose-woven shirt snagged on the thorns. He might have to rip the material to shreds just to put a good swing on the damn ball.

Then Johnny looked up and saw a narrow, bright opening, a slender tunnel to the outside world. He would have to follow through straight to the light. Now. His club slashing at the undergrowth, his quick wrists sent the ball on its way.

"Goodman, when he finally settled into his stance, could barely move without tearing his flesh on the needle-like briars," Lester Rice wrote. "He was in the clutches of a strange kind of octopus. He could swing his hands less than a foot without ripping them on the spines." Swallowed up in the thicket, Johnny was invisible to most of the gallery.

However, a few observant spectators noticed a dinner plate–size opening in the otherwise impenetrable bushes. Deep in the briars, Goodman had disappeared from view. Then the bushes rustled as Johnny executed the wristy, short-armed stroke. Suddenly, the ball shot through the barely visible escape route, and Goodman was on the green.

O. B. Keeler shook his head and burst out laughing. Openly stunned, Bobby Jones rocked back on his heels.

"That was the greatest golf shot I ever saw," the president of the USGA, Herbert H. Ramsey, gasped to Lester Rice. With a single blow, Johnny Goodman had held the line against Ouimet and finally won Ramsey's grudging respect.

Now the pressure was on Francis. Bunkered, Ouimet blasted out and settled for a four. Johnny rimmed his par putt, but still ended up with a halve. Once again, the recovery artist had fended off disaster.

Ouimet's backers grew quiet; Goodman's loyalists drew strength from Johnny's nervy recovery. They sensed the tide was turning, and they didn't think a little hooting and hollering was out of order.

Johnny's hair-thin lead lasted until the par-four, 428-yard fifteenth, where he dumped his approach into a trap and had to take a bogey. Playing meticulous golf, solid from tee to green, the players exchanged pars for the rest of the morning round, ending where they had begun.

Francis had struck the ball more consistently, but his fabled putting had been mediocre. Goodman had been wilder, and shorter off the tee, but he had invented one recovery shot after another to stay abreast of the champion.

Johnny ate a light lunch and hurried to the practice green, where he stroked putt after putt to keep his feel. After picking at his food, Francis strolled into a private room, settled into a chair, and closed his eyes.

The wind was blowing hard now, hard enough to build an invisible wall in the sky. Off the first tee, a 428-yard par four, Johnny hit his drive flush, only to see it die 220 yards away. His energy surging, he rushed his brassie and topped it, leaving him a full seven iron to the green. Nothing to it. He dropped it eight feet from the pin and knocked in his par for a halve. Nineteen holes, still dead even.

Golfers are so used to wearing the hair shirt, they often forget that the game's misfortunes are laced with light. Johnny expected to struggle, but he also expected streaks when he could do no wrong. In the U.S. Open he had broken the course record before Sarazen bested him with an even more brilliant round. Under pressure, he had ridden unearthly streaks in the Trans-Mississippi. He knew he would get hot, and now was the perfect time.

On the second hole, a 445-yard par four, both players hit 250-yard drives dead center, but Francis overshot the green with his two iron. Johnny rolled in a twenty-footer for a birdie to edge in front yet again. He was one up.

After halving the third, the players came to the fourth, a short par three, 163 yards, with the wind howling in their faces. Johnny drew a one iron from the bag, choked up, and hit a low screamer right onto the putting surface. Unable to negotiate the stiff breeze, Francis dumped his drive into a trap.

A pair of Johnny's backers whistled between their teeth. Frowning at the Omaha contingent, a Ouimet fan muttered, "Dirty pool." Johnny had forged ahead, two up.

The competitors halved the next two holes, but Francis found trouble on the sixth, a 575-yard par five, hooking his drive off the roof of a barn. The shot came to rest on the edge of the fairway, but Ouimet, after gaining a better angle by playing safe, blasted a strong brassie to reach the green in three.

On in regulation after a fine short iron left him close to the pin, Johnny dropped a ten-footer for another birdie. Three up.

Johnny was feeling it now. When he got hot with the short irons, he could sense every distance with the tips of his fingers; he could just lay them in there with his eyes closed.

On the short par-four seventh, only 374 yards, Goodman nailed a seven iron four feet from the pin, but Francis laid a partial stymie, effectively shrinking the hole to half its size. Working the narrowed line, Johnny knocked his birdie in anyway. Now he had forged ahead by four holes.

Ouimet just shrugged his narrow shoulders. Catching up with Goodman before the next tee, he remarked, "You don't let up, do you?" Johnny was almost embarrassed to be beating his graceful competitor.

At the sixteenth, a Baltimore priest remarked to O. B. Keeler, "This is the jinx hole. He [Francis] has played it badly all week."

Ouimet more than justified the Baltimore cleric's lack of faith. On the 422-yard par four, he was trapped. Flailing away, he failed to get out of the sand. He had one more chance. Sink the bunker shot or die. This time he hit a shot worthy of his talent, the ball landing gently on the putting surface and sweeping toward the hole, only to veer away at the last moment. The great Francis Ouimet had fallen.

"And then came that strange cry from the gallery of 2,000," O. B. Keeler wrote. "'Give Goodman the Walker Cup!'"

As the two men walked off the final tee, Francis grasped Goodman's hand and shook it firmly. "That was some fine shooting, Johnny. I'm impressed."

In his roundabout way, Ouimet was sending a message, Johnny thought. He had had no part in keeping Johnny off the Walker Cup team. But Johnny already knew that. "Any other day, you'd beat my brains out, Francis."

"Doubtful," Francis replied.

Grantland Rice offered this analysis: "When Ouimet seemed to be winning, he faced this devastating barrage on the next twenty holes. Read the record and weep for a gallant ex-champion: 3-3-3-4-4-4-4-5-4-3-4-3-4-4-3-4-4-3-4-4. Look at those figures — one 5, seven 3s and twelve 4s.

"The Nebraska youth with the spirit of a bulldog might have been using a rifle. He rarely left the line to the pin. He made almost no mistakes of any sort after he once caught the winning groove," Rice concluded.

Rice may have added one other significant figure. In the thirty-four holes he played against Francis Ouimet, Johnny Goodman didn't three-putt a single green.

When the Canadian Ross Somerville swamped the veteran Jess "Siege Gun" Guilford in his semifinal match, Johnny Goodman was the only American left standing. In a very real sense, before taking on Somerville in the finals, Johnny was already the American amateur golf champion.

He had fought his way through the tougher side of the draw, making good on his promise to vanquish every Walker Cup star in his path. Closing the melodrama by beating the Walker Cup captain, Francis Ouimet, he gave his performance a sense of finality. There was no denying him his rightful place on the team now, and the press reveled in his triumph.

The *Chicago Tribune*'s Westbrook Pegler crowed, "You may fancy the embarrassment of the genial commissars who govern the game of golf in the U.S.A. and keep a reasonably good job of keeping it sweet and clean and sporting when Johnny Goodman of Omaha, Neb., licked Francis Ouimet, in the semifinal of the national amateur championship . . . So tomorrow Johnny Goodman, who was overlooked, to put it in a nice way, but ignored, to put it more accurately, will be the final defender of the [U.S. Amateur] cup that has never crossed the American border since Harold Hilton . . . the Englishman, won it in 1911."

After the match, the supposedly taciturn Goodman was in high spirits and wasn't shy about sharing his feelings. United Press's Stuart Cameron caught a glimpse of the young star's suppressed emotions. "Johnny is different. Match over, win or lose, he'll talk by the hour, and he's lost plenty of times . . . But when he wins, as he did yesterday, he opens his heart. Bubbling over with the effervescent jubilation of youth Johnny will admit that beating a former champion is no small feat."

Gone was the careful language Johnny usually adopted for public consumption. In talking about the hard-fought match, Goodman expressed his sheer delight at the outcome, but also gave an insight into his strategic thinking.

"I was plenty pleased holding that lead. But I wasn't really satisfied until I was dormie three up," Goodman told Cameron. "I think I'm playing pretty good golf right now. Long as I can keep them fairly straight I won't kick. You notice I was satisfied to come close on the greens against Ouimet. I know I got three long ones, but what I try to stay away from is three-putt greens. Lordy, how I hate those three-putts."

Johnny's high spirits didn't last long. Soon enough, the usual slights began. First, he couldn't get permission to bring Stanley Davies and his other supporters into the dining room. Alone at the bar, he bought a scotch and soda and waited for a word of encouragement from H. H. Ramsey and the other USGA officials. After all, he was about to defend American honor against the Canadian, C. Ross Somerville, in twenty-four hours, but the USGA's top brass studiously avoided making eye contact with him.

A knot of well-wishers surrounded the defeated Francis Ouimet, including Bobby Jones and O. B. Keeler, his longtime allies.

Johnny tapped his fingers on the polished bar. He sipped his drink. Famished, he ordered a sandwich. Then he headed for the bathroom. A deadly silence followed him as he meandered among the tables and when he returned to the bar.

He chewed his ham and cheese fast now, and gulped his drink down. Unable to stand it any longer, he fled toward the door, where he ran into the sportswriter Paul Gallico.

According to the reporter, Johnny didn't try to hide his wounded feelings. "Goodman beat Ouimet and then got back to the clubhouse to find that Francis was the hero and himself ignored," Gallico wrote. "I saw him wandering, lonely and unnoticed, around the clubhouse and later found him sitting by himself in a cab. No one had even offered him a lift home. I talked to him. Naturally, he was bitter and resentful. But after he thawed out he talked a little too freely of how he had vanquished Ouimet. Or perhaps he talked too naturally. I don't know."

Goodman was perfectly capable of saying the right thing when the light was shining on him, but Gallico had caught sight of the private man and his private thoughts. Before thousands of spectators, Johnny kept a death grip on his emotions. Lauded for his icy demeanor in championship play, he couldn't yet mimic the stiff upper lip off the course, however much he tried.

He had sworn to himself that he would do a fine imitation of Bobby Jones in public, and like his idol say the right thing no matter how much he was provoked. Even as he boiled over with recriminations, he knew he had failed. He just didn't care anymore.

But he had played the best golf of his life. His swing had held up, and so had his nerve. No one could take that away from him.

In his column, Bobby Jones grudgingly gave Johnny his due. "If I had been offered my choice on the first tee I should have picked Somerville and Ouimet to meet in the finals. But Goodman played good golf throughout and managed to work out a score which was awfully hard to beat."

Grantland Rice had the final word: "Goodman is a grand young golfer with a fine swing and a cool head and a determined mind . . . Any golfer who can beat Seaver, McCarthy, and Ouimet on successive days needs no eulogy."

Less than three years had passed since Johnny had boarded the Fast Mail to California for his fateful meeting with Bobby Jones. Now, several months shy of his twenty-third birthday, he'd made his case. He was the best amateur golfer in America.

26

CROSS SOMERVILLE had torn through his draw at Five Farms, breaking the course record with a 68 against W. O. Blaney in the quarterfinals. The heir to a chewing gum fortune, the four-time Canadian Open champion did not speak much when he played golf, but unlike Johnny Goodman, he wasn't much for words in private either. Both men worked in the insurance business, though Johnny's office was mostly under his hat.

Bobby Jones hedged his bets, noting that while Somerville was longer off the tee, Goodman was putting like a demon. Johnny's caddie, Clarence "Reds" Neal, had no doubts about his man. "You polite fellers call it intestinal fortitude, but I call it 'Guts' and that's what is going to win for Johnny today."

On the first tee, the thin-lipped, hawk-nosed Somerville was greeted with polite applause. He wore a white flat cap, his shirt hanging loose over the brown trousers he favored over traditional knickers. By eschewing a tie, the Canadian added to his up-to-date, informal look.

Johnny Goodman appeared all in white, white shirt and white flannel knickers, offset by a pair of snazzy blue socks and brown-and-white golf shoes. For the final match, he wore a tie and a tie pin. He allowed a smile to appear on his lips as he acknowledged the frank cheers of his countrymen. Then he drew visibly inward, his features settling into an impassive mask.

The gallery for the Ouimet-Goodman match had been deeply divided, but now a love of country dominated the crowd. The Canadian Somerville was both a foreigner and a surrogate for the British Empire, and now Johnny Goodman had a chance to spit in John Bull's eye on behalf of the former colony. Spectators may not have known the details of Anglo-American golf history, but England, for most Americans, still reeked of musty aristocracy. As far as they were concerned, Johnny Goodman represented a straight-talking, clean-living American antidote to Old-World rot.

The USGA's highest circles were divided, however. C. Ross Somerville, with his comfortable fortune and buttoned-up demeanor, fit quite nicely into the social set of the fashionable American country clubs. And, if anything, the USGA's allies like A. H. Gregson had intensified their attacks on the sort of wrong people who were representing themselves as amateurs.

In a scathing 1931 *Golf Illustrated* editorial, he had cheered on the USGA's recent show of spine. "The annual meeting of the United States Golf Association was most encouraging to all of us who have at heart the best interests of the game and indeed, of all pure amateur sport. The most important question by far . . . was that of amateur status, whereof it was caustically and rightly stated that no matter concerned with the game has been productive of so much loose thinking . . . Far too long has the matter been allowed to drift along clouded by journalistic twaddle and with no consideration of standards . . . Any amateur game . . . which is going to remain free of professionalism must be in the hands of rulers who never allow these fundamentals to be obscured by any nonsensical pleading."

As always, Gregson's "fundamentals" were defined by a fundamentally sound bankbook. "If we have not the means and the leisure derived from those means, we have no right to be playing [amateur] golf." In another reactionary barrage, Gregson came as close as possible to naming Johnny Goodman, the freshly minted insurance agent, as amateur golf's chief malefactor. "Are we going to run our amateur championships so that they can be used as stepping stones to getting a position with . . . an insurance company with one's golfing acquaintances and fellow members as the prospects of the business?"

Johnny Goodman, who had imagined that gaining a foothold in the middle class would help him gain acceptance in the USGA's inner circle, read these fulminations with dismay. It seemed that no matter how correct his behavior, he could never satisfy his tormentors.

Standing on the first tee at Five Farms as the de facto king of American amateur golf, Johnny felt vindicated already. It was a bitter pleasure, but a pleasure indeed.

Like it or not, Johnny Goodman had become the face of American amateur golf. H. H. Ramsey and his friends did not like it at all.

Johnny knew his greatest adversary wasn't C. Ross Somerville. It was the elation he felt after beating Francis Ouimet, and a sense of justification that was all too sweet. He couldn't afford to be distracted by yesterday's thrills or that feeling of invulnerability, the victor's poisoned fruit. Overconfidence was his greatest enemy by far.

It was a perfect day for golf. A few clouds scudded across the bright sky. Only a gentle breeze blew across the first fairway. In fair weather, Five Farms would lose a few of its teeth.

In the morning round, the lead changed hands again and again. Somerville held a one-hole advantage through the first five, but on the 590-yard, par-five sixth hole, Johnny found his putting touch. After dropping his third shot eighteen feet from the pin, Goodman rolled it in for a birdie to tie the match.

The unruly gallery raced to the next hole, creating an impenetrable ribbon of humanity along the seventh fairway. Fashionable women in straw hats strained for a look at the players, especially the diminutive, white-clad Johnny Goodman. Older golf fanatics, huffing and puffing after negotiating Five Farms's hilly terrain, stabbed the spears of folding chairs into the turf and parked themselves in the front row.

After Somerville left his approach on the 349-yard par four on the upper level of the green, a full thirty-five feet from the hole, Johnny had an opening, but he failed to capitalize, sailing a niblick to the back of the green. No matter. He dropped a snaking forty-footer for another birdie to take a one-hole lead.

In Omaha, the Grain Exchange had a direct wire to the Goodman-Somerville match. From there news flashed to bond departments in banks all over town; tellers picked up the latest details and passed on blow-by-blow accounts. Phone operators at the department stores checked with the sports desks at the *World-Herald* and the *Bee* every few minutes, and news of who was up and who was down raced through the aisles of haberdashery and notions.

Still in his apron, Tony Goodman kept slipping out of the grocery to call the *Bee* from the pharmacy. A minor celebrity himself now, the handsome clerk affected an insider's mystery, doling out bits and pieces of action to breathless drugstore-counter jockeys. With every shift in the seesaw battle, Tony was seized by an attack of nerves, but he kept repeating his standard line: "Johnny told me he's got it in the bag."

Glued to her radio, which gave out fragmentary reports of the Five Farms battle, Josephine had resorted to manipulating her rosary beads to quell her fears. Every time she heard bad news she snapped off the radio, only to turn it on moments later to see if Johnny had turned the tide.

In the billiard emporiums, pool sharks normally dedicated to skinning marks were standing on the tables and swinging their cues like golf sticks. Cab drivers, who didn't know a niblick from knockwurst, grew irritated at the constant barrage of questions.

"Is he winning?"

"Down? By how many?"

"What hole? Is it close?"

"Where's our Johnny now?"

The Omaha papers always called him "our Johnny," and now the whole city felt that he was theirs too.

On the eighth, a 355-yard par four, Somerville "proved he was all to the mustard," according to the *Baltimore American*. After pulling his drive into the rough, Somerville hacked it out twenty feet from the hole and rammed his putt home for a birdie, tying the match again.

On the 179-yard, par-four ninth, Somerville, with an almost casual swipe, ran in a twenty-foot sidehill putt. As emotionless as his adversary, Goodman replied by rapping in his fifteen-footer.

Nose to nose, the stubborn competitors made the turn, but Goodman was riding one of his streaks. His mashie-niblick on the par-four, 378-yard tenth hole came to rest two feet from the cup. The partisan gallery whooped and hollered as he tapped it in for another birdie, his fourth in five holes. Goodman by one. Again.

Somerville ripped his next drive on the 424-yard par four past Goodman's on a fly. When Johnny came up yards short with a spoon, the Canadian stroked a three iron home and looked to have the advantage. Fighting back, Johnny stiffed his ten-yard chip. Unnerved by Goodman's brilliant short game, Somerville three-putted, handing Johnny another win. The Omahan was two up now.

The lead didn't last long.

On the twelfth, a 388-yard par four, Johnny was stymied — twice on the same green. Facing a forty-foot putt, he found Somerville's ball directly in his path. Forced to pop a niblick over the Canadian's ball, he managed to get within six feet. When Somerville laid a partial stymie, Johnny tried to nudge his putt around the edge of the impediment, only to rim the cup. His lead shriveled to one hole again.

Johnny had taken to smoking Chesterfields during his matches. Now he lit up, took a deep breath, and issued a cloud of gray smoke. Unfortunately, the cigarette didn't improve his play.

After dunking his tee shot into a trap on the par-three, 141-yard thirteenth, Johnny blasted out to eight feet, but he was stymied yet again, the third time in two holes. Forced to settle for another bogey, Goodman watched his opponent make a routine par. Johnny's lead had evaporated.

Stymies were part of the game. In fact, Johnny Goodman had laid a few himself — more than sixty years after his 1932 U.S. Amateur match against Goodman, Charlie Seaver was still haunted by several Johnny placed against him. But on consecutive holes Somerville, whether by luck or design, had blocked Goodman's short putts. It was galling.

Johnny gritted his teeth and marched to the next tee. The light breeze picked up steam, and dust rose from the dry fairways. The nationalistic gallery pressed up against the line formed by the 110th Field Artillery. A new convert to golf spoke up against the stymie rule, arguing its essential unfairness. He closed with an unassailable bit of logic. "It's our field, too."

A clutch of Baltimore patriots agreed.

By the time the two golfers came to the fifteenth, a par-four 424-yarder, the wind was blowing hard, flat in their faces. A driver and brassie still left Johnny fifteen yards short. Somerville, struggling, too, drove into the rough and lashed a long iron straight into a greenside trap. Now it was the Canadian's turn to flash his short game. Blasting out three feet from the pin, Somerville salvaged his par. Goodman bogeyed, and Somerville edged in front by one hole.

He promptly gave it back on the par-four, 402-yard sixteenth, missing a four-footer for par. After trading haymakers for seventeen holes, the two golfers were still standing toe to toe, slugging it out. Dead even.

On the eighteenth green, facing a fifty-foot sidehiller for birdie, Somerville lagged the sharp breaking putt with no thought of sinking it.

"It's going in," one onlooker gasped.

A collective intake of breath. Then the gallery, packed tight around the green island, watched the Canadian's ball roll and roll and nose straight to the bottom of the cup. Goodman, who had just blasted out to fifteen feet, snatched his ball from the putting surface and hurried to the clubhouse. He'd thrown everything he had against Somerville, and he'd still fallen one short.

Johnny was disgusted. Four birdies in five holes, and yet he hadn't been able to climb on top of his opponent. In the Canadian, he sensed a will similar to his own. Hard-bitten. Implacable. Somerville wouldn't crack. His game and his nerves were all too steady. He'd have to be beaten into submission.

Johnny wolfed down his lunch and scurried to the practice green. Somerville was already there, stolidly stroking putt after putt. The two men nodded to each other, but didn't exchange a single word. C. Ross Somerville was not Francis Ouimet.

Dry leaves blew across the first fairway. Women clapped their hands down on their brimmed hats to keep them from flying away. Johnny didn't bother to toss any grass in the air. He just raised the flat of his palm against the stiff breeze. It would be tough to reach the 424-yard par four in two now.

Both men lashed two irons on their approaches. Johnny struck his pure and into the heart of the green. Off-line, Somerville had to chip up, but he saved his par to hold on to his slender lead.

On the second, the wind was gusting behind the players. After a 275-yard drive, Goodman sailed his approach into a bunker. Popping one high out of the trap, he found himself stymied yet again, the third crucial stymie of the match, and he fell two down. It looked as if Somerville would slowly grind Johnny into the ground.

But at the par-four, 376-yard third, Goodman clawed his way back. Zeroing in on the pin, he dropped his approach ten feet from the hole. Falling short, Somerville chipped up, only to stymie Johnny yet again. But this time there was a hair's breadth of room around Somerville's ball and Johnny managed to lag a putt close and par the hole to get one back. He was only one down now.

As the two stone-faced fighters strode to the next tee box, a woman asked, "How can they stand it?"

"I can't," her companion murmured.

Then the frantic crowd swept them away.

After halving the next two holes, the players came to the gargantuan sixth hole, a 590-yard par five. Again Somerville faltered, skidding a brassie into a fairway trap. Playing with cool precision, Johnny pitched on in three and made his par, wiping out the Canadian's lead.

As Somerville trudged by, an American patriot let go a noisy raspberry. Another called out, "To hell with the redcoats."

The loyal Canadian contingent, engulfed by a sea of nationalistic Americans glowered. It seemed to them that a certain American element, a distasteful element, was getting the upper hand.

In a curious way, the Walker Cup was being played out again, in miniature.

With an unbending will, Goodman kept throwing pars at his suddenly erratic foe. On the par-four, 349-yard seventh, Johnny ripped a strong drive into the teeth of the wind, then flicked a neat short iron onto the green. Somerville lofted his approach into a steep bank behind a trap and left the difficult chip far from the hole. He could do no better than bogey, and Johnny took the lead for the first time in the afternoon round.

After halving the next hole, they came to the par-three, 179-yard ninth, the wind roaring in their faces. It took Johnny a full two iron to bang his tee shot on, but the ball landed safely on the carpet. White-lipped, the stolid Somerville took a mighty swing, trying to muscle a low three iron, but his tee shot fluttered twenty yards short. The miscue cost him yet another hole.

As they made the turn, Johnny had a shred of breathing room, a two-hole lead. More important, Somerville's wheels seemed to be flying off. In the last few holes, the Canadian had been off-line, wild and short, and he hadn't been able to knock down a single putt.

Johnny's confidence surged, and a subversive thought crept into his consciousness. He tried to beat it back, he didn't want to listen to the insistent inner voice, but the words rose in his mind against his will. He was going to win the United States Amateur.

Prickles of heat broke out on his face, and his hands tingled. His whole body was thinking the same thought, even the parts that couldn't think at all. Exercising all his mental strength, Johnny concentrated on forgetting.

But he was so pumped up he sailed his approach on the 378-yard, par-four tenth clear over the green. When he missed a six-footer for par, he surrendered half his lead. Still, a one-hole advantage was better than a one-hole deficit.

Settle down, it's a dogfight now, he told himself. One shot at a time. He knew how to win. Forget everything but the next shot and winning would take care of itself.

Back in Omaha, Tony Goodman had given up all pretense of working, once the pharmacist hauled a cabinet radio down from an apartment upstairs and installed it behind the soda fountain. Tony shuttled between a red leather stool and the pay phone, quieter now that the match had reached the homestretch.

No longer able to bear the play-by-play over the radio, Josephine threw on her flower-print dress, fumbled with the straps on her shoes, and then dashed from the house to a nearby Catholic church. Inside the great chamber, the cool air bore faint traces of incense. She surrendered to the soothing silence. Sprinkling herself first with holy water, she made her way down the aisle, knelt, and prayed that Johnny would make every putt ten feet and in.

C. Ross Somerville still seemed to have the jitters. Off the tee at the 424-yard eleventh, he hooked his drive right into the swollen gallery, the ball coming to rest in the trampled rough. Johnny slapped one in a good spot, and he breathed a sigh of relief. Let the Canadian beat himself. After Somerville punched one short of the green, Johnny promptly topped his brassie into a greenside trap.

The damn club was still plaguing him. He could hit every other stick in the bag, but the brassie still spooked him.

Somerville hit an indifferent chip, but swiftly reading his twenty-footer, he struck it hard, taking half the break out of the sweeping putt, and the ball curled in for a par. Johnny's lead had gone up in smoke.

But he didn't feel nervous. At least he didn't think so. Maybe a little lightheaded, maybe a little drained. But not nervous. Eight holes to go. Anything could happen.

They came to the 388-yard twelfth. With the honor, Somerville cracked a drive that faded gently around the right-bending dogleg. Johnny turned his head to loosen his neck. Then he whipped one straight, but rather short, a full twenty yards shy of Somerville's drive. His full mashie approach lost steam at the tail end of its flight and fluttered into a trap.

The gallery let out a collective groan. What was happening? Wasn't Johnny flying high a minute ago? Nervous coughs rippled through the gathering, but a single voice shouted out, "Come on, Johnny!"

Goodman dragged himself toward the bunker, his face expressionless. Suddenly, the gallery burst into applause. He nodded to acknowledge the friendly crowd, but it was a perfunctory gesture. He was concentrating.

The lie in the sand was perfect, though. Before climbing into the bunker, Johnny surveyed the green and picked a spot. Cutting the niblick under his ball, he looped the sand shot an inch from where he was aiming. Landing gently, the ball trickled toward the hole, where it came to rest two feet from the cup.

Now the cheers flowed freely. They came for Johnny's sand shot, for his courage, and for how much he'd given in every match. As he always did, Johnny glided quickly to his ball. After one glance at the break, he took the blade back and rapped the putt. Half the crowd broke for the next green, so they didn't see the ball rim the cup and spin out. Goodman looked down in disbelief. He'd blown the simplest two-footer in the world. A five-year-old could have canned it. It was almost too much to swallow. He'd slipped to one down now.

On the short, 141-yard thirteenth, the wind toyed with Johnny's tee shot and dropped it, cripple-winged, into yet another bunker. Somerville's drive died on the apron. Somehow, Johnny wiped the previous hole's misadventure from his mind. Yet again he cut a niblick out of the sand, yet again the ball curled toward the cup, but this time he rolled in his five-footer to save par. He'd pulled out of his tailspin, and held to only one down. Plenty of holes to go.

At the 565-yard, par-five fourteenth, Somerville aired one out off the tee, belting his drive a full thirty-five yards past Goodman's. But Johnny was in the fairway, and this time he caught his brassie flush. Both players hit clean mashies to the green and two-putted. Johnny was getting his rhythm back. He could feel it. He had pulled out of his nosedive.

After halving the fifteenth, the two men strode onto the sixteenth tee. Both of them had played brilliantly, both had suffered through bad patches, and both had recovered their bearings. Fans and reporters hadn't seen such a tight final match since way back in 1927, when George Von Elm squeaked past Bobby Jones.

Off the tee at the 402-yard sixteenth hole, the two golfers traded perfect 265-yard drives. Taking a mashie-niblick, Johnny hit first. Catching it a shade fat, he watched in dismay as the ball fell ten yards short. He'd have to stiff a chip. Somerville didn't do all that well, either, leaving his approach thirty feet short of the pin.

Johnny clipped a crisp shot off the turf. The ball hopped twice, then settled down and headed for the cup as if it had eyes. Finally, it came to rest right of the hole about four feet. An excellent effort. A makable putt.

Now it was Somerville's turn. The Canadian squinted, pressed his thin lips together. Taking a long, sweeping swipe at the ball, he sent

THE KING OF SWINGS

it on its way. It was heading straight for the hole, but did it have enough on it? Spectators craned their necks, stood on their toes. A woman in white linen couldn't stand the tension and covered her eyes.

Unwavering, the putt tracked straight at the hole and without pausing dropped to the bottom of the cup. A thirty-footer. Not a fatal blow. Just almost fatal. Somerville was now dormie two as they headed for the next tee. To stay alive Johnny needed a birdie on the seventeenth, a 155-yard par three.

Westbrook Pegler saw a "sylvan amphitheatre with the crowd, grown now to about 5,000, almost as many women as men, pressing close and breathing stertorously with the terrible suspense of the thing. Some of the elder members of the gallery were beginning to turn purplish around the ears with the pressure of their restrained emotions."

Somerville laid his iron shot thirty-five feet from the pin. Then Johnny came up just shy of the putting surface, but nothing to worry about — unless you needed a birdie to stay alive. Stoic, Johnny rapped a perfect chip at the distant pin. The ball was tracking right at the hole. Was it possible?

No, it was not. Running out of gas, the chip died a mere two feet from the cup.

Somerville struck yet another beautiful approach putt, the ball rolling inches below the hole before it came to rest. The struggle had come to an end. Goodman knew it before the bare fact registered on the spectators, who took the harsh turn of events in utter silence.

Johnny's mind raced along on two tracks. On the one hand, that two-footer he'd yanked past the hole throbbed like a toothache, and every mishit iron he'd pushed and pulled and hit fat over the final nine flashed before him. But he also knew he had a crucial role to play now: the graceful loser. He couldn't allow a shred of pique to show; he had to be restrained and gracious in defeat. The press would magnify every false step he made one-hundred-fold.

From his perch at the soda fountain, Tony Goodman conducted the postmortem. The marble counter, the shining implements for mixing malts, and the metallic grill provided an appropriate setting for dissecting the match. With professional detachment Tony drew out the cause of death, a single two-foot shot to his brother's heart, and held it up for inspection.

Gliding home from the church, Josephine did not yet know Johnny's fate, but she felt quieter now, shrouded as she was in the believer's stoicism. Win or lose, Johnny had performed a miracle as far as she was concerned, and there would be other matches, bigger still, she was sure.

Quickly, Johnny offered his hand to the victor, working up a weak smile as well. It had been a bitter loss, but he also felt a sense of relief. The terrible pressure had lifted. The match was over. A thin smile played on Somerville's hawkish face as he took his game opponent's hand.

Still the gallery didn't react. America's banner was dragging in the dust. The spectators couldn't seem to muster enough goodwill toward the northern invader to cheer his feat. It was awkward. Johnny held on to the Canadian's hand an extra moment, silently urging the crowd to show a bit of generosity.

Finally, a photographer broke the impasse. "Everybody cheer for the picture!" he shouted.

Now the applause broke out, and a few strained yelps as well. C. Ross Somerville, a Canadian and citizen of the British Commonwealth, was the 1932 U.S. Amateur champion.

After Somerville was awarded the cup, USGA president Herbert H. Ramsey drew Johnny aside, out of earshot of the throng of reporters. Bowing to the inevitable, he allowed that as far as the next Walker Cup was concerned, Johnny had nothing to worry about.

Johnny nodded slightly and whispered his thanks. It was all quite cordial.

27

BOBBY JONES HADN'T stroked a golf ball in competition in over two years, but if anything, he had grown in stature. His grand slam was beginning to take on a mythic status, and now his image was being projected in thousands of theaters all over the country so that Americans who never had the slightest interest in the vagaries of golf were being exposed to the Atlantan's graceful ball-striking and seductive Georgia drawl. *How I Play Golf*, the Warner Brothers' series featuring Jones wending his way through silly scenarios while imparting his secrets of the game, had been a smashing success. On screen Bobby had a natural presence, and having slimmed down to 175 pounds for his movie debut, he'd never looked better in his plus fours.

It seemed that Jones was everywhere, on the silver screen, reminiscing about his great matches on his own radio show, sharing tips in his golf column, and pushing goods in the pro shop, where his steel-shafted Robt. T. Jones clubs were offered for sale. This was a new Bobby Jones, the commercial colossus. Adding his piece of the take at the box office, he had more than realized the reported $250,000 Warner Brothers had guaranteed. To put this sum in perspective, during the same period an average family could get by, considering plunging Depression prices, on $1,500 a year.

That Jones had cashed in on his golfing prowess was hardly a secret. The Depression-era public, always eager to forget its own troubles and dream of better times, thrilled to the numbers printed next to his name, numbers that represented the most profitable scores of his life. During the winter of 1933, when fifty men were observed fighting over the contents of a single garbage can in Chicago, Warner Brothers picked up its option on Bobby Jones's contract, and he took a private car out to Hollywood to crank out six more shorts. *How to Break Ninety,* directed by George E. Marshal, was shot with the aid of recently invented slow-motion technology. Of course, it was a smashing success.

At this turning point in the culture of American amateur golf, when commerce was being legitimized by the greatest amateur of them all, Hollywood came knocking at Johnny Goodman's door. Remarkably, when Goodman was offered his own deal to star in a series of short instructional films, he turned it down flat. How much money producers waved in Goodman's face remains a mystery. Certainly, it was nowhere near the fortune the movie business was lavishing on Bobby Jones, but considering that Johnny's insurance venture had proven anything but a bonanza, and that he still couldn't afford his own apartment, Goodman's commitment to the amateur game could hardly be questioned anymore.

Goodman had been deeply wounded by the allegations that had been hurled at him over the years. His character and intentions had been called into question time and time again. The only way to prove that his motives had always been aboveboard was to sacrifice his commercial prospects. Unlike George Von Elm, he *was* willing to give up everything so that he could hear the starter say *Mr.* Goodman on the first tee of every tournament. In that sense Johnny Goodman was the most principled amateur of them all.

He also turned aside several propositions to turn pro. "Am I going to remain an amateur? You bet I am, and what's more I'm going to keep on trying to win the U.S. Amateur," Johnny told the Omaha newsman Ralph Wagner.

Johnny knew quite well how hard it was for a touring pro to make a living. He knew all about the grind on the road, and about the paltry purses. Still, after his gritty performance at Five Farms, with his name splashed across every sports page in the country, he might have pursued the sort of cushy club job that Tommy Armour and other top players had settled into. Despite the fact that country clubs had fallen on hard Depression times, there were jobs out there for the best amateur golfer in America, if only he'd take the money and surrender his amateur status.

Johnny also might have barnstormed like Hagen and Sarazen and chased endorsement deals as well. To understand what Goodman was giving up, consider how Gene Sarazen capitalized on his own sudden fame.

Sarazen set the standard for seizing his opportunities after he won the U.S. Open and the PGA in 1922. Barely out of his teens, and without a shred of business experience, he threw himself into every profitable venture he could lay his hands on. "When I became a champion in 1922, I was out to leave no stone unturned. I had spent too many years working for Indian nuts not to strike while my irons were hot," Sarazen wrote.

"In addition to my tie up with the Hearst newspapers, I endorsed everything from a new type of spikes to a cartridge for shotguns; I started a golf correspondence school under the aegis of Billy Gibson, Gene Tunney's manager; I made movie shorts with Linde Fowler; I wrote a book in which I set down my method for playing golf; I began my pleasant, profitable relationship with the Wilson Sporting Goods company as the first golfer on their advisory staff . . .

"I obtained a release from my contract with the Highland Country Club so that I could accept a salary at four times the amount they were paying me with the Briarcliff Lodge . . . I snatched up all the offers I could fit in to play exhibition matches at from $250 to $350 a performance. I tried to keep on the alert for the hundreds who lie in wait for any inexperienced person with earning power."

Few golfers could match Sarazen's whirlwind of activity, and many of Sarazen's creative ideas were novel for their time. Only Hagen, with his endless barnstorming and canny endorsement deals, had a similar eye for the main chance, though Sir Walter gambled and lost as often as he won.

But Sarazen's account of his moneymaking intrigues stands in stark contrast to Johnny Goodman's refusal to cash in on his own fame. However quaint it might sound today, Goodman stuck to his ideals. His commitment to the vision of the immaculate amateur cost him far more than most of the amateur game's practitioners who, like Travers, Jones, and Somerville, could afford their unblemished status.

However, in Goodman's mind, all the complex calculations about whether or not to join the professional ranks paled in comparison to one dream: maybe, just maybe, he'd become the next Bobby Jones. It may have seemed like a wild fantasy for a former South Omaha caddie, but perched on the pinnacle of America's amateur golf world, Johnny Goodman had earned the right to dream.

Clearly, his fixation on Bobby Jones had not abated. After negotiating perilous political waters by insisting to reporters that H. H. Ramsey had treated him "just fine," Johnny burst out with a grandiose plan.

If he was going to travel to England to play on the Walker Cup team in two years, he would have a shot at both the British Amateur and the British Open. "I want to pull a Bobby Jones and believe me I'm going to try for that end. That may sound foolish to some folks, but that's what I'm going to set my heart on doing," he told the *World-Herald*.

Unfortunately, as soon as Bobby Jones fell into Warner Brothers' embrace, the allure of the amateur ethic began to fade. The Depression made amateurism look faintly absurd. Once Americans had thrilled to Jones's modesty and self-denial. Now they got their vicarious kicks out of Bobby's big payday. Like courtly love, simon-purity had become archaic.

Just as amateurism was losing its luster, Johnny Goodman chose to embrace it all the more tightly. Like his worst detractors, H. H. Ramsey and A. H. Gregson, Goodman was defending the old values. He was allying himself with the USGA despite the best efforts of its higher ups to spurn him. In a striking irony that seems to have escaped his critics, Goodman had become amateur golf's last white knight.

No doubt Goodman believed that with the help of amateur golf stardom he could succeed in business, but his attempts to spin his fame into gold were always halfhearted. Making money would always play second fiddle to golf.

To serve what he had grown up believing was a higher code of behavior, Goodman acted against his own self-interest, and he knew it. In that sense, he was a true believer through and through.

While the press pursued its ritual search for the next Bobby Jones, it was difficult to see that the old ideals had gone out of fashion, but another man in Goodman's position, a man with just a trace of Sarazen's commercial acumen, would have taken hold of his opportunities. All Johnny Goodman could think about was winning the next big tournament — and the one after that.

While Johnny was selecting his vocabulary to please the USGA's potentates, the local papers were still happily stirring the fires of class conflict. In its 1932 U.S. Amateur postmortem, the *Omaha World-Herald's* Sportlog column fired one last shot at the golfing establishment. "Johnny's thorough subjugation of his fellow citizens on the Five Farms pastures was pretty generally regarded as a triumph of golf the game over *gahlf* the social accomplishment, even by those who received Johnny's achievement with sighs of regret and remarks to the effect that all was now lost because the bars were let completely down.

"The only section of golfdom that did not greet Master John's feat with delirious and reckless whoops was composed chiefly of the *gahlf* nuts, who like the bosses of the Republican party are hot for the prestige and prosperity of the favored few."

Bursting with regional pride, Sportlog went on to point out that midwestern golf was a far more democratic creature than its snooty eastern cousin. In Nebraska, the unsigned column asserted, bankers played with janitors, and businessman rubbed shoulders with the common man.

Of course, meatpackers couldn't afford the dues at the Omaha Field Club, and the lower middle classes had to seek out more modestly priced courses. Still, there was some truth in the *World Herald's* claim.

Omaha's emotional gravity held Johnny in its orbit. Josephine was there, as well as his brothers, his sisters, and his legions of boosters. In the months following his 1932 U.S. Amateur run, Johnny's name was everywhere. The Orpheum featured a film of his U.S. Amateur exploits. The posh Elms Hotel promised a golf weekend starring Johnny. A full-page *World-Herald* ad read "Omaha Is Proud of You, Johnny" and was graced by a picture of Goodman finishing a full swing. When Johnny bowled, it was news. When he caught a cold and couldn't play a match with Chick Evans, it was news. When he hit golf balls at the Brandeis Department Store, that was news, too.

As the Hoover regime ground to its close, the country was hit by the worst wave of bank failures in history. Bankers and Wall Street brokers, the most respectable figures of the previous decade, were hauled before the Senate Banking Committee, which presented a spectacle of stock manipulators, inside traders, crooked bankers, and architects of corporate pyramid schemes that would have been entertaining had its star players not fleeced an entire country.

All of the corruption that underlay the stock market crash was best summarized when Samuel Insull, the wealthy and influential utilities baron whose schemes had left investors in ruins, remarked: "What have I done that every banker and business magnate has not done in the course of business?"

Sometimes it seemed as if the only people thriving during the Depression were movie stars and bootleggers. A vibrant new genre, the gangster film, reflected the moment, and the winds of cultural change. In the 1931 film *Little Caesar,* Edward G. Robinson plays a rapacious criminal, Rico Bandello, who takes pride in his amoral business practices. Ultimately, Rico goes down in the usual hail of gunfire. The cold and crooked businessman of the past gets his comeuppance, and the audience derives the contradictory pleasures of identifying with the rebellious Rico and watching him eat lead for the evil of his ways.

Hollywood had discovered gold in preaching against acquisitive men.

Like most people living through the Depression's early years, Johnny Goodman didn't fully comprehend how much American conditions were shifting, and how fast. Only three years before, the stock market had been doing a credible imitation of El Dorado, and golf tournaments were awash in all the signs of unending prosperity: fine cars, beautiful clothes, lavish meals, docile servants, and society reporters eager to spread the word of the unending, if dignified, party.

By 1932, President Hoover was reduced to claiming that "nobody is actually starving." However, Congressman George Huddleston offered a more convincing portrait of the country's plight. "I do not mean to say that they are sitting down and not getting a bite of food until they actually die, but they are living such a scrambling, precarious existence, with suffering from lack of clothing, fuel and nourishment, until they are subject to being swept away, and many now are being swept away."

When the old laissez-faire medicine didn't revive America's fortunes, President Hoover's allies were puzzled. Confusion reigned on Wall Street and in the offices of the leading industrialists. On the farm, and in unemployment-ravaged cities, revolt was in the air. America's small bands of leftists and intellectuals believed they were witnessing capitalism's death throes, but couldn't agree on how to dance on the old system's grave. In defense of all that true Americans held dear, the Daughters of the American Revolution urged crossing guards to use green flags instead of red, so that children wouldn't be conditioned to obey the flag of revolution.

Few pursuits could have been less in tune with the times than amateur golf. No matter. Johnny Goodman stuck single-mindedly to his dream.

28

SUSPENDED ON SKELETAL IRON LEGS, an orange-striped black water tank loomed over the flat landscape of the North Shore Links in Glenville, Illinois. In the run-up to the first round of the 1933 U.S. Open, an early June wind as hot as a North African sirocco began to blow, but it brought no relief from the scalding sun. At best the breeze fluttered the dry, dusty leaves of the oaks, maples, and cottonwoods that dotted the thirsty fairways.

The heat was a dizzying, spots-before-the-eyes heat, striking spectators with a palpable force. Seated on white slats in the roofless bleachers at the ninth and eighteenth holes, the crowd itself was reflected whiteness, white shirts, white chiffon, white crêpe de Chine. Women in silk sports frocks offered up bare backs to the unforgiving sun, their white skin blistering for the sake of fashion. Men tipped white Panamas over their foreheads to make their own patches of shade.

The dryness coated tongues, parched throats, and sent spectators scurrying to the ice cream and beer vendors arrayed along the club's piazza, where bright-colored paper Japanese parasols were also for sale. The flimsy umbrellas did no good. Everywhere, the fiery sun prevailed.

North Shore stretched a full 6,927 yards and appeared to be a long-hitter's course, but the sun-baked track was hard as asphalt. A good drive could roll forever. However, North Shore was also dangerously tight. Accuracy would count for far more than raw driving distance. As wire service reporter Davis Walsh remarked, "The fairways start out narrow and then sharpen to a mere footpath, so that only the perfect tee shot avoids the rough. The rough is like a matted beard. Some say it needs a niblick. Perhaps I'd prefer a scythe."

Noting that most experts favored Sarazen, the previous year's champion, Walsh wondered if 1933 wouldn't be an outsider's year. Maybe Paul Runyon, Denny Shute, or Johnny Goodman would snatch the crown. Others mentioned Hagen, Cruickshank, or MacDonald Smith. Young stars like Craig Wood and Johnny Revolta came up as well. The Black Scot, Tommy Armour, was always in the mix, too.

In American professional golf's Holy Trinity, Hagen was the Father, Sarazen the Son, and Armour the Holy Ghost, Al Barkow observed. Armour's unique talent was rooted in his long, sinewy fingers. His whistling irons, the wonder of his time, had helped him win the 1927 U.S. Open, the 1930 PGA, and the 1931 British Open.

A machine gunner for the Tank Corps during World War I, Armour had lost the sight in one eye during combat. In his left shoulder he carried eight pieces of shrapnel. The Black Scot from Edinburgh's Braid Hills had a taste for eye patches, fine whiskey, and spicy tales. If he got a few under his belt, he didn't mind recounting how he had killed a German with his bare hands in the Great War. He could stand at a bar with Walter Hagen, knock back a string of drinks, trade tall stories, and if a suitable amount of money was on offer, extend his arm and hold the length of a pool cue perfectly erect using only his thumb and forefinger.

In the opening round at North Shore, Armour put on a demonstration of his formidable skills. In the crushing heat — temperatures hovered just below one hundred degrees — Tommy broke Al Espinosa's course record of 69 by one shot. After struggling through the inferno-like conditions, the Black Scot settled into the clubhouse's cool shadows, a stiff drink in hand. It was only the first round, but a five-shot lead did taste sweet. His nearest professional pursuers, Craig Wood, Johnny Revolta, Henry Ciuci, and Walter Hagen, could do no better than 73.

Hagen had won the 1932 Western Open, still considered a major affair, and on his southern swing during the winter of 1933, he had snagged the Charleston Open as well, but Sir Walter had been seized by an ailment that suited his age — the dreaded yips. The buccaneer who had never thought twice about banging ten-footers into the back of the cup began agonizing over the short ones. In desperation he shifted from his crouching, wide stance to Bobby Jones's more upright approach, but nothing much helped. He made brave predictions to the press about yet another comeback, but his killing stroke seemed to have deserted him for good. Sir Walter had become mortal.

The favorite and defending champion, Gene Sarazen, who had also swept the 1932 British Open, managed a two over 74, joining Ky Lafoon at six strokes behind the leader.

Stumbling out of the gate, Johnny Goodman blew three short putts, making the turn in a mediocre 39. In danger of shooting himself out of the tournament, Goodman fought off the slide on the back nine by balancing a pair of bogeys with two birdies for an even par 36. In the early going, he'd fallen a full seven shots back, but excepting Armour, he was only two behind the rest of the field.

At the start of the second round, only a handful of curious fans straggled along with Goodman after he cracked a straight drive down the first fairway. Josephine joined the threadbare gallery. She hadn't been able to bear listening to Johnny's 1932 U.S. Amateur battle on the radio, but now, watching him take this casual stroll over the close-cut grass, the golfing wars seemed more tolerable. In reality, the game wasn't all that tense, she thought. Announcers just exaggerated to make tournaments more exciting. The one thing she dreaded were those pushy reporters, but Johnny always did his best to protect her and keep her name out of the papers.

Goodman planned to stick to his program. Forget the bad shots, remember the good ones, and take a walk with Old Man Par. He didn't think about Armour or Sarazen or Revolta. If he played steady golf, he'd stay in the hunt.

His first drive had carried a fairway trap on the left of the 439-yard par four. A crisp long iron left him twenty feet from the pin. Following his swift routine, he deciphered the right-to-left line, took one practice stroke to measure the distance, and rolled the putt in. Nice start.

On the second, a short par five of 489 yards, he hit a perfect drive and followed it up with a sensational two iron. The ball bounced on the front edge of the putting surface and skittered to a stop ten feet short of the flagstick. His eagle putt just slid by the hole, but he tapped in for his second bird.

Johnny's solid mashie tee shot off the third tee settled four feet from the pin on the kidney-shaped third green. He barely paused before poking in his third birdie in a row.

Josephine noticed that two more onlookers had joined the gallery, a tall woman in a white linen dress and a bowl-shaped hat and a potbellied man with a big brush of a mustache. He looked like that comedian in the Laurel and Hardy movies, the one who always flew into a rage.

Up ahead, Tommy Armour had come back to earth. On the first hole, the rough, a greenside trap, and a balky putter had added up to a double-bogey six. Armour promptly bogeyed the second. Two birdies helped the Black Scot make the turn only one over, but he had a different look about him. He was waggling the club more, and his shoulders slumped as if he were carrying some extra burden. The pleasure had leaked out of his game. Tommy Armour was working at it now.

Goodman made his first error on the par-four, 447-yard fourth, dropping his approach into a trap. Blasting out without much trouble, he left himself an eight-footer for par. In a world of his own, he rapped the ball hard, taking the break right out of it. The ball was rattling around in the bottom of the cup before he looked up. When he was playing well he always tapped them firm. He was starting to feel it now.

A simple niblick to the green on the 353-yard, par-four fifth left Johnny with a seven-footer. The hole looked as big as a dinner plate now. He banged another one home for his fourth bird in five holes. When he lifted his head he noticed the excited gallery. Dozens of new faces were staring at him. Where had they come from? Where was Josephine?

Not wanting to distract him, Josephine had faded back behind the ranks of fresh onlookers. How did they find out Johnny was on a hot streak? Was there some secret telegraph wire running under the rolling hills?

As soon as Johnny dropped his fourth birdie, the mob broke for the next tee, trampling through a stand of woods, swirling around the next tee box, racing to line the fairway, humming like some human hive. Josephine stood on her toes to catch a glimpse of Johnny above the sea of straw hats, flat-brimmed hats with bright bands, snap-brimmed hats with dark bands. Even on this sweltering day some of the men wore long-sleeved white shirts and ties and the women long dresses that fell almost to their ankles. The days of rolled-down stockings and exposed knees seemed like a distant memory.

Suddenly there Johnny stood, his face burned by the sun, his blue eyes glinting. He looked serious but serene at the same time. Josephine wondered how he could stand to be so *exposed*. With all those eyes on her, she would just die.

"Armour's tanking," a man with a flushed face informed his neighbor.

Racing to the sixth tee, another golf fanatic burst out, "I heard Goodman's going low."

"Hot as a pistol," an onlooker informed him with the air of an insider passing on privileged information.

Josephine listened to these snatches of conversation with amusement. You'd think they were making all these impossible shots themselves.

Johnny glided through the next two holes in conventional fashion, but on the eighth, a 229-yard par three, an errant spoon sent his ball into a greenside trap. The ball was buried. Without much choice, he blasted out forty feet from the pin. Now he faced his first sure bogey. His best bet was to lag it close and take his medicine — he wanted to avoid a bigger number at all costs. For the first time that day he eyed a putt with apprehension.

Then he saw the swooping line with preternatural clarity and he didn't delay. Taking his long, fluid stroke, his putter low to the ground, he struck the ball right on the club's sweet spot. When he looked up he could see the dimpled ball holding the line like a planet in elliptical orbit. One more heartbeat and the black hole swallowed it up.

Starting on a low note, a roar rose step by step from the gallery. Josephine covered her ears. This was worse, much worse, than listening on the radio. She couldn't breathe; she couldn't escape the jostling crowd.

Up ahead Tommy Armour was struggling to put together a two-over performance on the back nine. Soon he would be in the clubhouse with a 75. By now the fickle fans had deserted the Black Scot en masse, swirling around Johnny Goodman instead. The defending champion Sarazen was falling completely out of contention after blowing sky-high with a 77.

One top player was coming on, though. Joe Kirkwood, the same trick-shot artist who had mesmerized Johnny Goodman when he was caddying at the Field Club, was blending five birdies and three bogeys to fashion a two under 70. And a more obscure young golfer, a twenty-one-year-old public course player from Texas, Ralph Guldahl, had crept into contention after adding a 71 to his opening round of 76. Olin Dutra and Craig Wood also stayed within striking distance of the lead.

After parring the ninth, a 408-yard par four, without incident, Goodman made the turn in a blazing 32. No one wanted to ask the question, least of all Goodman's Omaha contingent, but how could he possibly sustain the pace?

When he dumped another approach into a trap, this time on the tenth, a 446-yard par four, it looked as if he was in danger of going over par for the first time, but yet again his putter saved him, from twelve feet away.

The relatively short eleventh, a 349-yard par four, featured a hog-backed fairway that produced unpredictable bounces. Goodman struck a drive dead straight, only to find his ball nestled in a tough lie. He handled this obstacle with aplomb, then promptly three-putted for the first time.

Wielding a cane, an amateur expert in an opera hat declared that he knew what was coming next. Like every other golfer who played some holes over his head, Goodman would proceed to come apart at the seams. Josephine shot this detractor a sour glance, but her heart sank. For some mysterious reason Johnny had weakened in the stretch against Somerville. What would keep him from doing the same now?

But Johnny Goodman had found a stillness inside himself, a core of silence. Nothing could ruffle him now. Instead of buckling, Goodman reeled off three straight pars. At the 511-yard, par-five fifteenth, a dogleg left, Johnny hit a solid drive and followed it with a strong brassie, leaving him dead center with a niblick to the green. Taking a single practice stroke, he probed the air, sensing the distance. Then he clipped the ball, hitting it lower than usual in an attempt to run it up from the fringe. Landing precisely where he had aimed, the ball skipped right toward the pin. Dead at it.

Leaning against the back side of the cup, the flagstick acted like a backstop. With a soft click, the ball struck the pole and wedged itself halfway into the hole. Racing to the putting surface, Johnny and his scorer, Ted Payseur, an assistant basketball coach at Northwestern, surveyed the situation. Then, ever so gently, Payseur maneuvered the pin out of the cup and the ball dropped in for an eagle three.

And Johnny Goodman, so often accused of being too grim on the golf course, did an impromptu dance. Coming to his senses, he recognized a familiar round, cherubic face, a strand of black hair straying onto a broad forehead — the inescapable Bobby Jones. For a brief moment Johnny fixed his eyes on Bobby, who was covering the tournament for his syndicated column. Bobby offered a slight nod of recognition.

Then, within earshot of the Omaha contingent, Jones remarked to a USGA official, "Well, if he's going to win, we might as well give it to him with good grace."

"Luck, just luck," the USGA's man fumed.

The substance of this exchange was quickly communicated to Stanley Davies, who stormed to the defense of his protégé. After making his apologies for intruding on Jones and his companion, the tall, florid-faced golf pro went to the heart of the matter. "If you'll pardon plain English, that little fellow," he snapped, jerking his thumb in Johnny's direction, "has all the guts that this little fellow ever had."

His tone pure acid, Davies stared pointedly at Jones. Then, in his best Scotch accent, the Field Club professional added one more pointed remark. "And furthermore, if you want more comparisons," he said, nodding in Johnny's direction, "he hasn't had near the luck."

A welter of emotions drove Stanley Davies's outburst. First and foremost, he was responding to the USGA's shabby treatment of Goodman, but there was more than that behind his rage. A lifetime of observing the way the USGA concentrated its power in the East, and the august way it issued its often-contradictory rulings, also fueled his resentment. After making a perfunctory show of manners, Davies withdrew back into the gallery, scarcely believing what he had just done, but too angry to care.

Goodman, who never witnessed the confrontation, shook his head at his own good fortune. He'd been playing lights out, but the eagle was almost too much to ask for. He'd have to keep his bearings.

Half-joking, Francis Powers sidled up to the elated golfer and asked, "Has the heat affected you?"

"Something has, certainly," the grinning Goodman replied. How could he explain it? He felt so fluid. His weight shift, his timing, his extension were all one, a single thoughtless muscle in flight.

One under par on the back, Johnny came to the seventeenth, a 423-yard par four that had flummoxed several of the leaders that day. Goodman sailed his approach over the green, but again chipped it close to save par.

The eighteenth, another difficult par four, 437 yards long, would act as the final test. Five under as he strode to the eighteenth, Johnny thought it made sense to play for par and protect his lead. He smacked yet another strong drive, but the ball strayed slightly from the short grass, nestling just off the left side of the fairway. Johnny was presented with a peculiar lie, half in and half out of the rough.

His best bet would be a low runner. Just play it back and roll it into the heart of the green, he told himself. Taking a firm grip to keep the clubface from closing in the long grass, he hit a midiron and watched it strike short of the green, take one, then two bright hops on the sun-backed fairway, and roll dead at the pin. He felt no surprise. It was uncanny. Everything he did turned up aces.

The ball came to rest four feet from the hole. Several policemen maneuvered into the front ranks of the unruly gallery. An otherworldly look on his face, the slender Goodman marched onto the putting surface, then patiently waited while his playing partner, Billy Burke, lagged his approach putt close and tapped in.

Then Johnny drew his putter back and rolled in another bird, easy as pie. With that final nudge of his putter, he shattered the course record by two shots, tying Sarazen's U.S. Open record of 66 into the bargain. Better still, he had seized the lead.

Now the crowd surged toward him, swarming onto the green to get close to the diminutive man in white, to see his face, to touch his sleeve, to rub against him. Buried deep in the gallery, Josephine stood rooted to the ground in a state of terror, certain Johnny would get trampled.

Then the local cops sprang into action, fighting their way through the mob, pressing themselves tight around the dazed golfer and bearing him toward the clubhouse.

In the locker room, Johnny calmly submitted to a rain of questions from admirers and reporters alike. He smiled, signed autographs, chatted with newsmen, maintaining an eerie composure.

Reporters pressed him to relate his "best shot" of the day.

"The shot that felt best got me in trouble," he answered thoughtfully. "It was a perfectly hit iron to the fifth green, but it kicked into a trap."

"Who's the good-looking number following you around, Johnny?" another scribe demanded.

A dark look flashed across Goodman's drawn, tanned features. "No, you can't have her name. Can't a fellow have a date now and then without getting his girl in the papers?"

Then he spied Bill Schwartz, an old friend from St. Louis, and his mood shifted. "I sank another niblick, Bill," he called out. Now he was the picture of pure pleasure. He'd pulled off a small miracle, and he wasn't about to be shy about it.

"Did you get a bigger kick out of this round than the one at Pebble Beach?" a newsman called out.

Everybody knew what the sportswriter was talking about. The twenty-two-year-old Goodman might as well have had Bobby Jones's name tattooed on his forehead. "Yes, I know more now," Johnny replied.

The reporters knew exactly what Johnny was talking about. Experience had taught Johnny golf's perverse nature, making the game all the more difficult.

"If anyone had been rash enough Thursday to predict that Tommy Armour would be ousted from the lead before last night, that anyone would gain nine strokes on the Scot in one round, he would have been put off the grounds," Bobby Jones wrote in his syndicated column. "Yet that is what Johnny Goodman did in one of the most sensational uprisings in the history of the Open championship."

Whether influenced by his confrontation with Stanley Davies or not, Jones gave Johnny Goodman his due. Without striking a single blow, Bobby still hovered over the proceedings, but with these words he passed the amateurs' torch to his old tormentor. Modestly excepting himself from the equation, Jones went on. "For the past four or five years he [Goodman] has been about the most reliable performer year in and year out that the amateur ranks have been able to exhibit." In the mad scramble to anoint the new Bobby Jones, the Atlanta wizard had pronounced his own benediction.

But Tommy Armour stood only two strokes behind, and the trick-shot magician, Joe Kirkwood, was only three back. Olin Dutra, Craig Wood, and Ralph Guldahl all were within striking distance. Two hard rounds against the best players in the world had yet to be played.

29

AS REPORTS OF JOHNNY'S record-shattering round filtered back to Omaha, Pete Lyck, Johnny's boss and four-ball partner, paced up and back in his office. He had tried to do the right thing, to keep an eye on business instead of wasting time traveling to the big tournament, but now he could stand it no longer. Hanging an OUT TO LUNCH sign on the office door, Lyck raced to the municipal airport to catch the last flight to Chicago.

During Goodman's crucial rounds, Omaha merchants rolled up their flags and stayed inside their stores, catching the blow-by-blow accounts. The lights on the *World-Herald's* switchboard flashed madly. Everybody in town wanted to know the latest on Johnny. So jammed were the lines, reporters couldn't make outgoing calls all day. As the newspaper put it, "Many callers apparently didn't know a spoon from a butter knife, but they were excited anyway."

An early morning rain drenched North Shore's fairways and greens. To augment the downpour, the greenskeeper turned on the club's state-of-the-art $125,000 sprinkler system, hoping to soften putting surfaces that had turned so hard it was impossible to spin a ball to a stop on them. Unfortunately, a stiff west wind kicked up, quickly drying out the drenched grass. In the morning the greens were more receptive, but by the afternoon the midwestern track was hard and fast again.

Johnny Goodman's scintillating 66 had been ballyhooed and chewed to a pulp by the time he stepped up to the tee for the final two rounds. In his syndicated column, Gene Sarazen went so far as to say, "Given a few breaks today we may see another Francis Ouimet pop up and amaze the country with a triumph over the professionals. It would be a bit ironical if the man who beat Bobby Jones at Pebble Beach in 1929 should bob up to carry on where Bobby left off."

Sarazen, who had every intention of frustrating Goodman's assault on professional honor, had also suggested that his old rival, Walter Hagen, would do better to take to his rocking chair and watch the tournament from a restful vantage point. The Haig, who caught wind of this crack, wasn't amused.

After his mediocre performance in the first round, Hagen had commented that North Shore's fairways were pretty narrow. Sarazen jabbed the needle in a second time. "Well, they would look narrow to a man of forty," Gene opined.

No one had expected Goodman to go off like a skyrocket and sail into the lead, but now all eyes were on him; every shot he made would be dissected by experts and half-baked geniuses alike. Like every half-point leader of a major tournament, he was about to submit to a thirty-six-hole grindstone.

Johnny was joined on the first tee by his playing partner, MacDonald Smith, who had placed second in the U.S. Open two years before Johnny was born. Smith's older brother Willie had won the Open in 1899, and his brother Alex had taken the American crown twice, in 1906 and again in 1910 when he beat Mac in a playoff. (Alex was the author of the cheerful golf philosophy whose credo was "Miss 'em quick.") With roots going back to the first Scottish invasion of the American game, MacDonald Smith was a piece of walking history.

In the 1925 British Open at Prestwick, with his closest rival Jim Barnes in with a 74, Mac had needed a mere 79 to tie, and a 78 to win, a feat which for the Scot was "simple as stirring sugar," according to *The New Yorker* golf writer Herbert Warren Wind. Faced with this elementary task, Smith began to overthink every shot, blowing sky-high on the front nine with a 42. Worse still, with his adoring countrymen shouting encouragement and choking the fairways,

Old Mac had to wait ten minutes between shots on his way in to the clubhouse. Finally, he crawled off the course with a humiliating 82.

"The grim old bloodhound," as Wind called him, had come within three strokes of winning the British and U.S. Opens eight times. A ghost of frustrations past, Old Mac, whose career was well known to the autodidact Goodman, might have seemed like a bad-luck charm had it not been for his benign temperament.

The two men made a striking contrast on the first tee. The bare-headed Goodman, the picture of confident youth, appeared in an open-throated white shirt and gray slacks. Sensitive to changing styles, Johnny had left his favorite knickers in the closet. Not Mac-Donald Smith. In a traditional flat cap and fresh plus fours, Old Mac stepped onto the tee box, a cigarette dangling from his mouth.

With his controlled, modern swing, Johnny lashed a perfect drive. Utilizing his long flat stroke, a byproduct of a forgotten era, Smith produced the same result. An army of fans tramped after the two men, joining the dense lines of golf aficionados who crowded onto the edge of the first fairway.

Johnny Goodman had to do it all over again, and then one more time again. He knew he couldn't let up. After carding a par on the first, Goodman drove into the rough on the par-five second. After extricating himself from the long grass, he pitched to fifteen feet and promptly rolled in his birdie putt. The thousands-strong gallery erupted in cheers and applause. Omaha's Johnny was their Johnny too now. His putter still had the magic.

Old Mac matched Johnny's bird, and the two men strolled to the third tee. Goodman appeared far more relaxed than his tense Omaha boosters. Even if he could manage to keep his late collapse against Ross Somerville out of his mind, they could not. Johnny's mentor, Stanley Davies, with his eye for technique, watched for signs of tension, an aborted follow-through, a jabbing stroke on the green.

Innocent of golf's mysteries, Josephine kept a searching eye on Johnny's face for the subtle signs of emotion he hid so well from sportswriters and fans alike: lips pouting in self-disgust, V-shaped furrows deepening on his brow.

But Johnny just played golf, serenely sailing from the occasional mishap to the perfect recovery shot. On the 447-yard, par-four fourth, after a poor drive, he chose to play a safe shot. (Hearing later about Goodman's strategy on this hole, Gene Sarazen remarked, scornfully, that playing safe was not the way to win championships.) After a chip to five feet, Goodman missed the putt for his first bogey.

After parring the fifth, he needed a thirty-five-footer to save par on the sixth. Once again his putter rescued him — his exploits with the flat stick flirting with the miraculous by now — as the cross-country putt dropped in.

After shooting par on the seventh, he missed his tee shot on the eighth and had to settle for another bogey. No matter. On the 408-yard, par-four ninth, he laid his approach ten feet from the pin and stroked another one in for his birdie. His game well in hand, he made the turn in even par.

Meanwhile, Tommy Armour, his golf creaking and groaning, mixed bogeys and occasional birdies as he slowly gave ground. At the turn he was three down. Joe Kirkwood fared worse still, sailing to a full 40, four over on the front nine. Sarazen was conceding one stroke after another to par. Walter Hagen was fading, too, unable to raise the ghost of his former genius. Only Craig Wood and the obscure Ralph Guldahl were negotiating North Shore's glassy greens as well as Goodman.

Mac Smith, too, had fallen out of contention, contenting himself with enjoying his young partner's apparent march to victory. On the back nine, Johnny didn't disappoint the old bloodhound, or his raucous fans.

On the par-four tenth hole, Johnny hit a 250-yard drive dead center, a solid four iron to four feet, and dropped the short one for his third birdie of the round. On the 522-yard, par-five twelfth, he ran into a spot of trouble. Yanking his second shot into the rough, he had to contend with the long grass. From this unpredictable lie, the pumped-up Goodman muscled the ball clear over the green.

As he faced the long, delicate chip, spectators noticed a faint smile on the usually impassive golfer's lips. He seemed to know what was coming next. Cool and confident, he picked the ball clean and watched it die one foot from the hole. Every stroke seemed fluid, dreamlike. In this state, stone-dead sixty-foot chips felt routine.

On the next two holes, he was on in regulation but missed a ten-footer and a fifteen-footer in succession. He was almost surprised. Pars felt like consolation prizes. On the par-three, 160-yard sixteenth, he cut down his swing and punched a two iron through a stiff crosswind. The low shot had plenty of bite on it, spinning to a stop three feet from the pin. Somehow, he'd managed to hold a putting surface that had more in common with concrete than turf. Birdies came that easy.

As he stood on the eighteenth, Johnny needed one more par to come in at two under 70 for the morning round. Mac Smith shook his head in appreciation. The kid was in full sail, a wonder to behold. He'd seen that look before, on other faces in long-forgotten times. He'd even seen it once or twice in the mirror.

On the 437-yard, par-four eighteenth, Johnny's long-iron approach fell short. He took one glance at the lay of the land and formed a mental target around the hole. His sensitive hands fairly tingled. Then he put his long, silky stroke on the ball and it rolled true, never wavering until it died a few feet from the flagstick. The short putt was a foregone conclusion. A heartbeat later, the diminutive Goodman disappeared in a swirl of white shirts, straw hats bobbing on the surf of the roiling gallery.

In the second round, Goodman's putting had been otherworldly. In the third, his chipping had the stamp of genius. His 211 for three rounds left the rest of the field gasping for breath. Only the tall, slump-shouldered Ralph Guldahl had matched Johnny's morning round, but Guldahl, in sole possession of second place, had started well back of the leader and at 217 remained stuck, six strokes behind. Playing steadily, Craig Wood stood another shot back. The defending champion Gene Sarazen, Joe Kirkwood, and Walter Hagen had all fallen back, seemingly out of contention.

To some observers the real question now was whether Johnny would break the U.S. Open record, held jointly by Sarazen and Chick Evans. Two over 74 would do the trick, child's play the way Goodman was performing.

Johnny ate a light cottage cheese lunch. He didn't want to feel logy going out for the penultimate round. Goodman wasn't versed in Zen Buddhism, but he knew the virtue of keeping his mind blank, making himself feel like an empty shell. He'd gone weak against Ross Somerville because he'd thought it was in the bag if he played smart and careful. Well, he'd been too damn careful.

Then he caught himself. He wasn't supposed to think at all. He pushed another clump of cottage cheese into his mouth and swallowed. He could feel his windpipe tighten.

On the first tee, with a gallery ten thousand strong sucking the air out of the midwestern afternoon, MacDonald Smith tossed aside his cigarette, sidled up to Johnny, and said, "Let's do it again, John."

Somehow, with these simple words, MacDonald Smith, who went back to the days when cleek makers fashioned iron heads and joined Tennessee hickory to their handiwork, and whose Carnoustie roots tied him to the working-class Scots who made up golf's founding aristocracy, had cast a protective arm around his shoulder.

Johnny started out with a businesslike par. A string of them would certainly suit him fine, but he couldn't seem to help playing ungodly golf. On the 489-yard second hole, he struck a perfect mashie that darted straight for the flag, settling eight from the pin. Barely pausing, Johnny directed the ball into the center of the hole for a birdie. The third, a 167-yard par three, became the stage for more fireworks when Goodman laced his tee shot ten feet from the pin and dropped yet another birdie putt.

At this point, going back to his record-breaking second round, Goodman had played thirty-nine holes in ten under par, a streak worthy of Sarazen or the mercurial Sir Walter himself.

On the 447-yard, par-four fourth, Johnny's game sprang a small leak. Trapped on his approach, he blasted out and took two putts for his first bogey. It didn't seem to matter much after he made an easy par on the next hole. One under after five wasn't much to cry over. In another trap on the sixth, Johnny put a full stroke on the slightly buried lie and sailed the ball clear over the green. This one was troubling, the worst shot he'd come up with in three days.

As Goodman set up for his long chip shot, the crowd spilled over the apron, elbowing and jostling for a better vantage point. The raucous gallery pressed close, creating a narrow tunnel to the green. Johnny squinted, tried to line up, then stepped away. Oblivious to his distress, spectators elbowed each other to get an even closer look. Johnny was a Midwest kid, a plain straight-shooter. He was theirs, and they had a right to see him.

Without a word, Johnny lined up his shot a second time. As he was drawing his club back, a fan with more practice in Cominsky Park than a golf championship ambled directly across Johnny's line to the pin. Laughing, two of his friends seized him and dragged him back into the crowd.

Once again Stanley Davies sprang into action. Seeking out the nearest USGA official, Davies made his case. "This boy is doing what no one else has done in this tournament, and he deserves protection. It isn't fair to handicap him in this way."

Scurrying around, the official produced two stone-faced Marines in brown uniforms. Stationing themselves like twin bookends on either side of Goodman, they formed an invisible cordon around the Omaha golfer.

Davies and Pete Lyck deputized themselves to wave the gallery back a few feet on either side. Grudgingly, the spectators gave way. It didn't do much good. After an indifferent chip and two putts, Johnny had to settle for a double bogey.

Hard on the heels of this misadventure, he knocked his tee shot on the par-three, 229-yard eighth hole into yet another sand pit. Yet again he failed to get up and down and had to card another bogey. After an uncertain drive at the ninth, a 408-yard par four, cost him another par, Johnny made the turn with a three over 39.

As the *Chicago Tribune*'s Charles Bartlett put it, "Johnny acted as though he had been hit with a left hook when he was in front on points. There were traps and rough, rough and traps and more of the same. It appeared that he would take the count for he had finished the last four holes of the first nine over par."

Then over the invisible telegraph that ran from one nest of golf fanatics to the next came intelligence of an astonishing surge from the rear of the pack. Walter Hagen had gone wild, tearing apart the front nine with a 32. Resurrecting his once-magnificent short game, Sir Walter had picked up seven full strokes on Goodman in a mere nine holes. Bartlett evoked the turning point. "Meanwhile puffing couriers came to the clubhouse to report that Hagen the Great was doing tricks with the golf ball the likes of which had never been seen."

Worse still, word reached Goodman's huge following that the gangly Ralph Guldahl had turned in a one under 35, slicing four strokes from Goodman's once-insurmountable lead. The Texan was a mere two shots behind now, with Johnny Goodman fading fast. It seemed that the entire field, in one collective rush, was about to run Goodman over.

Johnny felt faintly drugged, his arms and legs suddenly slow and heavy. He thought it might be the heat or the long struggle itself, but he also couldn't quite extinguish flashes of his flameout against Ross Somerville from his mind. Knowing all too well that he had to douse these undermining memories, he shook his head, stretched his neck, fiddled with his club. Abstractly, he knew what he had to do: stop playing so damn careful. Attack the course again, head-on, come what may.

But he had lost that ineffable sensation he'd been riding for two days, the sense that every swing was pure timing, that every putt would find the bottom of the cup. The past was like some undertow beneath the fairway, threatening to drag him down, back into obscurity. Winning the U.S. Open would change his life, and he feared he wanted to win all too much.

Mac Smith didn't like what he was seeing. He had crumbled at Prestwick, and he didn't want to be party to another infamous collapse. On the tenth tee, he offered Johnny a cigarette, and as the gallery scampered up the fairway, he said, "Let's play some golf, Johnny."

"Yeah, I've been trying to steer it," Goodman acknowledged, shaking his head at his own folly. He drew the smoke deep down into his lungs. Hadn't he learned anything in the last round against Somerville at Five Farms?

Back in Omaha, at 2505 South Thirty-fourth Street, Johnny's brothers George, Bill, Tony, and Joe gathered around their sister Anna's radio, trying to follow the faint broadcast crackling over the airways.

Joining them was the hulking figure of their father, William, who had little comprehension of what was going on. William Goodman was back from wherever he'd been wandering. The children he'd abandoned just let him be.

When Johnny opened with a pair of birdies in the last round, the young men shouted and pounded each other on the back, but their mystified father simply grunted, "Yah, that's good." Then the broadcast switched to a horse race. U.S. Open updates came at fifteen-minute intervals.

As the announcer re-created the exciting dash of horseflesh, Anna muttered, "Who wants to hear about a horse race?"

"Get the tournament," Tony pleaded.

She spun the dial to no avail.

Johnny stepped up to the tenth tee to begin the fateful back nine. He had squandered most of his lead over Guldahl, but dwelling on that now would be fatal. Suppose he'd come from behind to take a two-shot lead? Wouldn't he feel entirely different, even if his position were exactly the same? And what the hell did Five Farms have to do with North Shore anyway?

Why not reach back to the moment when, as a kid too naive to know any better, he'd fought off a surging Bobby Jones at Pebble Beach? Or the way he'd made putts from every crazy angle against Francis Ouimet? Was hanging on at the U.S. Open any harder? Wasn't he the same man doing the same things with a bag full of golf sticks and a ball? He was leading the United States Open with nine holes to go. He ought to be jumping for joy. Inside, at least.

Out of earshot of the gallery, Mac Smith calmed his young companion. "You've got the goods, John. Show 'em now."

Almost inaudibly, Johnny offered his thanks. MacDonald Smith was a living link to the past, to featheries and rut irons and club heads forged by blacksmiths on the distant Scottish coast. Johnny sensed that Smith was saying, Relax, you're part of history already. You're connected, too. Just show us how.

Johnny felt quieter now. When he looked up, he saw Josephine's stark white face peering at him, worried, concerned, and for once his poker face cracked wide open and he smiled.

Uncertainly, Jo smiled back. What she really craved were the cool shadows of her church, but Stanley Davies, gesturing at the sunlit stage before them, told her, "He has the courage. He loves to fight."

Johnny slashed his next drive 270 yards down the fairway on the 446-yard, par-four tenth. A clean iron left him a twenty-footer. His strong approach putt hit the back of the cup and popped out, but he still made par to stop his skid — for the moment, at least.

On the eleventh, the short 349-yard par four, he promptly hooked his tee shot into the rough, yet another self-inflicted wound. This time, though, he lofted a niblick to thirty feet and got down in two.

On the next tee he lit another cigarette and exchanged glances with Old Mac, who nodded approvingly. In neat fashion on the par-five twelfth, he punched a pair of woods short of the distant green, chipped up neatly, and just missed his birdie putt. In the third round, that putt would have dropped, he figured, but three pars in a row were more than good enough. He followed up with a fourth.

On the fourteenth, a short par four of only 375 yards, he faltered again, and had to settle for a bogey five, but he fought off his demons on the par-five, 511-yard fifteenth. After two solid woods, he kissed a short iron six feet from the pin. In the morning, six-footers were as easy as putting into a soup bowl. Now the hole looked like the constricted end of a two-inch pipe. He took a deep breath and went through his routine. Line it up, take one practice stroke to feel the distance, and hit it on the sweet spot. The rest would take care of itself. His hands told him he'd picked the club up slightly, not quite getting a true roll, but he'd rapped it hard enough. The ball held the line and darted down the hole. Birdie four.

Now he was even on the back. It felt good. For a little while, anyway. On the par-four, 423-yard seventeenth, he dumped his approach into what seemed like the hundredth sand trap of the day. Only yesterday he'd been grinning when he climbed into these bunkers. This time he had a stony look on his face as he dug in. He had only one thought in his mind. Make sure you don't leave it in the sand. He didn't, sailing it past the flag a considerable distance. Putting defensively, he lagged the ball within a few feet and knocked it in for a bogey.

The par-four finishing hole, a healthy 437 yards distant, demanded a strong tee shot and a middle iron, even on the sun-glazed ground. Johnny's entire career depended on these last few shots, and he knew it. There was no use pretending anymore. With Hagen going hog-wild, and Guldahl picking par apart, he didn't quite know where he stood, but he was willing to bet one of the professionals was on a run.

When he took his practice swing, he had one thought. Shoot the works. He knew every inch of his swing, when he'd held back just a shade and when he'd stretched too far. If you weren't careful, tournament pressure made your muscles contract, whether you felt nervous or not. To fight your fears, you had to reach back a little farther just to get your usual extension. Anything less, and you short-armed it. Snap-hooked it.

He turned. And then turned an extra notch. He reached back, and then reached back some more. He could feel the tension in his legs, the trigger that sent him whirling back, and the sensation of striking the ball so pure it felt like nothing at all. Then he was corkscrewed in the opposite direction, balanced perfectly on his left leg, his drive streaking down the left side, unwavering and true. *Wham-ditty!*

A mashie in his hands now, he struck the ball one more time, pure muscle memory. He could tell before he looked up that he'd caught it just right, the club sliding through the grass and cutting a divot as straight as a rail. The ball took one hop on the distant green and then started running, and running some more. He held his breath, waiting to see if it would go on forever, until it disappeared over the far edge of the putting surface. Instead, it lost steam, coming to a halt six feet from the pin. *Wham-ditty!* Pure joy.

As he approached the final hole, thousands of onlookers swarmed up the fairway, swelling the ranks of the huge gallery pressing in on the green. Pushing and shoving, the unruly assembly threatened to pour over the putting surface. Buried in the crowd, Josephine pressed her arms to her chest. Stanley Davies stood on tiptoe. Pete Lyck elbowed his way to the front ranks to get a glance at Johnny as he strode up the narrow ribbon of fairway.

The six feet of grass between Johnny and the hole glistened in the sunlight. Straight down-grain. The ball would roll as fast as a marble on glass. For a moment, the bottled-up gallery managed a semblance of silence. Johnny didn't take any chances, cozying the ball up to the hole and letting it die for a tap-in and his par. One over on the back, he was in with a 76.

Pawing at the apron, the mob could barely contain itself. Bodies leaned on bodies; elbows flew. A whole contingent of U.S. Marines watched tensely. Then the dam gave way, a torrent of golf fanatics bursting onto the green. Forming a narrow phalanx, the Marines fought their way through the boiling mob, surrounded the diminutive Goodman, and bore him toward the clubhouse.

As they carried him away, Johnny Goodman knew one thing. Nothing had been decided.

30

ONLY WALTER HAGEN could have been out of contention and made himself the center of attention simultaneously. Hagen had started his final round so far behind, only his most devoted admirers bothered to follow him around North Shore, for what seemed like little more than a valedictory tour. Sir Walter would have none of it. With nothing to lose, he shot straight at every hole, and he tried to sink every putt, lightning-fast greens be damned.

For once his erratic drives stayed within the North Shore's narrow confines, and his old, miraculous putting touch returned. Hagen was holing everything from twenty feet and in, and they weren't crawling into the cup, either. They popped in, they rattled in defiantly, and when the Haig came to the sixteenth tee, he had already excised eight shots from par. In fifteen holes, he had fashioned eight birdies and seven pars.

Johnny Goodman had lowered the course record to 66 only the day before, matching Gene Sarazen's United States Open record as well. Now all Hagen had to do was par the last three holes, and he would post an unheard-of 64. But what if he kept up his barrage? What if he picked up just one or two more birds along the way? He might set a record that would stand forever.

While the old lion had already picked up an astonishing twelve strokes on Goodman, he could not catch the leader no matter what he did, but few in his entourage bothered to add up the numbers.

They were reveling in their aging idol's sudden metamorphosis, roaring on every sweet shot.

There was one golfer still out on the course, however, who had a realistic chance of nicking the front-runner at the wire. When the tournament began he had been the last man to attract the smart money, but slowly and steadily, Ralph Guldahl had been eating away at Goodman's wide margin. The six-foot-two-inch Texan had been feeding off long, accurate drives all day. In the morning he had matched Goodman's superb 70, but unlike the Omahan, he had continued to beat par in the afternoon. After making the turn one under, Guldahl picked up a birdie on the par-five twelfth. Six shots back at the beginning of the afternoon round, he had erased the entire deficit in one stirring charge.

The situation was very much in flux, though. With Goodman still out in the course in front of him, Guldahl calculated that he needed one or two more birds to win. Goodman might come out of his tailspin; he might go low on the last few holes. The Texan gave it everything he had, making par on thirteen and fourteen. But would simply conforming to par be good enough? Then the news filtered back to him.

Goodman was in the clubhouse with a 287. Guldahl did the math. All he needed were three pars to tie. But what about one birdie? For the first time the twenty-one-year-old public course phenomenon realized that he could actually win the United States Open. The game suddenly became much, much harder. With every golf fiend on the course racing to the Texan's side, Guldahl's pace slowed to a crawl.

In the locker room, Johnny Goodman lay on a bench, staring at the ceiling. An attendant waved a towel through the thick air. Omaha patriots alternately praised his strong finish and related, with righteous indignation, Stanley Davies's confrontation with Jones and that bigwig from the USGA.

None of these rationalizations could distract Goodman from the pleasures of self-flagellation. "I don't deserve to win after blowing such a big lead," he kept saying.

Pacing up and back in the locker room alcove, he took every report of Guldahl's progress as proof that he had blown the championship. "I'm too tired to care what happens," he muttered, but his anxious manner belied his resigned pose.

Alternating tides of hope and disgust washed through him. In the heat of battle he could maintain his impassive mask, but trapped in the confines of the locker room, his face, drained of blood, registered nothing but exhaustion and fear.

Walter Hagen lined up for his tee shot on the par-three sixteenth, drew his club too far inside, looped it back over the top, and uncorked a wild one. As the ball sailed out-of-bounds, the Haig shrugged. It had been one helluva run.

Constitutionally incapable of giving up, Sir Walter fashioned a three to add to his two-stroke penalty and then parred the next two holes to card a brilliant 66, tying Goodman's record.

In the clubhouse, Sir Walter added one final flourish. Finding a willing messenger, the Haig flashed some green and directed his minion to seek out an easy chair and deliver it straight to Mr. Sarazen with his personal compliments. Then Sir Walter headed straight for the bar, ready to tell, and retell, the story of his miraculous performance.

On the fifteenth hole, Ralph Guldahl hit a perfect approach that fluttered down four feet from the pin. Now he had his chance. A simple four-footer and he would take the lead. The ball sat in almost the same spot from which Johnny Goodman had made his birdie four and given his chances new life.

The lanky Texan hunched over the simple putt, the weight of the golfing world on his shoulders. It was the first time in his life that such a short one had had such great significance. Now, when he drew his blade back, it felt as if he were cutting through heavy water. Forcing the stroke to its follow-through, he pinged the ball, missing the putter's sweet spot and imparting a faint bit of sidespin. Mournfully, he watched the ball squirt wide of the target.

The tenacious Guldahl marched on, searching for the single

stroke that would transform his life. He added pars on sixteen and seventeen, but still couldn't quite break through. After seventy-one holes of brutal competition, Ralph Guldahl remained frozen in place, dead even with Johnny Goodman. When he reached the eighteenth tee, he was still groping for a breakthrough.

On a knob of land 437 yards away, the barely visible flag fluttered. Squinting into the setting sun, Guldahl set himself, fidgeted, and gripped his wood. Then, as he had done all day long, he launched a drive that rose in a graceful arch and settled down in perfect position, leaving a two iron to the putting surface. He had been lashing fine two irons all day.

But this one was freighted with a bit more meaning. Some analysts claimed that for a professional the U.S. Open victory was worth fifty thousand dollars in prize winnings, endorsements, film appearances, and exhibitions, not to speak of the alluring celebrity that came with it. Hell, you could end up having drinks in Hollywood with some sexy siren if you played your cards right. You'd get wined and dined in every country club in the country. Millionaires would sit at your feet while you dispensed the wisdom of the winner.

The Texan fell to concentrating on the small white ball at his feet. Then he drew the club back and fired.

Guldahl's swing looked like every other swing he'd made all day. The shot rose at a perfect angle, gaining altitude, hanging for a heartbeat high in the air. Then it began its descent. It looked just right, yet some slight shift in the Texan's downswing, perhaps a shade too much right shoulder, had sent the ball a few degrees offline. In its dying fall, the shot drew just a bit left and plunged into the sand.

The gallery groaned like a single, wounded creature. Guldahl put his head down and dragged himself toward the punishment that awaited him.

Some spectators in the front ranks crouched like catchers behind the plate. Others, peering across the undulating green, balanced on one knee. Up on a slight knoll, fans shaded their eyes against the penetrating sunlight.

The weary Guldahl climbed into the trap. Digging in, he flared open the face of his niblick and blasted out. The ball landed gently on the short grass, and as the onlookers gasped and whooped, it headed straight for the hole. Finally, it lost steam, settling four feet from the flagstick.

It was a superb shot, perhaps the capper to a superb round. The Texan had given himself one more chance. Make the four-footer and he'd force a playoff.

It looked like a straightforward task, but Guldahl had missed a similar putt on the fifteenth, cutting across the ball just a hair. Telling himself to stay down and make a smooth stroke, Guldahl did what golfers have been doing since the game's beginnings on the misty Scottish coast — the exact opposite of his sworn intention. He stood up, cut across the ball, and watched helplessly as the short putt refused to even kiss the cup.

On June 11, 1933, that single short stroke defined the difference between Ralph Guldahl and Johnny Goodman.

Moments later Stanley Davies and Pete Lyck invaded the locker room to inform their prostrate hero that he was the new United States Open champion. Goodman, who had been busy excoriating himself for playing it safe all too early, shot up from his bed of nails and began preparing for the presentation of the cup.

When he appeared on the lawn to await the awards ceremony, he was the picture of fashion in shirt, tie, and pleated pants, every hair in place, a smile pasted on his face. For those who hadn't seen him in the throes of self-abnegation just a few minutes before, he looked remarkably cool and untouched by his harrowing experience.

It hadn't taken long for him to banish the notion that he had backed in to take the title. Guldahl had missed two four-footers. Johnny had made his when it counted. A few feet of short grass separated the winner from the loser.

Time dragged on as Goodman, the reporters, photographers, newsreel cameramen, and the admiring gallery were kept waiting for the presentation. As the delay stretched on and on, the assembly grew edgy. Where were the USGA officials? What could be taking them so long? These events usually ran right on schedule.

The press peppered Goodman with questions, which he patiently answered one after another, but eventually they exhausted their inquiries. Heads turned toward the clubhouse. Feet shuffled. The smile froze on Goodman's face. Stanley Davies, Pete Lyck, and the rest of the Field Club loyalists fell to whispering as the tension grew more intense.

Finally, an enterprising cameraman went to seek out the officials in question. Surprisingly, they were huddled at the bar, nursing a few beers.

"Can't we have a picture of the presentation?" asked the cameraman.

"You can wait until we get finished drinking," the USGA official snapped.

Then the authorities turned their backs on the newsmen and made a show of immobility. The message was clear. For whatever reason, they intended to take their own sweet time.

Finally, the officials came forth, dragging the great U.S. Open cup. Unaccountably, USGA president Ramsey had made himself scarce. In the hubbub, few noticed his absence, but spectators versed in the ways of golf's ruling body wondered where in the world he might be.

Johnny didn't recognize the official gripping the great cup, a husky, smooth-faced man in a blue blazer, but he didn't wonder at Ramsey's disappearance. He knew what it meant.

When the photographers asked the USGA officers to pose with the winner, they flatly declined. For public consumption, Johnny Goodman didn't bat an eye, but quickly registering the insult, he pursed his lips and looked down at the ground.

The awkward silence lasted only a moment. Looking up, Johnny read the situation in a single glance. Then he reached out, seized both handles of the cup, and lifted it high. And so Johnny Goodman, the winner of the 1933 U.S. Open, had to crown himself, his only company a pair of Marines.

Ignoring the slight, Goodman bubbled over before the newsreel cameras. "Am I happy?" he asked ebulliently.

Then the burly USGA official who appeared to be leading the contingent stepped up and snatched at the trophy.

Confused, Goodman blinked at the man, then held on to his prize. "The photographers want more pictures," he protested.

"I don't care," the USGA officer said bluntly, prying the cup from the winner's hands and lugging it back to the clubhouse.

Still, nothing could dampen Johnny's enthusiasm. After the truncated ceremony, he patiently stood through a second barrage of questions. He didn't care what the USGA thought, he didn't care what his detractors said, he didn't care about much of anything except that he had won the U.S. Open.

The twenty-three-year-old couldn't — wouldn't — suppress his delight, and the press basked in his innocent glow. Speaking for his fellow newsmen, Paul Gallico wrote, "The finish of the thirty-seventh National Open golf championship at the North Shore Country Club here was a bit of a gripe to a great many parties on the heat-blistered fairways, but a source of pure and unadulterated joy to the merry boys of the press who do not have to worry about the social standing of the winner as long as he is colorful and good copy."

Grantland Rice, who had been writing about championship golf for decades, offered the best insight into Johnny's performance. "Any golfer who sets a smoking pace for thirty holes is usually due for a turn. The keen edge wears away. So outstanding credit is due Johnny Goodman for the brave rally that followed his sinking spell. He was skidding fast. His game was breaking up. It is a terrific burden to know that you have a big lead shot away, a sure, wide margin blown apart. Few can come back against such a hostile turn of events. Panic usually sets in. But under this strain Goodman played the last four holes in par, and he got his four where it counted most, on the final green."

One writer after another focused on Goodman's extraordinary touch, comparing his putting to the greatest of them all, Hagen and Jones. Francis Powers singled out Johnny's brave style — shooting for the back of the cup time and again, come hell or high water. Commentators also fixed on Johnny's deadly accuracy with the short irons, likening his approaches to precision marksmanship. With reckless abandon, sportswriters yoked the fateful phrase "the next Bobby Jones" to Goodman's name.

Jones had attended the 1933 U.S. Open in the flesh, but his spirit loomed even larger. No amateur could snatch the Open from the professionals without triggering the predictable comparisons. And so Johnny Goodman, who had dreamed the unlikely dream of becoming the next Bobby Jones, now found himself actually being mentioned in the same breath as the Atlanta wizard.

An Associated Press article typified the coverage. "Those big empty shoes of amateur golf, vacated three years ago by Bobby Jones after he had scored his grand slam, at last seem to be filled. Johnny Goodman, the orphan kid from Omaha and newly crowned king of American golf, has stepped into them."

An unnamed USGA official, perhaps making amends, seconded Goodman's anointment as the Second Coming of Saint Bobby. "He's another Jones, and make no mistake about that. He's got everything just like Bobby, including that magic putting touch that made Jones the greatest golfer the world has ever seen."

Noting that "the tea cups on the piazzas of the snooty country clubs are said to be rattling ominously," Frederick Ware suggested that Bobby Jones might be contemplating a comeback in order to dethrone Goodman and satisfy USGA reactionaries.

Navigating around the controversy, Goodman turned a scrupulously blind eye to every slight USGA officials had dished out. Choosing his words with care, he insisted that golf's ruling body had treated him graciously. He wanted to make the Walker Cup team, not start a social revolution.

What sportswriters didn't seem to understand was that, above all, Goodman wanted to play golf, not wave the populist banner. What Goodman didn't understand — or did his best to deny — was how difficult it was to envision him waving any other flag. Considering Johnny's background, and his fight against the stigma of his birth, how could sportswriters ignore the implications of his story? Certainly Johnny, who kept and carefully preserved voluminous scrapbooks, read every word.

The professionals, who didn't enjoy having first prize in their biggest tournament reduced to zero by yet another brilliant amateur, weren't terribly pleased by Goodman's exploits either, but they had a better sense of humor than the dour USGA officials.

Walter Hagen and Gene Sarazen were enjoying a drink in the clubhouse when word reached them that the young pro Guldahl had blown his last chance to claim the title. With a wry smile, Sarazen turned to Walter Hagen and said, "I guess I'll have to turn amateur."

"You aren't good enough," Sir Walter replied.

31

JOHNNY GOODMAN'S 1933 U.S. Open victory drew the public back to an earlier time when one amateur, Robert Tyre Jones Jr., terrorized and humbled the professionals year after year. Only five amateurs, Jerry Travers, Francis Ouimet, Chick Evans, Jones, and Goodman himself, had ever bested the pros in the U.S. Open, but Johnny's victory suggested that once again an amateur was going to toy with the honor of the professionals. In the excitement and confusion of the moment, no one, least of all Goodman, could imagine that he would be the last amateur to take the most sought-after professional crown.

The next Bobby Jones. The words rang in Johnny's ears. Who wouldn't have been intoxicated by the very idea of being compared to the most brilliant and charismatic golfer in history? On dusty Omaha fields he had pretended to be Bobby Jones; he had burned his name into the American imagination as the underdog who beat Jones; and now he was being mentioned in the same breath as his idol. It was an exhilarating, but disturbing, feeling. How could he live up to all that ballyhoo? In his more realistic moods, he knew he'd never hit the ball as far, or swing as gracefully, as the Georgia marvel. He'd never tap such a sweet flow of words, or move so smoothly among the country's chosen few. He would never be able to wipe away the stigma of his birth.

On the other hand, he was only twenty-three. It had taken Bobby seven years to break through to the big time. Johnny had snatched

a major championship after less than five years of top competition. Bobby had fought a balky putter for years, but Johnny's flat
stick had washed away his sins with the brassie again and again. If
his most far-fetched daydreams had already come into being, why
couldn't he pull off more-outlandish victories?

As far as smooth-talking the press, he was getting better and
better. Reporters were eating up his story. He could barely believe
how many articles he'd clipped from papers all over the country. And in the newspaper pictures, he didn't look half-bad either.
Maybe, after time, sportswriters would get tired of sticking him with
the hobo label, maybe they'd finally forget the boxcars and the
flivvers and let him be himself.

He had taken to correcting the reporters, even reshaping the facts
to make himself less the stark outsider, less the pariah from the bottom. For instance, while he had certainly spent one summer working in a slaughterhouse, Johnny began denying the tale. In subtle
ways, he suggested that the stories about his hardscrabble background were exaggerations. As long as his name was synonymous
with freight trains and slaughterhouses, he believed, he'd never be
accepted in the best circles.

His supporters, particularly his mentor, Stanley Davies, were also
involved in a concerted effort to clean up Goodman's image. Davies ripped into Paul Gallico's description of Johnny as an angry,
wounded outsider, going so far as to insist that articles such as
Gallico's should never be printed because they put athletes in a negative light. Davies, too, insisted that Johnny's humble beginnings
were being exaggerated by a press eager to sell papers. Too protective
by half, Johnny's backers hurt him as much as they helped.

More than anything, Goodman wanted to shed his old skin and
be seen as the Johnny Goodman he'd invented out of nothing. Cool,
confident, worthy of respect — a Walker Cupper down to his toes.

Unfortunately, although Goodman could win the U.S. Open, and
even fight his way onto the Walker Cup team, he couldn't revise the
sports page morality play. He and Bobby Jones had been turned into
symbols, flattened out, oversimplified versions of themselves. Nothing either man could do or say seemed to affect his fixed, mass-

media identity. Jones, the upper-class paragon, would forever be the selfless picture of grace; Goodman, the lower-class threat, would forever be the scrappy kid from the wrong side of the tracks. Jones could never live up to his reputation, and Goodman could never live his down.

What the mass media could not grasp was that Goodman's longing to be accepted as a figure in the mold of Bobby Jones was driven by his most admirable and least attractive qualities simultaneously. Johnny's devotion to the art of the game was worthy of Jones, but his stubborn desire to make himself palatable to the USGA kept him from speaking freely about its vicious campaign against him.

Goodman wanted to be welcomed into the elite country club world at all costs, and he paid dearly for his stubborn adherence to the eastern elite's vision of the perfect gentleman. At twenty-three, Johnny was simply too young to understand that his highest aspirations sprang, at least partly, from a wellspring of shame.

Of course the sports pages weren't interested in human beings; they wanted to tell fast-paced stories with neat, uplifting endings. The received wisdom may have been shifting with the times, but conventional thinking could never discern the forces that were pulling Johnny Goodman so violently in different directions.

In the flush of victory, Johnny could not know these things. In five short years, he had won so often — two Trans-Mississippis, three Nebraska State Championships, a second in the U.S. Amateur, and a U.S. Open title — it all seemed a blur. He was besieged by reporters, old friends, new friends, hucksters, operators, and fans. Exciting and dizzying by turns, the wave of adoration was sweeping him back home.

The familiar rituals unrolled once again. Omaha dignitaries met Johnny as his shiny Pullman rumbled into Union Station. When he stepped off the train holding Josephine's hand, he was met by a friendly, boisterous crowd. City fathers expressed their admiration and pride in the local boy, making it clear that Goodman's virtues and their own were one and the same. Johnny made his usual brief, shy speech.

But the truest emotions played out on Omaha's downtown streets. Riding in an open touring car, Goodman was trailed by newsboys and caddies who had a deeper reason to identify with their South Omaha hero. The *Omaha Bee's* W. E. Christensen evoked the revelry. "Newsboys chased Johnny's slow-moving, open car, shouting, reaching out, trying to touch his waving hand . . . Happiest of all the cheering thousands were the caddies from Omaha's golf courses who, afoot and on bicycles, followed at the rear tires of Johnny's car throughout the twenty-block parade and laughed at police attempts to make them keep a distance."

Not given to elaborate speeches, Goodman was generous with public gestures. As he rolled along, Johnny, perched on the folded top of an open Packard, reached out to the trailing boys and touched their hands. When the procession slowed, he signed scraps of paper; he slapped backs; he clasped his hands over his head; he shouted back to his old friends. The ragged caddies, joined by dozens of newsboys, danced and grinned and whistled through their teeth. A few took wild swings with broomsticks in emulation of their hero.

Johnny's popularity ran deep among working people who knew little and cared less about golf. Stenographers leaned out of office buildings and showered him with confetti. Two bleached blondes stepped out of a beer flat and clasped their hands over their heads in a gesture of triumph. Clerks poured out of the department stores and girls in starched uniforms jumped up and down as Goodman, waving from his open car, glided past.

Dinner at the Chamber of Commerce played out like a medieval pageant transplanted to the Midwest. A few notes of real feeling crept into the orations, though.

Mixing humor and outrage, Sam Reynolds put his finger on the real sore point. "Some people, including Bobby Jones, have said that luck had much to do with Johnny's victory," Reynolds said. "I am not setting myself up as a great golfer," he continued, "but there was a day when I beat Johnny Goodman, and that is more than Bobby Jones can say."

Sparked by Jones's remarks at the Open, Omahans had developed a decided animus toward the former amateur. In his column, Frederick Ware wrote, "In recent years — I suppose it began back in Pebble Beach — I've found my sentiments inclining away from Jones. He has displayed short sportsmanship more than once. That remark made in the presence of more than one Omahan at North Shore . . . is a fair example — 'Well, if he's going to win, I suppose we'd better give it to him with good grace.' ('We' failed to do so, however.)"

Ware lit into Jones for other transgressions, as well. He recalled Bobby's "radio slur on Goodman's expert, peerless play in the second round of the Open . . . one more of several reasons why my admiration for Jones the golfer has been shadowed by my disappointment in Jones the man. Jones was there. But he sulked on one of those little horseless saddles that have become very popular with the ladies in the gallery."

The image of an effeminate Jones "sulking" like some spoiled child is striking. In the millions of words written about the amateur paragon of virtue, Ware's outburst against Jones ranks among the most negative ever penned.

Increasing in vitriol, Ware's comments developed the "rich brat" theme further. "I should have liked to read that Jones was the first to congratulate Johnny last Saturday evening. That would have been the act of the true wonder man of golf. It's hard to think that Jones would be envious — he who has got almost everything without working very hard for any of it! Yet how else can one explain the abdicated emperor's conduct? Yes, I'm glad Sam Reynolds said what he said . . . I'm glad he fired that shot at Robert Jones."

Some of Jones's remarks about Goodman had been condescending, and he could have behaved more generously toward the new champion, but the claim that Bobby hadn't worked for what he'd achieved was patently absurd. Of course, Ware was correct that Jones had been born into comfortable circumstances, but despite his great advantages of wealth and talent, Jones had struggled long and hard before he learned to win.

Still, Jones had much influence within the USGA, and he hadn't gone out of his way to embrace Johnny Goodman, a worthy outsider who had done nothing to deserve the association's shabby treatment.

In his quiet, generous way, Francis Ouimet, as respected an insider as Bobby Jones, had behaved quite differently. As a competitor, he had treated Johnny warmly, and made a point of doing so in public. In private, he had signaled that he was on Johnny's side, and that he backed Johnny's Walker Cup aspirations. As events would prove, Francis had a very high opinion of Goodman, indeed.

Omaha's rage at Bobby was a decidedly hometown phenomenon. In the national press, Jones could still do no wrong. His image was impervious to criticism, and his defenders were legion.

As news of Frederick Ware's attacks on Jones filtered back east, Westbrook Pegler, who had previously chastised USGA officials for their snobbery, now turned around and, in a breathtaking display of journalistic hypocrisy, contended that the USGA had been reasonable all along in its treatment of Goodman. The writer who had previously claimed, with relish, that Goodman was "fighting the social battle of the downtrodden," now mocked the "well-meaning citizens of Omaha" who had "adopted for their banner the greasy overall and to have declared a class war on the U.S. Golf Association and some vague element known, for lack of any more particular identity, as those eastern dudes."

Pegler had done as much as anyone to throw gasoline on the Goodman fire. Now he cast himself as the defender of the eastern establishment, and in particular Robert Tyre Jones Jr. "An unfortunate part of all this milling around the *bastille* by Johnny Goodman's Omaha friends is that for no reason at all they are beginning to yell for the head of Bobby Jones."

Goodman, who didn't want to do anything to jeopardize his nomination to the Walker Cup team, kept insisting that the USGA had treated him just fine. For his part, Jones never commented on Ware's allegations. Yet neither man could escape the crossfire of a bitter era. The world of golf seems a strange stage on which to play out the wider social drama of the time, but it is a measure of just how desperate the Depression had become that its echoes could be heard so clearly in the sports pages.

One turn of events, though, was guaranteed to defuse tensions. Johnny Goodman could turn pro. By doing so he would surrender his pretensions to Bobby's vacant throne. More subtly, he would be admitting that his claim to amateur status had always been a ruse, that he'd been out to make a buck like the rest of those faintly unsavory characters like Hagen and his ilk, that he'd taken the amateur route because it was easier to gain attention competing against gentlemen who played for amusement, not grimy dollars and cents.

In fact, Goodman was busy fending off offers more lucrative than ever before. Gene Sarazen suggested a barnstorming tour, which, in the depths of the Depression, would have netted Johnny many times what a working man made in a single year. All the usual interests were after him as well: equipment manufacturers who wanted to feature his imprimatur, publishers who wanted to profit from the secrets of his game, purveyors of hair oils and cigarettes and wonder products yet to be marketed.

Naturally, if his run at the 1932 U.S. Amateur had sparked Hollywood's interest, his triumph at the U.S. Open — and all the loose talk about the rise of another Bobby Jones — made him a very hot commodity indeed.

In fact, Goodman, in his pursuit of Jones's mantle, had to embrace the amateur ideal to such an extent that he outdid his idol. As Jones had proved, the real money was in pictures, and he had made no bones about enriching himself and surrendering his amateur status accordingly. Meanwhile, Goodman stubbornly refused Hollywood's practiced seductions.

By 1933, exploiting the charisma of golf stars had become a Hollywood tradition. Bobby Jones's Warner Brothers deal had not come out of the blue. As far back as the early 1920s the picture business had rushed a starry-eyed Gene Sarazen.

Writing about his experience, Sarazen gets the tone of a Hollywood seduction, circa 1922, just right. "I swallowed everything they told me, and they couldn't tell me enough. I wasn't just another athlete for a two-reel stint, they said. I was star material. I could be groomed into another Valentino. Correction: I'd be bigger than Valentino. 'You have perfect camera ears,' I remember one agent raving."

As the center of attention, Sarazen had a fine time elucidating the proper swing for Norma Talmadge, Jack Pickford, and Buster Keaton, throwing in a few pratfalls for good measure, but his native instinct for self-preservation gave him pause, and one day he just packed his bags and fled the illusion factory.

Goodman didn't know about Gene Sarazen's misadventures in Hollywood, but he was well aware of Walter Hagen's contributions to cinema history. He'd also heard tales of Sir Walter's intimate relations with the film industry's most attractive stars.

In 1928 Hagen, a natural fit for Hollywood, actually starred in a feature-length film called *Green Grass Widows,* which also featured Hedda Hopper in her pre–gossip columnist days, and in 1929 he made a Mack Sennett film along with his pal Leo Diegel. While in town, the Haig held court at the Roosevelt Hotel's Blossom Room suite. Thelma Todd, Constance Talmadge, Bebe Daniels, and Bette Davis frequently stopped by for drinks and parties.

Not long after, at the 1929 PGA Championship at L.A.'s Hillcrest Country Club, Fay Wray, her mind drifting to a different aspect of Hollywood life, introduced Sir Walter as "The Opium Champion of Great Britain."

Johnny knew full well about Sir Walter's big payday, and his frolics with silver screen divas. He was well aware that he might never draw such frenzied interest from Hollywood again, and that in the face of the Depression, a film contract was a rare commodity indeed. However, Goodman stuck stubbornly to the path he had chosen years before.

In a wide-ranging interview with the *Chicago American,* Goodman insisted that he was sticking to his amateur status. "I have absolutely no intention of turning pro. I am going back home to make a living in my old job in the insurance business. Golf is a game for me, not a business."

Significantly, Pete Lyck, Johnny's middle-aged boss, was in the Chicago hotel room with Johnny during the interview. If Johnny Goodman had yet to attract too many clients, now that he'd won the U.S. Open, his potential value to the insurance man had skyrocketed. Not to speak of the prestige of being Johnny's local fourball partner. It is hardly surprising that Lyck would strongly advise Johnny to maintain his amateur status and stay in Omaha.

As an amateur, Johnny would still have to rely on Lyck's business for his supper; and Pete Lyck could say, "Johnny Goodman, he just won the U.S. Open? He works for me." As long as Johnny remained an amateur, Lyck retained power over him.

"I'm certain Johnny will never turn pro," Lyck assured the Chicago reporter. "All the years I've known him he has looked on golf as a game. He wants to make money in business."

How well Goodman was doing as an insurance agent is debatable. He may have intended to make a success in business, but golf always came first. However, his connection to Omaha's commercial world was quite vibrant in the days and weeks following his triumph. His name appeared in ads for WOW, an NBC affiliate, and for Woodmen of the World Insurance Company. The Chicago Lumber Company, the Pants Store, Roberts Milk, and Northwestern Bell all got into the act with display advertisements linking Johnny's name and their own wares.

Budweiser Malt, Gem Razor Blades, a certain Dr. Shepard, and the Chat 'n Nibble Restaurant all tied their names to the new U.S. Open champion's. A dry cleaner got into the act, too: "KING JOHNNY" *World's Best Golfer* DRESHER BROS. *World's Best Dry Cleaners*, a back-page pitch proclaimed.

The American Legion, the Kiwanis, and the Rotarians all sponsored affairs in Goodman's honor, and Johnny also made an appearance at Packers Park, thrilling the crowd with a drive from home plate that carried far over the center-field fence.

A more heartfelt, and more revealing, expression of hometown sentiment came in an anonymously penned *Omaha Bee* article directly addressed to Goodman himself. "We are Omaha people, and you are an Omaha man. Your fame is reflected on the entire city, and we bask in it. In a small measure we have all become celebrities; Omaha has become the city of the champion, which sounds very much like the champion city."

In the aftermath of his U.S. Open win, Goodman's symbiotic relationship with his hometown was sealed for the foreseeable future. From such a tight embrace, who could escape?

32

THE BRITISH KNEW exactly who Johnny Goodman was when he arrived at St. Andrews on May 1, 1934, for the Walker Cup competition. Recently, Gene Sarazen had left Johnny's name off his 1934 list of the world's top-ten golfers, triggering outrage in the London press. Any amateur who could beat the professionals struck a chord in English golfing circles, where aristocratic attitudes, while growing increasingly threadbare, still held sway. Ironically, while the Anglophile American upper class fretted that Goodman's manners might become a source of embarrassment, their English counterparts were lauding Johnny because he refused to play for pay. In the birthplace of golf, with its hallowed traditions and ingrained prejudices, it was the British who regarded Johnny Goodman as a gentleman.

Francis Ouimet, the American team's captain, stated his opinion of Goodman's game loud and clear. Johnny would play number one, pitting him against the best golfers the British had to offer.

Unlike Walter Hagen and Bobby Jones, who on their first trips across the pond hadn't adjusted their games to Scottish conditions, Goodman had spent months perfecting the shots he needed for the linkside elements. "I've been working hard to adjust my game to suit the climactic conditions of British courses," he told Francis Powers. "Every windy day this spring I was out on a course at home, learning to hit shots with and against the breezes. I understand that it is likely to be cold and windy in Great Britain. Should we encounter that sort of weather, I am all set. Also I have spent a lot of time perfecting a pitch and run shot, which I am told will be very valuable at St. Andrews . . . I'm just like a kid getting ready for his first circus," he added.

Powers seemed to understand exactly how much the Walker Cup meant to Goodman. "So there's no more romance in the world, eh?" he concluded. "Well, then you haven't talked with Johnny Goodman and seen the high roads of adventure that are spreading out before the little fellow from the cornfields of Nebraska."

Still, like every American invader before him, Goodman found the St. Andrews course mystifying. After a single round over the treeless track, Goodman discovered all his preparations had been for naught. "Just one round on this fine old golf course has been enough to convince me that we first-trip Americans will have our hands full in the Walker Cup matches in trying to play up to our scores at home," Johnny wrote for the Universal News Service.

"The strokes I thought I had mastered there are to some degree no good here; it's simply a different game, this golf they have to play at St. Andrews and, recognizing this, I've dug deeply into my cigarette money and bought myself a run-up iron and a heavy putting cleek. In this way I hope to eliminate an epidemic of three-putt greens."

As Johnny explained, the huge double greens allowed approach shots "to roll and roll." The high pitch, a staple of American golf, refused to bite on the rock-hard St. Andrews putting surfaces, and negotiating one-hundred-foot putts was a foreign art to stateside golfers.

Bobby Jones echoed Goodman's concerns. "St. Andrews needs a lot of knowing and a lot of experience in a kind of golf which cannot be had in America . . . On a typical St. Andrews day, when the ball goes scurrying across those vast greens, the British experience will count for a lot."

Johnny took time out from practicing to make a pilgrimage to the ruins of St. Andrews Cathedral. The old church grounds contain golf's most mystical shrine, the graves of Old Tom Morris and his son, Young Tom, who died a premature and tragic death.

Johnny felt a close kinship to Old Tom, who in the 1840s started out as an apprentice to the early professional Allan Robertson. Old Tom didn't remain a lowly apprentice for long.

He won the British Open in 1861, 1862, 1864, and 1867, then went on to become master greenskeeper at St. Andrews, where he also ran a shop that sold balls, handcrafted lofters, mashies, and niblicks.

Johnny spent a few hours wandering golf's sacred ground. He was particularly affected by Young Tom's statue, which depicts the young man addressing the ball, a Scottish bonnet on his head, his coat buttoned tight against the wild Scottish winds.

On the eve of play, Bobby Jones predicted the Americans were in for a difficult struggle. Calling the British team "an exceptionally good one," he praised Michael Scott, the previous year's British Open champion whose victory some had discounted as a fluke. "In addition to Scott there are Cyril Tolley, said to be playing better now than for some years, Roger Wethered, who is always at his best at St. Andrews, and Tony Torrance, perennial thorn in the American flank." Noting that only Francis Ouimet had considerable experience at St. Andrews, Jones struck an ominous note. "We cannot and ought not to expect to win forever."

In early May, there were still bare patches on the St. Andrews fairways, and the many divots, patched with sand, were still quite visible. Still, the greens were rolling well. Mercifully, they hadn't turned impossibly fast. Yet.

Bernard Darwin thought Goodman and Lawson Little were the most impressive players on the American squad. "I suppose the general view is in the Americans' favor," Darwin went on. "The British players certainly are not suffering from an inferiority complex," he added, a dubious assertion considering America's dominance in recent Walker Cup competition.

Partnering with the powerful Little in the opening match, Goodman provided a razor-sharp short game. The tone of the match was set on the very first hole, which the British surrendered with a three-putt. Goodman and Little worked smoothly together, knocking Tolley and Wethered back on their heels with consecutive birdies on six and seven. By the turn, the Americans had amassed a four-hole lead.

Local knowledge of the St. Andrews greens was supposed to be the British trump card. Instead, issuing a shower of three-putts, Tolley and Wethered went to pieces. Meanwhile, in clinical fashion, the Americans piled up par after par, surging to an eight-hole lead. In the afternoon, the slaughter continued. On the thirtieth hole, with Goodman and Little lying two, their opponents four, the rout came to an end, 8 and 6. For the British, it was a particularly humiliating end to a particularly humiliating match.

In the singles Goodman faced Michael Scott, the reigning British Amateur champion. Early in their match, a severe storm struck St. Andrews, but the confrontation went on anyway. Johnny still managed to pick up a pair of birdies before the turn. Playing brilliantly despite a driving rain, Goodman finished the front nine two up.

As the two competitors headed to the tenth hole, a solid curtain of rain descended, inundating the greens. Ground crews used shovels to scoop the water off the putting surfaces, to little avail. With the greens transformed into small lakes, and overall conditions verging on the impossible, both men's scores shot sky-high. Despite the conditions, Goodman held on to a two-hole lead.

Then the showers abated. In the afternoon the greens drained, and Johnny took off on one of his patented hot streaks, mixing birdies and pars to burst into a five-hole lead at the turn. He quickly added another bird, crushing Scott's hopes for a comeback. The end came soon, Johnny closing out his rival 7 and 6.

Once again the American Walker Cup team had crushed the British. A downcast Bernard Darwin termed Goodman's performance "appallingly good" in the Americans' 9½ to 2½ rout of his compatriots.

Naturally, as the number one American amateur, Johnny's showing was to be expected. The stories about his humble background and his treatment by the USGA, the colorful tales of boxcars and his house on wheels, were finally beginning to fade. Despite the anxiety of America's country club set, which had long done its best to ape aristocratic English manners, the sky had not fallen when the young

man from South Omaha had rubbed elbows with his British counterparts. Apparently, Johnny's pilgrimage to St. Andrews hadn't
caused Old Tom Morris to turn over in his grave.

Of course, Old Tom was from the servant class himself, but he
had turned himself into a craftsman, and a master of the golfing
arts. As the man the nobility looked to for advice on the royal and
ancient game, his position in the social constellation was of his own
making: lower, middling, and upper simultaneously. In the American firmament, Johnny Goodman had become Old Tom's worthy
descendent.

A keen student of golf, Johnny Goodman found pleasure in sensing
the flow of the game's history. He had carried Walter Hagen's bag,
and he had been close by during Sir Walter's final burst of glory in
the 1933 U.S. Open. He had seen Walter B. Travis chewing his cigar
in the galleries, and he knew how Travis's genius flowed through
Bobby Jones's hands and down the battered and taped shaft of Calamity Jane. The Black Scot, Tommy Armour, had imparted to him
the secret of how to strike an iron. He had contemplated golf's beginnings in the ruined cathedral at St. Andrews, and on the windy,
rain-swept Old Course.

The present fell away when he dreamed of his own place in this
history, and he knew he would have to win the 1937 U.S. Amateur in
Portland, Oregon, at the Alderwood Country Club, to fix it for all
time. A fixture among the favorites all through the 1930s, Goodman
had made it to the U.S. Amateur finals once, and to the semifinals
twice, before bowing out. Also, in the 1937 U.S. Open, Johnny had
been low amateur yet again, duplicating his feats of 1932 and 1933.
As George Trevor wrote, Goodman was "recognized as the best
shotmaker and most consistent scorer in the amateur ranks" of the
entire decade.

If he could only snatch the U.S. Amateur crown, he would join
the most exclusive club in all of golf, the handful of amateurs —
Travers, Ouimet, Evans, and Jones — who had won both the U.S.
Open and the U.S. Amateur.

Alderwood, designed by the Dublin-born Vernon Macan, re-

THE KING OF SWINGS

flected the golf architect's taste for the pitch-and-run shot, and his long-standing admiration for St. Andrews. His large and contoured putting surfaces often demanded the approach shot that was common currency in golf's birthplace.

"I design some of my greens to suit the run-up type shot. This is one of the great shots in golf, but very few of today's top players can execute it," Macan explained to the columnist Harry Young in 1963.

A Trinity College–trained lawyer as well as an expert golfer in his early years, Macan had lost a foot in the World War I battle of Vimy Ridge and eventually turned to course design. "Today, the uninformed believe a green should be constructed from back to front, so that it will retain the ball," he went on. "This is not the game of golf. Golf was not conceived as a mechanical operation but rather full of fun and adventure."

Set among dense stands of fir trees, Alderwood had its peculiarities. Macan had devised a front nine with three par fives and a par of 37, and a back with two more par fives and a par of 35. He added five par threes to the mix, leaving only eight par fours. Short, straight hitters like Johnny Goodman were penalized by the additional long hole, and rewarded by the additional short one. Overall, though, Alderwood, at 6,401 yards, was not a particularly long course, though when the fairways were soaked, as was often the case in the Pacific Northwest, there was little roll off the tee.

Macan spoke out of a deep love of the old game, but on the eve of the 1937 U.S. Amateur, Bobby Jones offered a different perspective on "fun and adventure." When pressed to name his favorites, Jones said, "I don't like anyone who isn't willing to settle down to a week of nerve punishment and hard work. That's what a championship is. It is mostly work — once you know how to swing the club and hit the ball. You've got to work on every shot and every hole. If you don't you can get lost in a hurry."

Of the pretenders to the crown, Bobby Jones liked Johnny Goodman best of all. Since the contretemps over his remarks about Goodman in 1933, Jones had gone out of his way to be photographed with Johnny, to invite him to his new Augusta, Georgia, tournament, the Masters, and to heap praise on Johnny's game, proving himself far more adept at public relations than his friends in high USGA circles.

Jones was not simply being gracious. Out of competition for seven years, he had had the opportunity to step back from the fray and take an objective look at who rose to the top in the U.S. Amateur time and again. Jones cared too much for the game to let any petty feelings cloud his judgment.

After observing Goodman for nine years, he had grown to respect ability. "I like the way Johnny Goodman hits the ball. He's sound. His swing is compact and under control. He knows what he is doing."

By now Bobby had settled into his new life. Deeply involved in the design of Augusta National and the inner workings of the Masters, he was also learning the ropes as a member of several corporate boards. His fame as a golfer inspired these sinecures and underlay his success as a lawyer as well. Eventually, he was able to buy a house in Atlanta's most exclusive neighborhood. His wife, Mary, dubbed their Italianate home "Whitehall," and it was there that Bobby Jones settled into the life of the southern squire.

Jones was still a fixture at the great tournaments, but ever so slowly he was becoming a figure from the past. As Bobby faded into the background, the American amateur game was undergoing a quiet revolution. Competitors at Alderwood included machinists, file clerks, office machine repairmen, unemployed cabbies, waiters, indigent college boys, and more than one golfer who owed his job to President Franklin D. Roosevelt's Works Progress Administration. *Collier's* magazine contended that "amateur golf, once the sanctuary of the select, has become as democratic as the Union Station washroom."

Although *Collier's* was overstating the case quite a bit — prohibitively expensive and socially exclusive country clubs thrive to this day — the amateur game had undergone a startling transformation. Frank Strafaci, a real threat to win the 1937 Amateur, was a plumber from Brooklyn. Ray Billows, the New York State star, had made his way to his first Empire State championship in a fifteen-dollar car that wheezed its last breath just before it wobbled up to the country club gate. Joe Thompson and Bill Holt had ridden to the 1937 Western Open in a trailer with a lean-to. Paul Leslie couldn't afford a caddie, so he brought along a friend to carry his sticks at the Western. Leslie and his buddy must have worked well together. He swept the prestigious meet.

For the fourth time in six years, Johnny made his way into the semifinals, this time against an obscure Tacoma player named Bud Ward.

The young Ward was built for football. Although he had never hurled his husky body at a lineman, Bud had starred as a high school basketball player in Olympia, Washington. Ward had touch on the hardwood and exceptional touch on the green. As Dick Metz remarked, Ward had "great hands. They are strong, well-built hands, and they always work together. He putts as well on one type of green as another . . . Ward savvies roll and break to perfection, and there never is any variation to his smooth putting touch."

As predicted, Ward put on a short-game clinic, but it was Johnny Goodman who left his mark on the Alderwood greens. His work with the flat stick in the semifinals is considered remarkable to this day. Out of thirty-six holes, Johnny one-putted fifteen to finally subdue Ward, who fought bravely to the end. On the slender margin of one up, Johnny Goodman slipped into the finals of the 1937 U.S. Amateur.

In his battle for the U.S. Amateur crown, Johnny was slated to battle one of the amateur game's new breed, Ray Billows. Billows was a gangly young man with big ears and a receding chin. Pale, thin, and hollow-chested, he looked utterly harmless, but he had a marvelous, relaxed temperament. "I'll tell you this about Billows. He has less tension than any good golfer I know, and this includes Walter Hagen," Grantland Rice commented.

Noting that the slender Billows weighed no more than 130 pounds, Rice wrote, "He isn't any too long, but he is straight. He never plays a careless shot . . . He knows he can lay a chip stone dead — and he can putt. He seems to get more fun out of golf than most anyone."

Portland provided a cloudless day for the penultimate match. With its fairways dried out, Alderwood became more vulnerable.

After his enervating battle with Bud Ward, Johnny Goodman had good reason to weaken or at least go through an unsteady patch. Instead, he continued his faultless play in the morning round against Billows, shooting a one under 36 on the front and a one over 36 on the back. Even par, however, was not enough to shake the loose-limbed Billows from his tail.

After the morning tour, Goodman held a two-hole lead. Against a player of Billows's quality, two up hardly qualified as a lead. In the afternoon round, on the 501-yard, par-five first hole, the purportedly short-hitting New Yorker demonstrated just how dangerous he could be.

With an overflowing gallery of five thousand fans pressed together like subway riders on either side of the fairway, Billows launched a wind-assisted, 280-yard drive that gave him an opening to the green, though his line was partially obscured by a massive tree.

Bobby Jones, Goodman's ever-present shadow, looked around for a good vantage point from which to watch Billows's second shot. Accompanied by Charlie Yates, Jones wandered over to a mound at the corner of the fairway.

Just as Billows was preparing to hit his brassie, a stranger strolled over and stood next to Jones. Billows proceeded to draw a line-drive shot that veered around a pair of looming traps at the last moment. When the ball landed on the green, it headed straight for the hole before losing steam a mere six inches from the cup.

Jones turned to Yates and said, "You know, Charlie, that's the most amazing golf shot I've ever seen. I don't believe anybody could play that shot just like Billows did."

Irritated at this display of ignorance, the stranger snapped, "Mister, you don't know what you're talking about. Bobby Jones could play that shot better than Billows."

Jones replied, quietly but firmly. "Well, I'm certain he couldn't."

Looking askance at Jones, the stranger shot back, "Mister, did you ever see that sonofabitch play?"

Preferring the pleasure of anonymity, Bobby Jones did not dispute the point.

Goodman conceded Billows's eagle, and the match tightened up good and proper.

Johnny came back quickly on the 449-yard, par-four second hole, his par good enough for the win. The two matched birdies on the 510-yard, par-five third, but Goodman slowly forged ahead with a birdie on the 559-yard sixth, where he chipped to seven feet. After ten holes, Goodman had built a formidable four-hole lead with only eight to go.

Johnny seemed to have the 1937 U.S. Amateur well in hand. The less-experienced, twenty-three-year-old Billows was showing signs of strain. He had three-putted the seventh and yanked a shot into the rough on nine, striking a spectator. In other words, it was a perfect moment for the leader to take a nosedive, and Goodman did his best to comply.

On the 182-yard, par-three eleventh, Johnny's drive landed short in a nest of dense, tangled grass. Chipping out, he sailed the ball clear over the green, a full fifteen feet from the pin. When he failed to get down, his lead had shrunk to three holes.

On the 510-yard, par-five fifteenth, both players hit superb approaches. Goodman pushed his eight-footer a hair, though, and the ball shaved the cup. Going to school on Goodman's misjudgment, Billows took the break out of his putt, jamming it into the heart for his bird and cutting Goodman's lead to two holes.

Johnny promptly threw away half of his margin on the 207-yard, par-three sixteenth when he failed to get up and down from sixty feet. With two holes left, Johnny found himself clinging to a one-hole lead.

Billows hooked his approach on the par-four, 410-yard seventeenth into a mound, but he caught a bit of luck when the ball careened onto the green, a long fifty feet from the pin. Johnny left himself a similar lag putt, but his supporters groaned when he failed to give the ball a good ride, leaving it a full four feet short. All he had to do was blow this one, and he'd find himself dead even going to the eighteenth.

But Goodman had been depending on unshakable putting all week, and his confidence held up one more time. He went for the center of the hole, hard. The gallery was so quiet that the sound of the ball rattling into the cup seemed like the only sound in the world.

Billows had one more chance. His happy-go-lucky demeanor was gone now. His face was a mask of pallor. His mouth had turned into a white line of determination. Still, he let loose a graceful swing, rocketing his tee shot down the fairway at the 561-yard, par-five eighteenth.

All day, Billows had been outdriving Goodman, but this time Johnny took the club back a shade farther, he spun back a bit faster, and he matched his opponent's blast foot for foot, a full 280 yards off the tee.

Hitting his brassie first, Goodman came up sixty yards short of the green. Billows had his chance now. One solid blow and he could reach the green in two, giving him a chance to force a playoff. The New Yorker took a long backswing. Then he whipped his club down with every ounce of strength he had.

In dismay, he watched the shot take off in the right direction only to fade at the end of its flight. The gallery scrambled to get out of the way, but the ball disappeared in a welter of arms and legs. Shaking his head, Billows traced the white pellet into an orchard of pear trees. Then, to his relief, he realized that he had a wide-open path to the green.

The ball lay half-perched in the long grass. It would be tough to stop it out of that lie, so he planned to run it and hope for the best. Meanwhile, he had to wait for Goodman, who stood far behind him in the fairway.

Goodman didn't give Billows much of a chance. "The final shot that Johnny Goodman played to the pin on the thirty-sixth was a masterpiece," Grantland Rice wrote. "Facing the possibility of defeat again, after he had apparently packed the match away, his perfect head-and-hand action carried the sixty-yard pitch to within seven feet of the cup."

Billows still had a chance, though. The way the ball came out of the grass would determine his fate. He had to hit it hard enough to catch the apron and hope it would roll to the pin without too much energy, but he had to guard against dumping it short into the long grass. Fearing he would lose his chance to force a playoff, the New Yorker gave his stroke a little extra; the ball came out hot and ran thirty feet past the pin.

Billows was still away, far away on a green that had lost all its moisture under the beating sun. All week the putter had felt like a feather in Ray Billows's hands. Now it felt like a bludgeon. He held its neck as if he were choking it and blasted his lag putt too far and way too wide. When he missed yet again, he conceded the match.

Grantland Rice captured the dual significance of Goodman's feat. Johnny had taken the 1937 U.S. Amateur, but in doing so he had joined a circle so select that it contained only four members. "It took Bobby Jones, the greatest golfer of this or any other era, eight years to win his first amateur crown. It took Johnny Goodman, the finest amateur golfer in the world today, an extra year to join the four American immortals of golf — Francis Ouimet, Jerry Travers, Chick Evans, and Bobby Jones — who were good enough to win both the Open and the Amateur crowns in both medal and match play."

Rice understood the deeper meaning of Goodman's triumph as well. "This is the ultimate test — the final proof of form and heart, of skill and nerve control. No upstarts ever crack the entry to this portal."

What Rice could not know was that Johnny Goodman would be the last amateur to ever pull off the remarkable feat.

The championship cup was a huge, gold affair. Goodman stood, beaming, while John G. Jackson, the USGA president, made the presentation. Pressing the cup into Johnny's hands, Jackson looked thoroughly delighted. No longer camera shy in Johnny's presence, the USGA had made its peace with its most gifted whipping boy.

And then Goodman, as cool and calm as he had been on the course, lauded his opponent. "I'm sorry, Ray, there aren't two titles awarded."

The following year, Goodman graced the cover of *Time*, which praised his golfing prowess but made sure to point out that he was still a bit rough around the edges. Johnny Goodman's battles with the USGA had defined his journey, and the question of whether or not he would take a dollar to play the game he loved defined golf in his time.

Still, it is indelible images that tell the story: Johnny and his friends climbing onboard the Cowboy Pullman to St. Louis, the nervy kid lashing his first drive into the morning fog at Pebble Beach, the elegant Bobby Jones fighting back, the ebb and flow of the struggle along the edge of the sea; Francis Ouimet casting his arm around the outcast's shoulder; Old Mac, victim of so many bitter defeats, urging Johnny on over the perilous last holes at the U.S. Open, and Johnny's final march over Alderwood, a track dreamed up by a wounded man who never stopped dreaming of the Old Course and its immense, rolling greens.

EPILOGUE

OMAHA. June 26, 2004. Jack Atkins, Johnny Goodman's nephew, is sure he can find his uncle's grave. We follow him as he tramps around St. John's, the modest South Thirty-sixth Street cemetery where Goodman was buried in 1970, but among the stones, chiseled with names like Stankiewicz, Macheski, and Lodz, his monument eludes us. In his sixties, Jack insists that he recalls Goodman's 1970 funeral, and precisely where his uncle was laid to rest, near a certain tree, but there aren't many in the few open acres of ground, and none of them yields Johnny's marker.

Her cameras swinging on her neck, my wife, Rose, wanders off in one direction. I try another path. Jack surveys the landscape, squinting in the wash of sunlight.

A burly, flushed-faced man bursting with colorful stories of Omaha's past, Atkins has given us a tour of what were once the city's rough-and-ready spots, Johnny's Café, the red-light district, the ground where the great slaughterhouses once roared night and day. But Omaha is an insurance town now, a Great Plains center of higher education and up-to-date technology. The packinghouses are empty hulks. The Grain Exchange is being converted into condominiums. In a burst of commercialized nostalgia, the Old Market has been turned into a nest of boutiques and quaint restaurants. In South Omaha, you are more likely to find a good plate of *arroz con pollo* than fresh kielbasa.

We renew our efforts, segmenting St. John's with the precision of surveyors. Jack takes one section, Rose another, and I inspect a third. Time grinds on. Despite the fact that the cemetery is modest in size, we can't seem to locate Goodman's grave. We search row after row of stones to no avail. Even Jack, who was so sure of himself before we launched into our search, wonders if we should give up. Perhaps the tree he was looking for has fallen down; perhaps his memory is faulty.

Then Rose shouts for us. She's found it. Relieved, we hustle to the spot, but there is no monument, no stone. Rose appears to be staring at a section of grassy, flat ground. On her knees, she brushes away the dry weeds. Then I see the brass plate, approximately three feet long and a foot wide. Noting that Goodman served in the Quartermaster Corps during World War II, the metal rectangle offers Goodman's date of birth and the date of his passing. It is no wonder we could not find his marker. It is almost invisible in the overgrown plot.

Next to the first plate, we discover a second, this one commemorating Josephine and Johnny. Made of granite, it is a shade more substantial, but also quite modest in size.

I didn't expect a grandiose mausoleum, but Goodman's grave is startling in its obscurity. His story had been one of the most compelling of his time; he had been the subject of hundreds of articles in national newspapers; his picture had graced the pages of *Life* and *Time;* his voice had been broadcast over the radio; his image had been captured in newsreels. I couldn't help but wonder what had happened to him after the glory days.

Tabloids have conditioned our imaginations with tales of how the mighty destroy themselves through drugs, drink, and carnal excess. If Johnny Goodman had flamed out in the usual ways, he might have gained a permanent place in the American firmament. In fact, the real story is far more subtle, and more revealing about who we were and who we've become.

After his great run in the 1930s, Johnny Goodman lived a rather settled life. Leaving the insurance business behind, he worked as a representative for Hamm's beer, distributed by Josephine's brother-in-law, John Atkins. Eventually, he managed Atkins's successful club, the Burchwood.

In 1938 he married Josephine at St. Stanislaus Church — Lawson Little stood as best man — and moved into his mother-in-law's house with his bride. Despite his celebrity, he and Josephine could not afford a place of their own.

Part of Goodman's problem was the Depression. All the promises in the world weren't going to materialize while business remained so tight and so many couldn't find work. But his difficulties were also rooted in his devotion to amateur golf. His commitment, both a virtue and a curse, made it impossible for him to capitalize on his fame.

He and Josephine were finally planning to build their own house, when the Japanese attacked Pearl Harbor. Although he was already thirty-three, Goodman joined the service and was posted to New Delhi, India. One snapshot shows Johnny in a white T-shirt standing beside a turbaned golf pupil. Johnny didn't much like the military. He felt lonely and isolated. He hated the intense Indian heat.

Soon after he came home he was driving on an icy road. Catching the vague shape of an animal in the corner of his eye, he swerved and ended up wrecking his car. He broke his arm in so many places, he never quite recovered his golf swing. Although Goodman could still play at a high level, he'd lost his edge. He was thirty-eight years old.

After World War II, professional golf came into its own. The play-for-pay game was full of appealing stars, Sam Snead, Jimmy Demaret, Byron Nelson, Ben Hogan. Amateur golf, which had been ceding ground to the professional game all through the 1930s, lost its ascendancy for good.

Johnny Goodman's values became a relic of a lost time. In our own money-driven moment of American history, the idea that amateur athletes have an innate purity that is lacking in professionals sounds so quaint as to be incomprehensible. Today, scouts crawl all over talented junior high school basketball players, and we think nothing of it. And when a senior in high school drops out to try his hand at making the professional golf tour, we are interested as long as he wins. If he doesn't make a dollar, we forget him fast.

Riddled with hypocrisies great and small, the amateur ideal has always been problematical, but the idea of playing the game for the sheer love of its challenges and beauty has an appeal that survives, however diminished, to this day. As the embodiment of that ideal, Bobby Jones, with all his grace, power, and artistry, excited the imaginations of an entire generation. In Jones's thrall, Johnny Goodman held fast to the amateur ideal during the most productive years of his life, but eventually his fame began to fade. By 1950, when he was no longer a hot commodity in Omaha, he and Josephine decided it was finally time to get out of town.

She had always hated the cold winters; he told his closest friends, cryptically, that in Omaha he had had "too many bosses" and too little to show for it.

Eventually, along with their son, three-year-old John junior, they settled in a three-room apartment in South Gate, California. For a number of years Goodman worked as a representative for Canada Dry, but when the company was downsized, both he and his boss were laid off. Jobless and without a pension, Goodman was at sea.

Not long after, when he was fifty, Johnny Goodman almost died of cirrhosis of the liver. After recovering, he never took another drink. His brush with death led him to meditate on how he wanted to spend his remaining years.

His desire to make golf his life only intensified. He could no longer summon the strength to be competitive in the big tournaments, but he could still turn in a fine round or two. More important, he had keen insights into the game, which he yearned to pass on. Unsure of how many years he had left to live, Goodman decided to return to his natural home, the golf course.

In order to teach what he knew, Johnny Goodman, at fifty years of age, had to surrender his amateur status. While he never competed for prize money, he did begin teaching at the Bellflower Golf Center, a nine-hole, par-three course and driving range. Occasionally, his old friend Bing Crosby sent him an actor in need of emergency golf therapy, and Goodman's good humor and patience brought him a modest following. Most days he spent teaching and playing a bit. On weekends he would take John junior to play a round, but he was so unpretentious about his achievements that his son didn't learn about his father's brilliant past until he was in his late teens.

After turning sixty, Goodman, who sensed that he didn't have long to live, told Mary Kersigo Miklas that he had no regrets. "Mary, I've done everything I ever dreamed of doing, I've traveled all over the world, and if I go soon I know I've lived a good life."

"Johnny, don't talk that way," she admonished him, but Goodman's presentiment soon came true.

On August 1, 1970, just eight days before he passed away, sixty-year-old Johnny Goodman returned to the Omaha Field Club to play a round with his nephew, Jack Atkins. Thin, bespectacled, pale, Johnny looked his age. At the second hole, he topped his tee shot. The ball shot down across an asphalt-covered cart path and smacked into a bank near the ladies' tee box. Jack suggested that his uncle hit another one — they were just playing a friendly round, after all — but Goodman gave his nephew a frosty look.

"I don't believe in mulligans. I believe in playing golf the way it's supposed to be played. I'll play the ball where it lays."

Johnny's errant tee shot had come to rest alongside the cart path, a dozen feet below the fairway. Goodman climbed down into the small ravine, took out a fairway wood, and hit a perfect shot, two hundred yards to the top of the hill. He followed this recovery with a short iron to six feet from the pin and sank the putt for par. For the next few holes, Goodman refused to say a single word. Eight days later, on August 8, 1970, back at home in California, Johnny Goodman died in his sleep.

Every year at the U.S. Open an amateur turns in a fine round or two, then fades from the leaderboard. The professional field is deep with artists who can shape every shot in creation, players who can sink million-dollar putts on greens as fast and smooth as ice. Seventy-three years have passed since Johnny Goodman bested the greatest pros of his time, Sarazen, Armour, Burke, Wood, Hagen, and Guldahl, but he still stands as the last amateur to pull off this unlikely feat. It's a record that might last another seventy-three years — or forever.

ACKNOWLEDGMENTS

MY EDITOR, Susan Canavan, deserves all the credit in the world for seeing the book through its many drafts. Without her close reading, incisive comments, and unstinting support, this project would have been a far different, and thinner, affair.

Susan's crackerjack assistant, Will Vincent, close reader, fast responder, and expert golfer, kept track of all the loose ends and tied them together.

Sally Wofford-Girand, my agent, suggested I try my hand at narrative nonfiction. Out of my otherwise clueless ideas, she seized on the Johnny Goodman story and guided me through the proposal-writing process.

As always, Rose Mackiewicz was my co-creator in spirit and in reality. She knows all my shopworn tricks, and never lets me get away with a single one.

Many thanks to John and Helen Goodman Jr. for their generous support. John's mother, Josephine, had preserved voluminous scrapbooks that tracked Johnny Goodman's entire career. When John and Helen granted me access to this material, I knew I would be able to draw a detailed, nuanced picture of Johnny Goodman and his times.

Jack Atkins was a tireless supporter and contributor to this project. He knew Johnny Goodman's career and the man as well. His love of the colorful side of Omaha's history also informed much of this story.

Mary Kersigo Miklas welcomed me into her home and spoke freely about her relationship with Josephine and Johnny.

Rand Jerris, director of the USGA Museum; Doug Stark, head USGA librarian; and Patty Moran, also at the USGA library, provided invaluable advice and guidance. The USGA library is the premier resource center for the golf historian. It is simply invaluable.

The Omaha Field Club assisted this project by opening its files, as well as giving me access to intriguing photographs and early plans of the golf course. Thanks to the membership for all the kind treatment.

The Douglas County Historical Society was a great help as I familiarized myself with Omaha's history and infrastructure. Particular thanks to Don Snoddy, who knows everything about the history of the railroad and much more.

Frank Morley at the Western Golf Association sent me a copy of a rare piece of film from the 1933 U.S. Open. Your contribution was much appreciated, Frank.

Rex Schultze, a fellow Johnny Goodman historian, generously shared his archive on Goodman and offered keen insights into the golfer and his times. Many thanks, Rex.

Gary Kastrick, a historian of South Omaha, helped me understand the ethnic nature of South Omaha in the 1920s and 1930s, as well as the dynamics of long-forgotten street games.

Jim Schoeller, pro at the Stamford Golf Club, helped me analyze Johnny Goodman's swing after viewing Pathe newsreel footage of the 1933 U.S. Open.

Library staff at the State University of New York at Oneonta have been helpful throughout the creation of this work. Librarians answered my every question, no matter how self-evident or trivial. I promise to keep asking in the future. Many thanks.

Thanks also to Don Ende, who answered my casual question about great upsets in golf history by mentioning Johnny Goodman's battle against Bobby Jones. Thanks to Paul Stratigos, fellow links addict, who tolerated all the usual moaning and groaning that mixing book-writing and golf entail. Next year, we'll both stop hooking, Paul. Thanks to Chip Walden for that putting tip. One of these days, we'll break 80 again, Chip. Thanks to the rest of my friends at the Stamford Golf Club, that hidden treasure in the Catskills, where I play, and fail, all too often.

A NOTE ON INTERVIEWS

MOST OF THE PRINCIPALS in this story had passed away when I began this project. However, I did conduct many useful interviews. John Goodman Jr., Helen Goodman Jr., Jack Atkins, Mary Kersigo Miklas, Tom Goodman, Doris Goodman, Bob Astleford, and Harl Dalstrom were all generous with their time. Any quotes attributed to them in the text were taken during these interviews. In addition, I relied on Walter Curtis's interviews with Josephine Kersigo Goodman and Matt Zadalis.

SELECTED BOOKS

Allen, Frederick Lewis. *Only Yesterday: An Informal History of the 1920s.* New York: Harper and Row, 1931.

Allen, Frederick Lewis. *Since Yesterday: The Nineteen Thirties in America, September 3, 1929–September 3, 1939.* New York: Harper and Row, 1940.

Barkow, Al. *Golf's Golden Grind: The History of the Tour.* New York: Harcourt Brace Jovanovich, 1974.

Brendon, Piers. *The Dark Valley: A Panorama of the 1930s.* New York: Knopf, 2002.

Clavin, Tom. *Sir Walter: Walter Hagen and the Invention of Professional Golf.* New York: Simon & Shuster, 2005.

Curtis, Walter J. Sr. *Johnny Goodman: The Last Amateur Golfer to Win the U.S. Open.* Richmond, Va.: W. J. Curtis Sr., CLU, 1997.

Darwin, Bernard. *Golf Between Two Wars.* London: Chatto & Windus, 1944.

Darwin, Bernard. *Bernard Darwin on Golf.* Guilford, Conn.: Lyons Press, 2003.

Fountain, Charles. *Sportswriter: The Life and Times of Grantland Rice.* New York: Oxford University Press, 1993.

Frost, Mark. *The Grand Slam: Bobby Jones, America, and the Story of Golf.* New York: Hyperion, 2004.

Frost, Mark. *The Greatest Game Ever Played: Harry Vardon, Francis Ouimet, and the Birth of Modern Golf.* New York: Hyperion, 2002.

Hargreaves, Ernest, with Jim Gregson. *Caddie in the Golden Age: My*

Years with Walter Hagen and Henry Cotton. London: Partridge Press, 1993.

Hotelling, Neal. Photography by Joann Dost. *Pebble Beach Golf Links: The Official History.* Chelsea, Mich.: Sleeping Bear Press, 1999.

Jones, Robert T., and O. B. Keeler. *Down the Fairway.* Atlanta: Longstreet Press, 1927.

Jones, Robert Tyre Jr. *Bobby Jones on Golf.* New York: Broadway Books, 1930.

Keeler, O. B. *The Bobby Jones Story.* Chicago: Triumph Books, 1953.

Kennedy, David M. *Freedom from Fear: The American People in Depression and War, 1929–1945.* New York: Oxford University Press, 1999.

Kyzig, David E. *Daily Life in the United States, 1920–1940.* Westport, Conn.: Greenwood Press, 2002.

Labance, Bob. *The Old Man: The Biography of Walter J. Travis.* Chelsea, Mich.: Sleeping Bear Press, 2000.

Larsen, Lawrence H., and Barbara J. Cottrell. *The Gate City: A History of Omaha.* Lincoln: University of Nebraska Press, 1997.

Lowe, Stephen R. *Sir Walter and Mr. Jones: Walter Hagen, Bobby Jones, and the Rise of American Golf.* Chelsea, Mich.: Sleeping Bear Press, 2000.

Mayo, James M. *The American Country Club: Its Origins and Development.* New Brunswick, N.J.: Rutgers University Press, 1998.

McElvaine, Robert S. *The Great Depression: America, 1929–1941.* New York: Times Books, 1984.

Parrish, Michael E. *Anxious Decades: America in Prosperity and Depression, 1920–1941.* New York: W.W. Norton, 1992.

Sarazen, Gene, with Herbert Warren Wind. *Thirty Years of Championship Golf: The Life and Times of Gene Sarazen.* London: A&C Black, 1990.

Sinclair, Upton. *The Jungle.* New York: New American Library, 1960.

Wind, Herbert Warren. *The Story of American Golf, Its Champions and Its Championships.* New York: Knopf, 1975.

GLOSSARY OF GOLF TERMS

brassie: Two wood.

mashie: Five iron.

mashie niblick: Seven iron.

match play: Two players play head-to-head, with each hole worth one point. The U.S. Amateur follows a match-play format. However, to qualify for the U.S. Amateur, players must compete for two rounds of medal play.

medal play: Players' total individual score are posted each round. Professional tournaments are scored in this manner.

midiron: Two iron.

niblick: Nine iron.

spoon: Three wood.

stymie: An archaic rule followed in singles play until 1952. If a player's ball blocked the line of another player on the green, and was more than six inches away, the ball that impeded the putt did not have to be marked. This rule forced players to chip very short distances, often just a few feet, in order to loft shots over the obstructing ball.

INDEX